MISSING
LETTERS TO
LUTHERAN
PASTORS

Edited by
Herman J. Otten

Foreword by
Jacob Ehrhard

Lutheran News, Inc.
New Haven, Missouri

MISSING LETTERS TO LUTHERAN PASTORS

Library of Congress Card
Lutheran News, Inc.
684 Luther Lane
New Haven, MO 63068
Published 2014
Printed in the United States of America
Lightning Source, Inc., La Vergne, TN
ISBN #978-0-9832409-7-6

Comments

Of great interest was Herman Sasse's letter of April 18th, 1960 found on pages 19 to 21. In that letter he discusses the Herman Otten case in which the St. Louis seminary agreed to show cause why student Otten should not be certified. Sasse writes, "Everybody knows that some of your professors have publicly taught things not reconcilable with the Lutheran Confessions." It was obvious from Sasse's comments that had he been on the Board of Appeals the vote would have been 6-5 that the seminary had not shown cause, even as it would have been 7-5 had this reviewer been on that Board.

Of interest in that same letter was Sasse's comment about one of the professors at the sem of whom he wrote, "as I am convinced is certainly concerned about the whole case." Sasse did identify this professor as he closed the letter. It was Martin Franzmann, this writer's most esteemed professor.

On page 43 Sasse again brought to the attention of his readers the ancient struggle in Rome, who has the final authority, pope or councils? At Vatican II it was the pope. The council had voted to discuss a document drawn up by conservatives on two sources of Revelation and on inerrancy and inspiration. It was the schema, the pope withdrew it from discussion.

On pages 71-73 Sasse discusses what he thinks are shortcomings in the Brief Statement. A very interesting read, he would have agreed with those from the WELS, their president, a Franzmann brother, and faculty back in the early 60's when this young pastor accompanied Prs. Romoser, Mackenzie, Kretzmann, Burgdorf, and Dr. Becker to discuss church and ministry at the WELS seminary in Thiensville.

—Pastor Walter Otten

This essay makes use of Herman Sasse's monumental book "Was Heißt Lutherisch" ("What Does It Mean to Be Lutheran") to assess the status of confessional Lutheranism within the LCMS. Sasse's analysis of the unique identity of the Lutheran Church as "the confessional church par excellance" serves as a timely reminder that Lutheranism, alone among the denominations of Christendom, defines itself solely by its doctrine - that which we believe, teach and confess. Unlike all the others, for whom polity, liturgy, institutional identity, magnitude or antiquity are decisive, Lutheranism must be defined by the faithful confession of the pure doctrine of the Word of God, no matter what the cost of that faithful confession may be, institutionally or personally. The content of Sasse's book is presented in summary. The relevance of Sasse's words to the contemporary circumstances of the LCMS, whose self-styled Confessionals have been all too willing to sacrifice theological integrity for institutional control, is nothing less than remarkable. Herman Sasse embodied Lutheranism's fearless commitment to the Truth and was content to pay its cost, scorning the world's recognition and fame, to offer the good confession.

—Pastor Laurence White
Our Savior Lutheran Church
Houston, Texas

"While at the seminary, many teachers formed me confessionally: Preus, Scaer, Marquart, Weinrich, Wenthe. While out of the seminary, no teacher so continues hewing me confessionally as Herman Sasse. I was present in the study of President Harrison (back at Westgate, Iowa, in the early '90s) a number of times as he was working on the Sasse translations of The Lonely Way, never knowing what comfort these words would give me in these past 14 years of shepherding on the lonely way."

"May our Lord continue to raise up confessional teachers to guide the Church Catholic along the straight, narrow, and often, lonely way."

—Pastor Michael C. Brockman
Associate Pastor for Hispanic Outreach
Grace Lutheran Church, Wichita, Kansas

Lutherans Commemorating Sasse's 100th Birthday

Sasse said CN editor should be thanked not condemned
Christian News, June 26, 1995

Left to right: Dr. David Scaer, Dr. Hermann Sasse, Professor Kurt Marquart. This previously unpublished photo was taken by the editor of *Christian News* in 1959 at the Lutheran Church-Missouri Synod's convention in San Francisco when Marquart, Scaer, and the editor took Sasse out for lunch. After the Lutheran Church-Missouri Synod's Council of Presidents repudiated *Christian News* in 1969, Sasse wrote: "Somebody should rise and publicly thank Herman Otten for his brave fight. We all were not sometimes fully agreed with him. He has made blunders. But why was it left to a young pastor to speak where others should have spoken?" Sasse is regarded throughout the Lutheran world as one of the greatest Lutheran theologians of the twentieth century. LCMS President Jack Preus subscribed to *Christian News* for Dr. Sasse.

Acknowledgements

Thanks to Luke Otten for arranging the publication of this volume and to Naomi Finck and Natalie Hoerstkamp for type-setting and Alvin Schmidt for helpful suggestions.

Sasse at the LCMS's 1959 Convention

A Theological Convocation in San Francisco prior to the 1959 Convention of the Lutheran Church-Missouri Synod where Dr. Hermann Sasse made a presentation. How many of the famous Lutheran theologians and leaders in the photo below can you identify? Dr. Alfred Fuerbringer, president of Concordia Seminary, St. Louis is at the lower left. Dr. Jackayya from India is at the podium. Drs. Noack, Hoopmann, and Sasse from Australia are at the inside of the table to the right. Professor Kurt Marquart is "the young kid on the block" in the rear with the clerical collar. Some others on the photo are Lutheran theologians and leaders from the Lutheran Church-Missouri Synod, the Evangelical Lutheran Synod, the Wisconsin Evangelical Lutheran Synod, Brazil, and England. Some of them are Dr. Martin Franzmann, Dr. Herman Harms, Professor Elmer Moeller, Dr. Theodore Nickel, Dr. Arthur Nitz, Dr. George Pierce, Dr. Herbert Boumann, Dr. Roland Wiederaenders, Dr. Paul Zimmermann, Dr. George Beto, Dr. William Danker, Professor Julian Anderson, Dr. Oscar Naumann, Rev. Herbert Schmidt, Professor Frederic Blume, and Dr. Thomas Coates.

[Arrows pointing to Kurt Marquart (L) and Hermann Sasse (R)]

The following statement is taken from the June 22, 1959 Convention Bulletin of the 1959 San Francisco Convention of the Lutheran Church-Missouri Synod. It should be noted that Dr. Sasse at the LCMS's 1959 Convention strongly supported the adoption of the controversial Resolution No. 9 which reaffirmed the Brief Statement of the Lutheran Church-Missouri Synod. Although Dr. Sasse's church was a member of the LWF, Dr. Sasse opposed membership in the LWF. The editor of *Christian News* spoke with Dr. Sasse at the 1959 convention.

The following statement is taken from the June 22, 1959 Convention Bulletin of the 1959 San Francisco Convention of the LCMS:

Dr. Hermann Sasse, professor of the United Evangelical Lutheran Church's seminary in Adelaide, Australia, made a *90-minute presentation* at the Friday evening session of the convention on Lutheran ecumenicity. "The Missouri Synod is one of the *last fortresses of Lutheranism,*" he said. After characterizing true ecumenicity as "the quest for the true Church," the noted church historian pointed out that in free America, the quest for the Church became the quest for unity. He said that in America the ecumenical movement has stemmed from two sources the federation program of Reformed Protestantism, and the plans for organic unity as espoused by the Anglican tradition and implemented by the Lambeth Conference. Both alternatives fail, the German-Australian theologian said, because they reject the sovereignty of the Scriptures and its emphasis on salvation by faith alone, and, in the case of the Reformed tradition, devaluate the Sacraments. He warned that "we must not be Pharisees in approaching these problems ... *we must not despair.* We know our duty. We have to go back to Scripture and the Confessions of the fathers. We have missed opportunities, and have not worked as hard as we should have... Inside the Lutheran World Federation or outside, we must work, not as enemies, not in hostility, but as those who seek and ask for the truth of God, and ask that such efforts be blessed. Many lonely theologians of the world are looking at us. *May God bless all* endeavors to rediscover the Lutheran Biblical doctrine of the Church ... the way of the Church is the way of the Cross." Dr. Sasse, whose church body is a member of the LWF and not in fellowship with the Missouri Synod, also participated in the theological conference which preceded the convention. —*Christian News,* September 25, 1995

Dr. Hermann Sasse to Herman Otten, 1959

Dr. H. Sasse
(please do not abbreviate South Australia — the name of the state)

"63 Pirie Street
Prospect, South Australia
2ᵈ December, 1959

My dear Mr. Otten:

Please forgive my failure to reply at once. I am in a terrific situation here resulting, my wife seriously ill so that I had to do all the house work in addition to my many duties at the end of the academic year. For many years this is the first Christmas when I have to work alone to cope with urgent obligations towards editors and printers. So today I can just drop a line to tell you that I have not forgotten you. As to Charlemann's paper, I agree with you. It is very superficial and untenable, Anglican rather than Lutheran. I enclose our thesis on the question. This is mainly my work. I think the Brief Statement, written by Pieper 30 years ago, does not answer all of our questions and contains even such a doubtful statement as that "man had a ____ overship. Now—

ledge of nature. It must be translated into the language of our time. Part of it. has a section & it should go the proper way as indicated in San Francisco. I am making a list for them. Unfortunately my contributions are no longer available in print. They are at St. Louis (Reformed Theol. Review, Melbourne). What I can find I shall send you, but you must keep them for me. In the whole controversy I am on your side against Pieper. It is a grave violation of Christian love to present such teachers to the young students of tomorrow. You leaders know what grave mistakes have been made. — I am just receiving the volume of documents; I am shocked by the treatment you had to undergo. Are you still being victimized. Please let me know about your personal situation and your whole situation. If necessary I shall intervene with Dr. Behnken. You cannot be punished for the sins committed by Dr. _____. God bless you brother. I shall help as best I can. Best wishes and kind greetings

Yours in communione fidei, H. Sasse.

I am in a great hurry. Please tell me fully and frankly what I shall do to help you.

Concordia Theological Seminary

6600 N. Clinton St. / Fort Wayne, Indiana 46825-4996 / (219) 481-2100

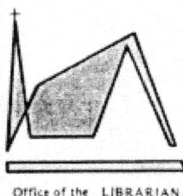

Office of the LIBRARIAN

Christian News
P.O. Box 241
Washington MO
63090

Oct. 30, 1990

Dear Rev. Otten,

Some few months ago an archive was established at Walther Memorial Library to collect the letters and papers of Hermann Sasse. I am writing you to ask whether you might be willing to help us in this regard. I know of several significant letters which were published in *Christian News*. Would you be willing to copy the correspondence you exchanged with Sasse and send these copies to us? Whatever you may send to us will be filed in the archive.

Thank you for your kind consideration,

Matthew Harrison
Ref. Asst.

P.S. We can cover the cost.

Enclosed is my Sasse file. Please copy what you want and return to me. You will find more material in Christian News and the Christian News Encyclopedic. Check Index

God's blessings.

Herman Otten

Mailed
11-13-90 KP

TABLE OF CONTENTS

Foreword

I was first introduced to Hermann Sasse as an undergraduate student at Concordia University—River Forest, Illinois. Along with C.S. Lewis's *Mere Christianity* and Gene Edward Veith's *The Spirituality of the Cross*, Sasse's *Here We Stand* was a gateway to a depth of Christian thinking I had not experienced before. Sasse's historical survey of the Reformation reveals him to be a masterful Church historian. It's not just that he knows names and dates and places and events. He narrates Church history. And he does so in such a way that we Lutherans are not on the outside looking in, but are caught up in the story. For Sasse, the Lutheran Church did not originate in 1530 with the presentation of the Augsburg Confession, or in 1517 with the nailing of Luther's Ninety-five Theses to the door of the Castle Church in Wittenberg, Germany. It begins with Christ sending out a handful of men to be His witnesses to Jerusalem, Judea and Samaria, and to the ends of the earth.

In these letters, Sasse again shows himself to be the exceptional Church historian. Of great importance for the Christian of 2015 is his statement on abortion. The question of life from conception to birth is not a problem that the Church began to wrestle with after *Roe v. Wade* in 1973. Sasse brings us to the early Church and weaves our story with theirs, showing how the Christian Church of the first centuries distinguished itself from the world and the pagan religions by its concern for the life of pre-born children. This was not a philosophical idea for the early Church, but one grounded in the revelation of the Holy Scripture, and that God Himself was incarnate as a fetus in the womb of a virgin mother.

For Sasse, to be Lutheran is to have a distinctly Lutheran confession. In a letter to Herman Otten, Sasse writes, "What you need, or rather what we all need, is that Holy Scripture and the confessions of our Church are regained as the living truth which our time needs" (Personal letter dated 1 December, 1968). It is not enough to have the Scriptures, but we must also agree as to what the Scriptures say. Unity is found in confession, and for Sasse, that unity is expressed in the seventh article of the Augsburg Confession: "For the true unity of the Church it is enough to agree about the doctrine of the Gospel and the administration of the Sacraments" (Augsburg Confession, VII. 2). Time and again he returns to this simple, yet profound, confession of what the Church is and where it can be found.

This confession is what guided Sasse in his work in the Ecumenical Movement. The earlier union movements in Germany between the Lutheran and Reformed Churches provided a backdrop for the early to mid-twentieth century effort to unite the various Christian Church bodies under one umbrella. The movement, however, was bound to fail because of its reliance on uniting in works of service while minimizing the doctrinal differences of the Churches' confessions. "Doctrine divides, service unites," was the watchword of the Ecumenical Movement, but the *satis est* of the Church's unity, the sufficiency of true ecumenism of the seventh article of the Augsburg Confession, is found precisely in agreement concerning the doctrine of the Gospel and the Sacraments. Lacking this agreement, there can never be true, churchly unity.

Much of this present volume deals with what the sainted Dr. Ronald Feuerhahn calls a "lacuna" in Sasse's teaching, namely his view of Holy Scripture. "On the Doctrine *De Scriptura Sacra*"—Sasse's fourteenth letter to Lutheran pastors—presents a learned and in-depth treatment of the "pure fountain and source of God's truth," the Holy Scriptures. However, with respect to the teaching of the inspiration of Scriptures, Sasse wobbles. He confesses the inspiration of Scripture, but allows that only the theological portions of Holy Scripture are inspired. Matters treating of historical data or pertaining to a particular ancient world view could and did contain errors and even contradictions, though he maintained that such errors were minor in nature.

Shortly after the circulation of this letter, which was written in 1950, Sasse changed his mind. That he changed his opinion is interesting enough, but the way in which it changed has more to say to the Church today. It was not until he came to Australia and found himself in the middle of the fellowship discussions between two Lutheran Churches, that his views on Scripture became more aligned with the traditional Lutheran view. By theological conversation and a common agreement, the "Theses on Scripture and Inspiration," which were integral to the merger of the two Lutheran Church bodies of Australia. When asked about his former view of inspiration, Sasse pointed not to his own private view, but to the common agreement of his Church. The lesson of Sasse's biography is that not every theological error (and what theologian is without his own theological lacuna) is indicative of systemic heresy. Furthermore, the solution to what Francis Pieper calls a "felicitous inconsistency," is also found in the mutual conversation and consolation of the brethren in the Church (Smalcald Articles, III.IV).

But even though his views on Holy Scripture and its inspiration changed, his "Letter 14" continued to be circulated and published without his permission. Several of his private letters to Herman Otten reveal his displeasure that he continued to be appealed to by those who would attack the inspiration and authority of the Holy Scriptures. A detailed history and examination of the saga of Sasse's view of Holy Scriptures can be found in the Concordia Seminary Monograph Series: *Scripture and the Church: Selected Essays of Hermann Sasse*, edited by Jeffrey J. Kloha and Ronald R. Feuerhahn. The personal letters in this present volume serve to round out the story.

Given the extended controversy over his view of Holy Scripture, some Lutherans may be skeptical of his writings. But perhaps a word from one of my own teachers, Professor Kurt Marquart, himself a student of Dr. Sasse as a young pastor in Australia, might offer a critique and solution to Sasse's Scripture problem:

> Nevertheless, it is true that a certain ambiguity

haunted Sasse's writings on this subject. If a grateful pupil be permitted to conjecture about a venerable and learned master's oversight, I would say that Sasse never succeeded in applying his deeply incarnational, Chalcedonian theology of the cross to Holy Scripture with the same consistency with which he had applied it to the sacraments and to the Church. The theology of the cross demands that the mysteries of God acting under earthly "masks"—including, therefore, Holy Scripture—be taken not at their apparent face value, in terms of human phenomena, but at their real face value, as given by God in His Word. Theology, also bibliology, must be done "from above," that is, in reliance on God's authority alone, without substantive admixtures "from below," that is, from the wisdom and philosophy of the world ("Theological Observer: 'A Tale of Two Books'", *Concordia Theological Quarterly*, July-October 1986).

Sasse provided his own solution to the Scripture problem, even if he never quite saw it clearly for himself. The Christian faith revealed in Holy Scripture is a faith of God coming to man, clothed in humility, masking His glory. Reason alone can never find the Son of God under the flesh of Jesus. It can never find God's goodness hidden under suffering and the cross. It can never see Baptism as something other than plain water. It can never conclude that the true body and blood of Jesus are present in the bread and wine. Reason only sees things according to their outward appearance. But not so with the things of God. "God does not see as man sees, because a man looks at the outward appearance, but the LORD looks into the heart" (1 Samuel 16:7b). In the heart is where faith resides, and it is only through faith that we can see, contrary to our own reason and strength, that the words of Holy Scripture are truly the words of the Holy Spirit.

Jacob W Ehrhard, Pastor
Trinity Lutheran Church
New Haven, MO

PREFACE

Hermann Otto Erich Sasse was born in Germany on July 17, 1895, the eldest of five children. He died on August 8, 1976. Sasse entered the German army in 1916. He was awarded the Iron Cross, Second class, the second highest honor in the German military at that time. Only six out of 150 of the men Sargent Sasse brought into the Battle of Passchendaele survived. He was ordained in St. Matthew Lutheran Church, Berlin, on June 13, 1920. He served as a pastor for fourteen years. A large double parish at St. Nicolai had some 10,000 member. Sasse retained a pastoral heart, a love for people, even after he became a world famous theologian. He was a true *Seelsorger*, a carer of souls who visited people.

In 1924 he married Charlotte Naumann. A year later he went to Hartford Theological Seminary in the U.S. on a Master of Sacred Theology program. His doctoral supervisors at the University of Berlin were Adolf von Harnack, Karl Holl, Reinhold Seeberg, and Julius Kaftan. Later Sasse participated in the anti-Nazi cause.

The first meeting of the Lutheran Church-Missouri Synod President John Behnken with Sasse was at the Sasse home in Erlangen, Germany, in November 1945. Behnken asked Concordia Seminary, St. Louis, to invite Sasse to lecture at the seminary. Professor Ronald Feuerhahn writes in *Hermann Sasse - A Man for Our Times*: "Professor F.E. Mayer was a member of the small committee of the faculty which sought to block the invitation. The reasons offered by the faculty are not merely interesting; they also may indicate something about the changing theological climate of the Missouri Synod which is very instructive for today. In the end he (Sasse) was invited and arrived on 5 June 1948.

"Once in St. Louis, discomfort with Sasse's opinions continued. His 'pessimistic' view of things in the German Churches, noted in the faculty concerns, stood in sharp contrast to the optimism of the St. Louis theologians. It is perhaps significant that on this visit Sasse was given more time for lectures for the Wisconsin Synod and the American Lutheran Church than for his hosts" (p. 19, *Herman Sasse - A Man of Our Times)*.

In 1933 Sasse was called to the chair of Church history and symbolics at Erlangen University in Germany. In 1949 he moved to Australia, serving on the faculty of Immanuel Theological Seminary in North Adelaide. Feuerhahn concludes his essay by quoting Richard Jungkuntz: "But there are Lutherans in America, as there are in Europe and Australia, who today thank God that from Hermann Sasse they have learned – in a better way than they knew before – *'was heist Lutherisch'*: what it means to be Lutheran" (p. 29, *Herman Sasse - A Man of Our Times)*.

The back cover of *Hermann Sasse: A Man for Our Times?,* published by Concordia Academic Press in 1998, has these testimonials:

"Here is a fascinating review of 20th century international Lutheranism as dramatically personified in the Germanic jeremiad of one of its most controversial and influential participants, Hermann Sasse..."

--William H. Lazareth, Bishop Emeritus
Metropolitan New York Synod, Evangelical Lutheran Church in America

"Hermann Sasse, through his writings, continues to influence confessional Lutheranism around the world..."
--Ralph May, President,
The Lutheran Church-Canada

"It is evident that Hermann Sasse is indeed a theologian and a man for our time. The theological issues that he dealt with continue to be the issues that the Lutheran Church is wrestling with...."
--Roger D. Pittelko, President Emeritus
The English District, The Lutheran Church-Missouri Synod

No Narrow Minded Lutheran

When *Encounter*, a youth magazine in Australia, published Sasse's article "The Sacrament of the Altar" in 1970, it commented: "Dr. Sasse is not a narrow-minded Lutheran — one who knows and understands only one point of view . . . He has been studying sacramental theology and the history of the sacraments for about 40 years in close connection with theologians of various Churches, Eastern Orthodox, Roman Catholic, Anglican, Reformed and Presbyterians, among them the greatest experts of these Churches."

This book has several articles on Sasse's death. Although the official publications of the major Lutheran Church bodies in the U.S. and their seminaries virtually remained silent at the time, Dr. Carl McIntire, president of the International Council of Churches and editor of the *Christian Beacon,* reported Sasse's death and highly commended Sasse and his long battle for the truth of God's Word. Sasse and McIntire had exchanged letters. Dr. David Hedegard, a Lutheran theologian from Sweden, who was a vice-president of the International Council of Churches, was close to Sasse. A *Festschrift* honoring Hedegard includes a chapter by Sasse titled "Luther and the Bible."

Otten first met Hedegard in the 1950s when Hedegard was teaching at Faith Seminary in Philadelphia. When Hedegard was a guest in the Otten home in New Haven, Missouri, Otten introduced him to William Beck, translator of An American Translation of the Bible. The two soon found they both supported Luther's principles of translation. While Sasse and Hedegard took issue with the Reformed theology of McIntire and others in the ICCC, both sided with the ICCC in its battle with the World Council of Churches. Hedegard served as a reporter for *Christian News* at a WCC Assembly. ICCC leaders placed a copy of Otten's *Baal or God* in the registration packet of each one of the more than 1,000 delegates coming from many nations at the ICCC Congress in Geneva, Switzerland, in 1965. There Otten met with Lutheran theologians such as Hedegard and Uuras Saarnivaara. They sided with Sasse's position. Otten also promoted Sasse's scriptural and Lutheran position at ICCC congresses and executive committee meetings in New Jersey, Pennsylvania, Florida, Amsterdam, the Netherlands, Berlin, Germany, and Santiago, Chile, where he was invited to speak. While Sasse's position was not appreciated by the WCC, the National Council of Churches, and Lutheran World Federation, it was championed by the ICCC.

The Old American Lutheran Church (ALC)

Sasse recognized some sixty years ago that there were still some confessional Lutheran theologians in the American Lutheran Church. He spoke at some of their seminaries, including Wartburg and Capital. At the time Otten preached in an American Lutheran Church (ALC) congregation when he worked for a farmer whose wife had graduated from the ALC's Capital University in Ohio, which still had some confessional Lutheran professors. *Lutheran Hour* speaker, Walter Maier, also recognized that the ALC had truly Lutheran professors such as Herman Preus, Leupold and Reu, who walked in the footsteps of Charles Porterfield Krauth, author of the *Conservative Reformation and Its Theology*, published by Augsburg and then reprinted by the LCMS's Concordia Publishing House (CPH). Dr. Lawrence Rast, now president of Concordia Seminary, Ft. Wayne, Indiana, is the editor of the latest printing of Krauth's book.

Sasse took sharp issue with *Dialog: Lutheran Journal of Theology*, published in the U.S., which listed as editors and contributors many of the world's leading Lutheran theologians. Carl Braaten, an editor of *Christian Dogmatics*, published by Fortress Press, was one of the first editors of *Dialog*.

When Sasse left the liberal Lutheran Church in Germany and went to Australia, the move from Germany to Australia came at great financial sacrifice. He left a well-paying position and assurance of a good pension for a small Church body, which could only pay a small salary and a $300 a year pension. Sasse wrote to Otten when he retired that he had to cancel his subscription to all publications except *Christian News* because of his financial situation. Concordia Seminary, Springfield, Illinois, President Jacob Preus first subscribed to *Christian News* for Sasse urging Sasse to read *CN* (then *Lutheran News*) to keep up with what was happening in Lutheranism.

Otten and Marquart Meet Sasse in 1959

Kurt Marquart and Herman Otten met Sasse in 1959 at the LCMS's convention in San Francisco, where, thanks to LCMS president John W. Behnken, Sasse was the convention essayist.

Marquart, Otten, David Scaer, Kenneth Fisher, and Walter Otten went to the 1959 convention to inform LCMS leaders that there were professors at Concordia Seminary, St. Louis, who denied the inerrancy of the Bible, promoted the destructive notions of Biblical higher criticism, were open to evolution, and denied direct messianic prophecy. Marquart and Otten also met with other overseas theologians who attended the 1959 convention, including Australian Lutheran Church leaders.

Behnken later asked Otten to come to his home office in St. Louis. There he showed Otten a call he had from an Australian Church for Otten. Behnken asked Otten to withdraw what he had reported about the theology of several St. Louis seminary professors, declare all professors were orthodox to get certified by the seminary, and then accept the call to Australia. While Otten was not adverse to going to Australia, he said it would not be honest to say all the St. Louis professors were orthodox Lutheran theologians. Since the St. Louis seminary still insisted Otten had not told the truth about the seminary, Behnken could not give Otten the call.

Letters from Sasse in this volume show that Sasse was willing to plead with Behnken for Otten's certification. Otten had sent Sasse documentation of the "Seminary vs. Otten" case, which Otten and Marquart had prepared while Marquart was serving as a pastor in Weatherford, Texas. It included "A Specification of Doctrinal Issues" in this volume (pp. 2-9).

When the "Seminary vs. Otten" case was heard by the LCMS's convention's elected Board of Appeals, (five attorneys and six pastor-theologians), Marquart, Otten's lead counsel, could not submit letters from Sasse since it would not be possible for the seminary's attorneys to examine Sasse. The Board of Appeals traveled five times to St. Louis to hear the case. Professors and students testified under oath, and documents were submitted. A court reporter took down every word. The 1,050 page transcript is at the Concordia Historical Institute.

Letters from Sasse show that he remained a strong supporter of Otten and *Christian News* until his death. When Trinity Lutheran Church, New Haven, Missouri, won its case with the LCMS after being expelled from the LCMS for calling Otten to be its pastor, Sasse rejoiced that a congregation won over the bureaucracy. Sasse wrote that *Christian News* was about the only publication regularly reporting the truth about what was going on in Lutheranism. He hoped *CN* would receive the necessary support to continue.

Sola Scriptura *(Cover and masthead, pp. 124-126)*
This volume includes a previously unpublished essay which Sasse had sent to *Sola Scriptura* for publication. Sasse was an editorial representative of *Sola Scriptura*. This theological journal was published by Lutheran News "a non-profit organization at Trinity Lutheran Church, New Haven, Missouri." Some of the others listed on the masthead were such *Christian News* subscribers as Robert Preus, John Warwick Montgomery, Robert Hoerber, Alvin Wagner, Laurence Faulstick, Walter Lammerts, William Oesch, Neelak Tjernagel, Glen Peglau, David Hedegard, Eugene Klug, Vernon Harley, J. Val Andreae, Reuben Redal, John Baur, Bjarne Teigen, Marcus Lang, Waldo Werning, Kent Spaulding, Paul Schnelle, Walter Dissen, Roy Guess, Arnold Jonas, Harry Marks, Oswald Skov, Dan and Jean Simpson, Eugene Kaufield, Carl Baase, Siegbert Becker, Bruce Adams, Marku Sarela, Richard Hanneberg, Elmer Reimnitz, Alvin Schmidt, and other U.S. and overseas readers of *Christian News* interested in an international Lutheran theological publication which promoted uniting true Lutherans around the world.

A Current Formula of Concord

This present volume includes letters from Sasse commenting on the LCMS's *Brief Statement* and the inerrancy of Scripture. When Marquart and Otten were roommates at Concordia Seminary, St. Louis, they promoted a 20th Century Formula of Concord which would reaffirm the ancient creeds of Christendom, the *Book of Concord* of 1580 and also speak to such current issues as evolution, abortion, historical criticism, the nature of truth, homosexuality, the ordination of women, etc. *Christian News* later recommended that such confessional Lutheran theologians as Sasse, Wilhelm Oesch, Robert Preus, Marquart, Siegbert Becker, Henry Koch and others work on such a statement. It should cover more than the LCMS's *Brief Statement*.

Letters and articles in this volume show that Sasse's view on the inerrancy of the Bible changed through the years. Kurt Marquart in 1988 wrote in "A Tale of Two Books" in this volume: "Nevertheless, it is true that a certain ambiguity haunted Sasse's writing on this subject. If a grateful pupil were permitted to conjecture about a venerable and learned master's oversight, I would say that Sasse never succeeded in applying his deeply incarnational, Chalcedonian theology of the cross to Holy Scripture with the same consistency with which he had applied it to the sacraments and to the Church." "Where, after all, is the theologian who has no 'blind spot'?"

Matthew Harrison, Sasse and *Christian News*

Matthew Harrison, President of the Lutheran Church-Missouri Synod, wrote this year in the preface to Volume III - *Letters to Lutheran Pastors, 1957-1969*: "WITH THIS THIRD VOLUME of Hermann Sasse's *Letters to Lutheran Pastors*, an effort of nearly a quarter century comes to a close. There is, to be sure, much more of Sasse to translate and publish, and others have and are taking up the challenge. What a journey this has been for me! With two volumes of *The Lonely Way* and with three volumes of *Letters to Lutheran Pastors*, we have now put into print some 2,500 pages of Sasse" (xi).

Harrison wrote to *Christian News* on October 30, 1990 from Concordia Theological Seminary, Ft. Wayne, Indiana: "Dear Rev. Otten, Some few months ago an archive was established at Walther Memorial Library to collect the letters and papers of Hermann Sasse. I am writing you to ask whether you might be willing to help us in this regard. I know several significant letters which were published in *Christian News*. Would you be willing to copy the correspondence you exchanged with Sasse and send these copies to us? Whatever you may send to us will be filed in the archive. Thank you for your kind consideration, Matthew Harrison, Res. Asst. P.S. We can cover the cost."

CN replied: "Enclosed is my Sasse file. Please copy what you want and return to me. You will find more material in *Christian News* and the *Christian News Encyclopedia*, check Index. God's blessings, Herman Otten."

The letters and articles in the Sasse file in *CN*'s research center sent to Harrison are in this volume on *Missing Letters to Lutheran Pastors.* Hardly any of it is in the 2,500 pages of the books published by CPH and edited by Matthew Harrison. It is simply not politically correct in the Lutheran Church-Missouri Synod to recognize that such confessional Lutheran theologians as Hermann Sasse and Kurt Marquart, supported the work of *Christian News*, insisted that Otten won his case with Concordia Seminary, St. Louis, and that the seminary and the LCMS bureaucracy broke the by-laws of the LCMS when they refused to recognize the ruling of the LCMS's Commission on Appeals.

Why This Volume

Those who today are regularly reading *Christian News,* as the Australians Hermann Sasse and Kurt Marquart did, know that today Concordia Seminary, St. Louis, has departed further from the text of the Bible than it did when Marquart and Otten first informed Sasse in 1959 about what was going on at the St. Louis seminary and elsewhere in the LCMS. At that time the seminary never would have invited a pro-lesbian, universalist, non-Trinitarian theologian like Dr. Daisy Machado from Union Theological Seminary, New York, to lecture at the St. Louis seminary on how to do mission work. The seminary never would have invited the long line of liberals who support the pro-abortion, pro-homosexual, and pro-evolution position of their denomination to lecture on how to preach. The seminary would never have accepted money from the pro-theistic evolution American Association for the Advancement of Science. The AAAS only funds those who do not insist on a six day and young earth creation. The seminary would never have recommended as its alumni book of the year a book by pro-evolutionist Bishop John Polkinghorne.

The seminary's theological journal would never have published articles by pro-evolutionist Matthew Becker and editorials praising a higher critic on the Seminex faculty like Fred Danker. The seminary's theological publication would never have published a eulogy by David Benke, now praised by Harrison, of Father Richard Neuhaus. *CN* has often documented the fact that Neuhaus denied the inerrancy of the Bible, promoted Rudolf Bultmann's demythologizing of the Bible, rejected justification by faith alone, and was a pro-homosexual universalist who joined the Roman Catholic Church.

When Marquart and Otten first told Sasse about the theological liberalism at the St. Louis seminary, no professor had attacked the actual text of the Bible as St. Louis seminary Provost Jeffrey Kloha has now done. *CN* published Kloha's essay first presented in Germany promoting a plastic text of the Bible. *CN* published the entire conclusion of Kloha's 719 page 2006 doctoral dissertation prepared at the University of Leeds, England. *CN* commented on a *Festschrift* prepared by Kloha and another higher critic of the Bible in honor of J. Keith Elliott, Kloha's doctoral advisor. Kloha's contribution to the *Festschrift* is "Elisabeth's Magnificat, (Luke 1:46.)" Sasse in his writing agreed with the Bible that Mary said the Magnificat and not Elisabeth. Sasse fled from the destructive higher criticism still promoted in Europe and went to Australia. While *CN* has published essays by such confessional Lutheran scholars as John Warwick Montgomery, Jack Kilcrease, Jack Cascione, and Brandt Klawitter exposing the false doctrine in Kloha's writings, *CN* knows of no LCMS professor or bureaucrat who has publicly said Kloha's writings contain false doctrine.

Today the St. Louis seminary has claimed that Dietrich Bonhoeffer was the greatest Lutheran theologian since Martin Luther. This volume shows what Sasse said about Bonhoeffer's "schwäermerei." The index to the St. Louis seminary's *Concordia Theological Monthly* (*CTM*) from 1930-1959 shows no reference to Bonhoeffer or any writing by Bonhoeffer. The only reference to Bonhoeffer *CN* has found in the *CTM* is in a brief item in a German section of the *CTM* warning against Bonhoeffer.

Kloha – Sasse – Scharlemann – Marquart

"Kloha – Sasse – Scharlemann – Marquart", an article in the April 13, 2015 *Christian News* noted:

The editor and Kurt Marquart met Sasse in 1959 at the LCMS's convention in Denver. They took Sasse out for lunch and spoke at considerable length about the denial of the inerrancy of the Bible by various professors at Concordia Seminary, St. Louis. Sasse shared the concerns Otten and Marquart had.

He was thrilled that the 1959 convention reaffirmed what the LCMS's *Brief Statement* said about the inerrancy of the Bible. The March 30, 2015 *CN* photographed a few of the letters Sasse sent to Otten. After the LCMS's Council of Presidents and LCMS President Jacob Preus condemned *Christian News* as untruthful, some 850 laymen and pastors gathered at a testimonial banquet for *Christian News* in a Chicago hotel. They were *Christian News* readers from 10 states and Canada. The keynote speaker was Alvin Wagner, a member of the LCMS's Commission on Theology and Church Relations (CTCR) and one of the LCMS theologians in correspondence with Sasse. After noting that Hermann Sasse wrote that "Somebody should rise and publicly thank Herman Otten for his brave fight," Wagner said: "That from one of the worlds' ablest Lutheran scholars can hardly be tabbed Repudiation. It is APPRECIATION of the highest order coming as it does from one of the keenest observers of the historical Church scene past and present. When he hears – as he undoubtedly will –that you, the concerned of Illinois, did rise and publicly thank Herman Otten and his gifted wife Grace for their 'brave fight,' his heart will rejoice." Sasse asked: "But why was it left to a young pastor to speak when others should have spoken?"

Since none of the letters Sasse sent to *CN* and articles *CN* published by Sasse are in the CPH volumes of Sasse's *Letters to Lutheran Pastors*, even though they were sent to Harrison, *CN* is being urged to publish volume IV of Sasse's letters with these letters and articles.

Jeffrey J. Kloha and Ronald R. Feuerhahn are the editors of "Scripture and the Church: Selected Essays of Hermann Sasse, Concordia Seminary, Monograph Series, 1995". The foreword says that "Jeffrey Kloha, as a graduate student, was responsible for the bulk of this research; his work has been thorough and to the highest standard" (v).

Kloha is the author of "Hermann Sasse Confesses the Doctrine De Scriptura Sacra" on pp. 337-423. He writes about Sasse's "Letter 14," the only letter Sasse ever withdrew and some essays by Concordia Seminary Professor Martin Scharlemann. Major sections of them together with some articles by and about Scharlemann are in the *1961* and *1962 State of the Church Books of Documentation* compiled by Otten before *Christian News* began. Kloha mentions that the April 15, 1969 *Christian News* published letters from Sasse and Scharlemann. Otten publicly challenged Scharlemann' denial of the inerrancy of Scripture when Scharlemann gave his essay on "Revelation and Inspiration" at a Missouri District Pastoral Conference in 1959, at a Missouri District Convention at Concordia Seminary, St. Louis, and then at the LCMS's 1962 Convention in Cleveland.

Scharlemann changed his position. In 1973 he was one of the signers of "Crossroads", a document which affirmed the inerrancy of the Bible and opposed the liberals in the LCMS. Scharlemann, at a meeting held at Concordia Seminary arranged by Walter Hoffmann, president of *Affirm*, withdrew all the charges he had made vs. *Christian News*. He helped *Christian News* with the publication of An American Translation of the Bible by his close friend and associate with the Lutheran Scholar and at the graduate school at Concordia Seminary, William Beck.

Kloha concludes his essay, "Sasse Confesses *De Scriptura Sacra*": "Sasse made it clear, however, that he did not represent a position identical with, or similar to, fundamentalism or even the theologians of Lutheran Orthodoxy." "He was concerned to understand the Scriptures as both divine and human, not separating the two or emphasizing one at the expense of the other, but attempting to understand clearly the relationship with them" (pp. 422-423).

x x x

Kloha in his essay "Text and Authority: Theological and Hermeneutical Reflections on a Plastic Text" presented in Oberursel, Germany, in November 2013 in a section titled "Theological Reflection on a Plastic Text of the New Testament" approvingly cites Sasse's "Letter 14," which this book shows Sasse repeatedly asked the seminary not to publish and use.

A 42 page pamphlet published by *Christian News* in 2015 includes Kloha's essay, together with responses by Jack Cascione, John Warwick Montgomery, and Brandt Klawitter.

(* See note on page 234)

Marquart and Sasse

The editor has just finished preparing the questions for Volume VIII of *Marquart's Works* on the Bible and Historical Criticism. Marquart, who served as pastor in Australia for 12 years, had more direct contact with Sasse than anyone else in the LCMS. What he says in Volume VIII should settle the controversy about Sasse, inerrancy, and the *Brief Statement*. Marquart made it clear in his work that what Kloha now writes is contrary to scripture and scientific fact.

In no way would Sasse ever have supported Kloha's radical attack upon the Bible expressed in some of his essays and particularly in his 2006 719 page doctoral dissertation. The March 2, 2015 *CN* published sections of this essay where Kloha speaks about many "corruptions" and Kloha's entire conclusion. It's unfortunate that the computer addicted dummy down clergy refuses to subscribe to and read *Christian News* to get the facts. They treat *CN* like poison. They never urge members of their congregations to read and support *CN*.

Kloha, who has been acting president of Concordia Seminary, St. Louis, has the solid support of the seminary's faculty, Board of Regents, the LCMS Council of Presidents and the LCMS's Praesidium. How many of these dignitaries have read Kloha's doctoral dissertation? Kloha says he is glad the *CN* editor is not a member of the LCMS and that his views are not tolerated in the LCMS. *CN*'s long record shows that *CN*'s position is the position of Scripture, Luther, the Lutheran Confessions and that of the LCMS as affirmed by Walther, Pieper, Stoeckhardt, Arndt, Ludwig Fuerbringer, Maier, Beck, Engelder, Laetsch, Surburg, and others. Kloha, in his article "Elisabeth's Magnificat (Luke 1:46)" on pages 200-219 of Texts and Traditions: Essays in Honour of J. Keith Eliott, edited by Peter Doble and Jeffrey Kloha maintains that Elisabeth spoke the Magnificat. Sasse agrees with Luke 1:46 and insists these words came from the mouth of Mary (p. 66 of this book). Kloha's position is further from Scripture than was the position of those who formed Seminex and yet there is hardly a word of protest from the bureaucracy and the organized conservatives supporting the bureaucracy.

They refuse to read *Christian News*. They prefer to remain ignorant as they sit at their computers.

The Lasting Legacy of a Real Christian Gentleman

While Hermann Sasse had to endure many hardships during his long battle for God's truth, he always remained a real Christian gentleman, even in the midst of controversy. Theologians, who have at times been quick to attack before careful thought, can learn from Sasse.

Dr. L.B. Grope noted in his "A Tribute to Dr. Sasse" at the death of Sasse in 1976: "Despite the irreparable loss that we have suffered, Dr. Sasse, though dead, will continue to speak to us through his writings in the years that lie ahead. He will continue to encourage us to be confessors, whether we be pastors or parishioners, professors, or presidents. He will continue to call us to be faithful: ..."

Dr. S.P. Hebart concluded his sermon at Sasse's funeral: "Hermann Sasse knew that he would live on, enshrouded, as Luther once said, in the mind and memory and Word of God, in the presence of God, even though he slept the sleep of those who have died and who look for that great awakening, the resurrection of the dead and the life of the world to come."

Seeking Advice from Sasse

New Haven, Missouri
November 5, 1959

Professor Hermann Sasse, D. Th.
63 Clifton Street
Prospect, So. Australia

Dear Professor Sasse:

Perhaps a re-introduction will first be in order. This summer four students had lunch with you one afternoon at the San Francisco Convention. I am one of those students and also the student to whom you remarked, immediately following the vote on the *Brief Statement* resolution, that you have seldom seen laymen testify as they had at S.F.

Recently the Western District Pastoral Conference heard an essay delivered by Dr. Martin Scharlemann. This enclosed essay has been delivered to several large conferences throughout our Synod. Although the author does not mention your name in the written essay, he did remark that you would support his views on inerrancy and, in general, gave the impression that you would not seriously criticize this essay. Dr. Scharlemann has met considerable opposition in several districts and apparently mentioned your name to calm the fears of our leading administrators.

As you read the essay you will immediately recognize that the author has merely copied from a few of the current popularizers of Barth. I have detected whole sections taken from John Baillie, Robert Grant, G.E. Wright, etc. Actually I do not believe that the author himself realizes the serious implications of the Kantian epistemology he has copied. Finally there can be no real revelation at all.

At the Western District Conference I had an opportunity to ask several questions and also state that you would not now defend the views Dr. Scharlemann ascribed to you. According to him, it would be impossible for you to accept the *Brief Statement*'s doctrine of inerrancy.

This enclosed resolution which our congregation passed on the S.F. action on the *Brief Statement* will show you that there has been considerable opposition to the convention resolution. Under separate cover I am also sending you a confidential matter. While at the convention we considered discussing this with you but then decided not to take up your time. My friends and I would appreciate your frank evaluation on this case and any suggestions you may wish to offer.

You will know how to handle the Scharlemann essay.

With kindest regards,
Sincerely,
Herman Otten

Study Questions

1. What did Sasse tell Otten at the LCMS's 1959 convention in San Francisco? ____
2. What did Otten send to Sasse? ____

1

§

A SPECIFICATION OF
DOCTRINAL ISSUES

Sent to Hermann Sasse by Herman Otten on November 5, 1959
(This 1959 document is in "Concordia Seminary, St. Louis vs. Otten
Case – Book of Documentation Arranged by Kurt Marquart")

This statement is not a list of charges, but a presentation, side by side, of (A) Synod's historic position as I have learned it from the Catechism and other authoritative sources, and (B) positions of St. Louis Professors, defended publicly in class and in some cases elaborated in discussions with me.

In listing the two sets of positions I am not asserting irreconcilable conflict. A thorough, incisive examination, which I as a student was of course in no position to carry out, may reveal some apparent differences to be merely matters of terminology or emphasis. My listing of the two sets of positions is not a charge of false doctrine, but an allegation that such and such positions are being held and taught. All I am stating is the need to clarify scrupulously the relation between the old *modus docendi* and the new.

I. De Scriptura

Position A
1. Holy Scripture is the verbally inspired written Word of God. (*Brief Statement.* #1)

2. "Scripture is the inspired Word of God and the only infallible rule of faith and practice." (*Mutual Responsibility*, A)

3. Therefore the Holy Scriptures "contain no errors or contradictions, but . . . are in all their parts and words the infallible truth, also in those parts which treat of historical, and other secular matters." (*Brief Statement.* #1)

4. "We reject the doctrine . . . that Holy Scripture . . . does, or at least might contain error." (*Brief Statement* #5) "Whether a person takes the Christian attitude toward Scripture and lets Scripture be the Word of God, is seen at once from the attitude he takes as to the possibility of error in Scriptures." (Pieper 1, p. 280)

5. "It is absolutely necessary that we maintain the doctrine of inspiration as taught by our orthodox dogmaticians. If the possibility that Scripture contained the least error were admitted, it would become the business of *man* to sift the truth from the error. . . . The least deviation from the old inspiration doctrine introduces a rationalistic germ into the-

2

ology and infects the whole body of doctrine." (Quoted in *Walther and the Church*, p. 14)

Positon B
1. Holy Scripture is the verbally inspired written Word of God.[a]
2. Scripture is "the inspired Word, of God and the only infallible[b] rule of faith and practice." (*Mutual Responsibility*, A)
3. But Scripture contains errors and contradictions.
4. We cannot *a priori*, dogmatically deny the possibility of errors. Inerrancy is an open question.
5. The old dogmaticians, also Pieper and Engelder, took extremist positions on inspiration and inerrancy.

Notes:
a) Since those who deny the inerrancy and plenary inspiration freely subscribe to "verbal inspiration" (Cf. Appeal. Appendix C, 49, 2 and Exhibit G, pp. 1 and 2), the term "verbal inspiration" by itself is meaningless.

b) Expressions like the U.L.C.A.'s "the inspired Word of God . . . the only infallible rule and standard of faith and practice" (Constitution, Art. II, sec. 1) do not confess the inerrancy, nor touch the real issue, for at the same time the U.L.C.A. declares through its commissioners: "Our commissioners were unable to accept the statement of the Missouri Synod that the Scriptures are the infallible truth 'also in those parts which treat of historical geographical, and other secular matters.' We find the words quoted not in accordance with our Lutheran Confessions...nor with the Scriptures themselves." (C.T.M., Vol. X, Jan. 1939, no. 1, p. 65)

II. De Satisfactione Christi

Position A
1. The *vicarious satisfaction* means that Christ has, as a Substitute of mankind, fully appeased God's wrath for sin and satisfied the demands of His justice. (Pieper, II,344ff)
2. "Vicarious satisfaction" is not a "picture" but a literal reality. "Not merely the 'basic idea,' as the moderns say, is correct, but the whole matter is entirely Scriptural." (Pieper, II, 347)
3. "'A change of attitude *on the part of God* is meant.' . . . a change took place, not in men, but in God." (Pieper, II, 346)
4. "In lucid and exact language the Formula of Concord teaches that the *obedienta Christi activa* is an integral part of His substitutional satisfaction . . . Restricting the *obedienta activa* to the 'willing assumption of suffering' is here expressly rejected." (Pieper, II, 374)
5. The Ransom of Matt 20:28 was paid to God. (Pieper, II, 380)
Position B
1. One should hesitate to affirm that God's wrath was appeased, since He still has wrath over sin.
2. The "vicarious satisfaction" is one of the Biblical pictures of the

3

Atonement.

3. Since God is immutable, there cannot be a change in the mind of God.

4. The theory of Christ's active obedience has no Scriptural support, the usual passages being inapplicable.

5. We do not know to whom the Ransom of Matt. 20:28 was paid, since Scripture does not specify this.

III. De Ecclesia

Position A
1. The Church consists of all those and only of those who have saving faith. (*Brief Statement*, #24)

2. An isolated believer (e.g., one on a desert island) is just as much in the Church as any other believer, namely solely and alone by virtue of his faith.

3. Hypocrites and other unbelievers are in no sense members of the Body of Christ (i.e. the Church, properly speaking) though they are mixed with the Church in external Christendom, which, however is not the *corpus Christi* but a *corpus mixtum*. (*Kirche und Amt*, Thesis 2)

4. The Church *qua* Church, i.e. "the Church, in the proper sense of the term, is invisible." (*Kirche und Amt*, Thesis 3)

5. The Church is not a Platonic dream..., but a concrete reality.

Position B
1. The Church consists of the Christians.

2. From the New Testament point of view a Christian is in the Church only when he stands in a relation of active communication with one or more other Christians.

3. Hypocrites are, in a sense, part of the Body of Christ.

4. The Church is invisible, that is, it is not an external polity, but "invisible" does not mean "cannot be seen."

5. The Church is not a Platonic dream, but a concrete reality.

IV. De Anima et de Resurrectione

Position A
1. Man is a dichotomous (or trichotomous) being consisting of a body and a spirit or soul.

2. Man's spirit or soul is immortal and survives physical death.

3. The Jehovah's Witnesses' denial of immortality is anti-scriptural.

4. The Bible teaches:
    a) the immortality of the soul, and
    b) the resurrection of the body.

5. Resurrection means the reconstitution of all human corpses and the glorification of the bodies of believers on Judgment Day. (Pieper I, 475

4

ff; III, 507 ff)

Position B
1. Man is a psychosomatic unity.
2. The immortality of the soul is not a Christian, Biblical teaching. Hence several hymns in *The Lutheran Hymnal* ought to be taken out.
3. With regard to immortality, Jehovah's Witnesses are more Biblical than traditional Lutherans.
4. The Bible teaches
    a) no immortality of the soul, but only
    b) the resurrection of the body.
5. It is doubtful what the *"body"* is. The corpse that is buried is not the body, but the mask of the body. The corpse itself is buried never to rise again.

V. De Creatione

Position A
1. God is the Creator of all things.
2. "Where Scripture speaks historically, as, for example, in Genesis 1-3, it must be understood as speaking of literal historical facts." (Synodical Conference Statement on Scripture, Proceedings, 1958, p. 44)
3. Adam and Eve were two real, historical,[a] human individuals, created directly by God. ". . . all men are Adamites, i.e. Adam is the first man and the progenitor of all mankind. This is no theological problem, but a doctrine clearly revealed in Scripture." (Pieper, 477)
4. It is anti-Scriptural and impermissible to hold that man's physical nature originated or may have originated by means of (albeit "theistic") evolution from some other species. "Evolutionism and all that is involved is thoroughly treated and refuted in *Lehre und Wehre*, 46, 8-239; 55, 289-550." (Pieper, I, 470, n 5)
5. Genesis 1 and 2 contain no contradictions.

Position B
1. God is the Creator of all things.
2. A symbolical interpretation of Genesis 1-3 or even 1-11 is permissible.
3. Adam and Eve may be taken as symbols of mankind, and not necessarily as real persons.
4. The theory of evolution, viewed as God's means of creation, cannot be dogmatically denied, but should be left a permissible opinion. (Possible qualification: personally we do not believe in evolution.)
5. Genesis 1 and 2, taken literally, are contradictory.

    [a] An ambiguity may arise here by virtue of the distinction between ordinary, phenomenal, "calendar" history and some sort of transcendental, noumenal "Urgeschichte." Thus, in this sense, Adam and Eve may be said to belong to "real history" (tacitly defined as

5

Urgeschichte"), though their actual existence in the literal sense of Genesis 1-3 may be denied.

VI. De Vetere Testamento

Position A

1. Whatever the N.T. asserts about the hermeneutics or isagogics of the O.T. or any part thereof, is in principle *ipso facto* the dogmatically binding position, to the exclusion, *e limine*, of all other interpretations.

2. St. Matt. 22:41-45 and Acts 2:14,25-31 demand the affirmation, on dogmatic grounds, of the Davidic authorship of Psalms 110 and 16 respectively.

    a) Neither Scripture nor Christ in His humiliation ever taught error.

    b) The theory of accommodationism is to be rejected.

    (Pieper, I, 473)

3. The O.T. directly and consciously predicts a personal Messiah. Jn.12,41; Acts 2, 30-31.

4. The O.T. teaches a blissful immortality for God's believers.

    ". . . Holy Scripture . . . clearly affirms the resurrection of the body in the Old Testament." (Pieper, III, 534-535)

Position B

1. Matters of isagogics and hemeneutics cannot be settled a priori, dogmatically, from the N.T., but, since they belong to the Bible's "history-side" rather than its "faith-side" must be settled on the basis of scientific evidence.

2. St. Matt. 22:41-45 and Acts 2:4,25-31 do not demand the affirmation of the Davidic authorship of Psalms 110 and 16, because

    a) We must take seriously the Knechtsgestalt of Scripture and Christ's state of humiliation.

    b) Christ accomodated himself to rabbinical hermeneutics and to the prevailing isagogical views.

3. The O.T.. contains no rectilinear, predictive prophecies of a personal Messiah.

4. The O.T. teaches no distinction between the fates of the good and the evil after death: Both languish as shades in Sheol.

From *"Theologische Hermeneutik. Leitfaden fuer Vorlesungen,"* CPH, 1912:

Translations by Brandt Klawitter:

"#28. *Die voellige Uebareinstimmung der Schrift mit sich selbst muss bei ihrer Auslegung in voraus feststehen und darf in keinem Falle aufgegeben werden, da bei ihrem goettlichen Urheber eine Inkonsequenz des Denkens, Wollens, und Redens, ein Selbstwiderspruch oder ein auch noch so geringer Irrtum unmoeglich ist . . . . Es ist darum falsch, wenn behauptet wird, dass ein wirklicher Widerspruch in der Schrift vorkomme oder auch nur vorkommen koenne."* (p. 15)

"#28. The complete agreement of Scripture with itself must be granted prior to its interpretation and may not under any circumstances be given up. For with its divine author any inconsequence of thought, will, and speech, any contradiction or even the smallest error is impossible...It is therefore false, when it is asserted, that a real contradiction in Scripture may be brought forward or even could be brought forward." (p. 15)

"#34. . . . *Der christliche Exeget muss darum festhalten, sowohl dass mit dem als Erfuellung der Weissagung berichteten Ereignis Gottes vorbedachter Rat und Plan hinausgegangen ist, als auch dass fuer Verstaendnis und Auslegung der Weissagung der Bericht ueber die Erfuellung entscheidend ist . . . . Bei der Auslegung eines prophetischen Spruches oder Abschnittes des Alten Testaments hat man sich danach umzusehen, ob im Neuen Testament ausgesprochenermassen ueber ein Ereignis als Erfuellung dieser Weissagung berichtet ist. Ist dies der Fall, so ist dem Exegeten die weitere Arbeit und Untersuchung gleichsam abgenommen und auch die Bedeutung einzelner Worte sichergestellt.*" (p. 18)

"#34. ...Therefore, the Christian exegete must maintain not only that God's foreordained council and plan has gone forth with the reported occurrence of the fulfillment of a prophecy. He must also hold that the report about the fulfillment of the prophecy is determinative for its understanding and exegesis...With the interpretation of a prophetic saying or a section of the Old Testament one must also observe whether an event in the New Testament is reported as the clear fulfillment of that same prophecy. If this is the case, then the exegete is unburdened of further work and investigation even as the meaning of particular words is made certain." (p. 18)

" . . . *An dem richtigen Verstaendnis messianischer Weissagungen darf sich der Exeget auch dadurch nicht irremachen laasen, dass sie oft ganz unvermittelt neben zeitgeschichtlichen Reden stehen; vgl. die Umrahmung von Jes.7, 14 Micha 2,12.13 und dazu Luther XIV,1025.1026. Ebenso muss er auch hueten vor der Verkehrtheit mancher Ausleger, die gerade bei solchen Weissagungen einen zwei oder mehrfachen Sinn annehmen und die direkte messianische Beziehung in Abrede stellen,*"(p. 19)

"...with regard to the correct understanding of messianic prophecies the exegete must not allow himself to go astray due to the fact that they often appear quite suddenly next to talk of other contemporary history (e.g. the context of Isaiah 7:14, Micah 2:12-13 and also Luther XIV, 1025-1026 [St. Louis ed.—cf. *Luther's Works, American Edition* 18:227-228]). At the same time he must also beware of the error of many exegetes, who accept two or more meanings of such prophecies and thus deny the direct messianic connection. (p. 19)

From C.F.W. Walther's **Die Evangelisch-Lutherische Kirche die wahre sichtbare Kirche Gottes auf Erden.**

"*Brentiu: 'Wenn Paulus diesen* (18.) *Psalm von Christo auslegt, so ist keine andere Auslegung, selbst nicht eines Engels anzuerkennen.'*

Derselbe: "Da wir apostolische Zeugnisse haben, welche der Grund der Kirche sind, dass dieser (2.) Psalm von Christo, dem Sohne Gottes zu verstehen sei, so ist selbst kein Engel, geschweige ein gottloser Rabbiner, der etwas anderes lehrt, su hoeren." (p. 78)

"Aeg. Hunnius.... 'Allerdings ist derjenige ein Ketzer, welcher einen Artikel des Glaubens leugnet; aber nicht nur dieser, sondern auch derjenige, welcher eine geschichtliche Erzaehlung des heiling Geistes leugnet.'" (p. 122)

"Brentiu: 'When Paul interprets this (18th) Psalm about Christ, no other interpretation, not even that of an angel, is to be recognized.'

From the same: "As we have apostolic witnesses—which are the foundations of the Church—that this (2nd) Psalm is to be understood as pertaining to the Son of God, therefore no angel, much less a godless Rabbi who teaches something otherwise, is to be heard." (p.78)

"Aeg. Hunnius… 'Nevertheless that one is a heretic, who denies an article of faith; not only that one, however, but also he who denies any historic report of the Holy Spirit." (p. 122)

VII. De Praedestinatione

Position A
1. Election is to be understood in the narrow sense as an election unto final salvation which always embraces the "ordo salutis."
2. The Scriptural term "elect" refers to:
    a. only those who will finally be saved;
    b. not Zeitglaeubige
    c. not all men.
3. The "elect" can fall temporarily, but God will surely restore than and bring them to final glory. (*Brief Statement* and *13 Theses* of 1881)

Position B
1. Election is to be understood in the wider sense as an election unto eternal life which believers have now by faith; but which can be lost. Any formulation needs to take seriously all warnings against a false sense of security.
2. The Scriptural term "elect" refers to:
    a. those who will finally be saved, and
    b. also *"Zeitglaeubige"* but
    c. not all men.
3. The individuals to whom the Scriptures apply the term "elect" can

fall; whether permanently we know not and say not.

VIII. The *Brief Statement*

Position A
1. Public teachers of the Missouri Synod are sworn to the Sacred Scriptures and the Lutheran Symbols.
2. Therefore public teachers are bound to the *Brief Statement* as an authoritative statement, in the face of contradictory interpretations, of how the Missouri Synod understands the Scriptures and the Symbols. (Respective resolutions of 1932, 1947, 1956; *Lutheran Witness,* Nov. 10, 1953, p. 7 (379); Oct. 7, 1958, p. 15 (471)

Position B
1. Public teachers of the Missouri Synod are sworn to the Sacred Scriptures and the Lutheran Symbols.
2. Therefore public teachers are not bound to further elaborating and safeguarding formulations, such as the *Brief Statement*.

Respectfully submitted,
Herman Otten
February 8, 1959

Study Questions
1. Some St. Louis seminary professors taught that the Bible contains ____ and ____.
2. Some St. Louis seminary professors taught that we do not ____ to whom the ransom was paid.
3. Some St. Louis seminary professors taught that when it is said that the Church is "invisible" this does not mean the Church cannot be ____.
4. Some St. Louis seminary professors taught that ____ is buried never to ____.
5. Some St. Louis seminary professors taught that the Bible does not teach the ___ of the soul.
6. According to some St. Louis professors, the theory of evolution may not be ____.
7. Evolution and all that is involved is thoroughly refuted in ____.
8. What is "Urgeschichte?" ____
9. Whatever the N.T. asserts about the hermeneutics of the O.T. is in principle ____.
10. Matt. 22:41-45 and Acts 2:4, 25-31 demand on dogmatic grounds that David wrote Psalms ____ and ____.
11. The O.T. directly and consciously predicts a personal ____.
12. Some St. Louis professors taught that the individuals to whom the Scriptures apply the term "elect" may permanently ____.
13. Are public teachers in the Lutheran Church-Missouri Synod bound to the *Brief Statement*? ____

9

§

SASSE OFFERS TO HELP OTTEN – SHARES CONCERNS
Dr. Hermann Sasse to Herman Otten
December 24, 1959

Hermann Sasse
63 Clifton Street
Prospect, South Australia
December 24, 1959

My Dear Rev. Otten:
Please forgive my failure to reply at once. I was in a horrific situation this semester. My wife was seriously ill so that I had to do all the house work in addition to my many duties at the end of the academic year. For many years this is the first Christmas that I have to work in order to cope with urgent obligations . . . so today I can just drop a line to tell you that I have not forgotten you. As to Scharlemann's paper, I agree with you. It is very superficial and untenable, Anglican rather than Lutheran. I enclose our theses on that question. This is mainly my work. I think the *Brief Statement*, written by Pieper 30 years ago, does not answer all of our questions and contains even such doubtful statements that Adam had a perfect scientific knowledge of nature. It must be translated into the language of our time. But if Scharlemann has objections he should go the (?) way as indicated in San Francisco. I am working ____ for them. Unfortunately my contributions are no longer available in print. They are ____ (*Reformed Theol. Review*, Melbourne). What I can find I shall send you, but you must keep them for me. In the whole controversy I am on your side against Scharlemann and Piepkorn. It is a grave violation of Christian love to present that to the young students of Missouri. Your leaders know that grave mistakes have been made. I am just receiving the volume of documents. I am shocked by the treatment you had to undergo. Are you still being victimized?

Please let me know about your present position and your whole situation. If necessary, I will interfere with President Behnken. You cannot be punished for the sins committed by Dr. Sieck. God bless you brother. I shall help as I can. Best wishes and kind regards.

Yours ____,
H. Sasse

I am in a great hurry. Please tell me whether I should implore Dr. Behnken.

Editor's Note: The volume of documents Otten sent is in "Concordia Seminary, St. Louis vs. Otten Case – Book of Documentation – Arranged by Kurt Marquart" now available from Christian News. It includes "A Specification of Doctrinal Issues" signed by Herman Otten on February 8, 1959 and prepared with the help of Kurt Marquart.

* * *

AUSTRALIAN THESES OF AGREEMENT
Sent by Hermann Sasse to Herman Otten
December 24, 1959

7.

(a) Among the signs of the latter times (cf. *Theses on Eschatological Matters*, Preliminary Statement a. par. 2), we must also include the appearance of the Antichrist (Dan. II; 2; Thess. 2:1ff.; 1. John 2:18 and 22; 4:3; 2. John 17; etc.). We recognize that in the interpretation of these passages no full agreement has existed or exists. Such differences of exegesis need not be Church-divisive, provided the interpretation offered does not contradict any clear word of Scripture (cf. *Theses on Principles Governing Church Fellowship*, 4 d and e).

(b) The Confessions of the Lutheran Church teach that "the Papacy is a part of the kingdom of Antichrist" (Apol. XV, 18), because "the marks of the Antichrist plainly agree with the kingdom of the Pope and his adherents" (Tractatus 39), yea, that "the Pope is the very Antichrist, who has exalted himself above and opposed himself to Christ, because he will not permit Christians to be saved without his power" Smalcald Articles, II, iv, 10); cf. also Apol. VII-VIII, 4; XXIII, 25, German text; Tractatus 31-53, 57-59; Formula of Concord, Sol. Declaratio, X, 19-23. We, too, recognize that the Roman Papacy bears the distinguishing features of the Antichrist in greater number, more distinctly, and with greater soul destroying force than in any other known historical person and phenomenon, because

1. The Pope has anathematized the Gospel of the sinner's justification by faith alone;
2. The Pope has introduced into the Church the cult of human beings;
3. The Pope has made himself the Vicar of Christ, claiming infallibility for his arbitrary definitions in matters of faith and morals, even if they are contrary to Scripture or without any Scriptural basis, claiming also absolute rule over the Church and the obedience of all mankind.

(c) In saying this we do not identify the papacy with the whole Church in which it has established itself. With Luther and the Lutheran Confessions (Art. Smalc. I) we recognize that even within the Roman Church remnants of the Gospel and of the true Sacraments of Christ have remained and therefore also true believers in the grace of God in Christ are to be found there. Nor do we deny that there have been and are other persons and phenomena in the world which also bear essential marks of Antichrist (1. John 2:18; 4:1-3; 2. John 7).

(d) The Church cannot definitely state how and in what form the prophecy on Antichrist may still be fulfilled in the future in the Papacy and/or elsewhere. For the sake of their soul's salvation all Christians should at all times be on their guard against the Antichrist and the antichrists and their lying and deceit, recognizing them by the marks whereby they may be known according to the Word of God.

* * *

VIII
THESES ON SCRIPTURE AND INSPIRATION

On December 14th 1950 the Joint Intersynodical Committees resolved to interrupt the discussion on Eschatological Matters by taking up the doctrine of the Scriptures and Inspiration. The seven Joint Meetings and many more subcommittee meetings during 1951 busied themselves with this doctrine. On December 13, 1951, the Joint Committees adopted the following ten Theses, which are herewith presented to our pastors and people for careful study. Any criticisms should be forwarded to the respective secretaries.

*

1. We solemnly reaffirm the Scriptural principle of Luther and the Lutheran Church that "the Word of God shall establish articles of faith and no one else, not even an angel" (Smalc. Art. Pars II, ii, 15; Trigl. p. 467) and declare with the Formula of Concord: "We believe, teach and confess that the sole rule and standard according to which all dogmas together with all teachers should be estimated and judged are the prophetic and apostolic Scriptures of the Old and the New Testament alone" (Epit., de compend. regula 1; Trigl. p. 777).
   We therefore accept the Scriptures, i.e. the canonical books of the Old and New Testaments as the only source and ultimate judge, rule and standard of all doctrine of the Church, also in the doctrines on the Holy Scriptures and on inspiration. In so doing we reject all attempts which have been made even since the Reformation, or may still be made, to introduce into the Church under whatever name other sources of doctrine besides Holy Scripture. cf. Theses on Principles Governing Church Fellowship, 1-3.
2. We teach that the Holy Scripture is the Word of God in writing. As the written Word, the Bible is inseparably bound up with the Word Incarnate and the oral Word. Its proper and essential content is the Eternal Son of God, the Word who was made man in the person of Jesus Christ

12

(John 1:1, 14; 1. John 1:1f; Rev. 19:13; Heh. 1: 1ff: John 20: 20: Luke 24:27; Acts 10:43; 2. Tim. 3: 15ff.). This content it has in common with the oral Word either preceding or following the written Word. Although, therefore, the Word of God is not identical in its totality with Scripture, Holy Scripture is, without limitation, God's Word. Everything which Scripture says is God's Word. On the other hand nothing can be proclaimed as Word of God which is not taught in Scripture.

3. We believe and confess that Holy Scripture does not only contain the Word of God, but that it is God's Word as a whole and in all its parts. We reject as unjustified the attempts made to distinguish between that which is Word of God in the Scripture and that which is not, whether this be done on the plea that Scripture consists of various writings: Old and New Testaments; Law, Prophets and Holy Writings; Euangelion (gospels) and Apostolos (other New Testament writings); or on the plea that a fundamental distinction must be made in the whole of Scripture between the Law and the Gospel.

4. We confess that in the entire Holy Scripture, both in the Old and in the New Testaments, even where it is not immediately apparent, God the Father through God the Holy Ghost proclaims the Son, Jesus Christ, as Savior and Lord (John 3:34; 17:6,14; Matt. 22:44f; John 5:39; Heb. 1:1ff.; Acts 10:43; John 16:13f.; 1. Cor. 2: 3; 2. Tim. 3: 16).
Our belief in the Bible is faith in the Triune God, who speaks to us in the Scripture.

5. We teach with the Confession of the Lutheran Church that Holy Scripture can be rightly understood only by those who believe in Jesus Christ as the Savior of sinners.
We believe that only the *sola fide* (by faith alone) leads to the right understanding of the *sola scriptura* (the Scripture alone), that justification by grace through faith in Christ, the "chief topic of the Christian doctrine .... is of special service for the clear, correct understanding of the entire Holy Scriptures, and alone shows the way to the unspeakable treasure and right knowledge of Christ and alone opens the door to the entire Bible" (Apol. IV, 2 German text; Trigl. p. 121; cf. Theses on Principles Governing Church Fellowship, 5).

6. We teach with the Nicene Creed and with the whole true Christian Church that Holy Scripture is given by inspiration of God the Holy Ghost ("*theopneustos*") 2. Tim. 3:16; 2. Peter 1:19ff. Inspiration in this sense was the unique action by which God the Holy Ghost gave to men He chose His Word of revelation for oral proclamation or for written recording, so that of this their spoken or written word it must be said without limitation that it is God's own Word. 1. These. 2:18.

7. We teach inspiration in this sense not only of the individual oral or written words of the prophets (2. Peter 1: 19ff.), of the apostles (1. Cor. 2:13; 1. Thess. 2: 13), of the psalms (Matt. 22:43; Heb. 3:7) and of the Law (Matt. 5:17ff.), but of "all Scripture" (2. Tim. 3:16), i.e. the Scriptures as a whole (John 5:39; 10:35; 2. Tim. 3:15) and in all single passages (John 2:22; 7:38; Acts 1:16; 8:32) and words (1. Cor. 2:13) of the Old and New Testaments (2. Peter 3:16).

13

8. We teach the verbal and plenary inspiration of the Scriptures (2. Tim. 3:16); 2. Peter 1:21; Rom. 3:2; 1. Thess. 2: 13; 2. Thess. 2: 15; 1. Cor. 2:13; 1. John 1:1-4; Rev. 2:7,11,17; Jer. 1:9), but we reject the various theories (mere divine enlightenment, mechanical dictation, etc.) which have been offered as an explanation of the "how" of inspiration, or by which the verbal and plenary inspiration is in any way limited or denied. Scripture teaches the fact of inspiration, but is silent on the "how," i.e. on the manner or method. The latter has not been revealed and therefore remains an inaccessible divine mystery; we cannot know how God the Holy Ghost worked the miracle that human words became His Word.

9. We confess that Holy Scripture as the Word of God written by men is at the same time both divine and human. In defining the relationship between the divine and human side of the Bible we could use the analogy of the divine and human nature of Jesus Christ, the Word Incarnate; of the divine and human word in absolution; of the real presence of the body and blood of Christ in, with, and under the bread and wine in the Sacrament of the Altar. But we limit ourselves to what Scripture clearly teaches about the divine and human character of the prophetic Word. God is the prime and absolute source and origin of all revealed truth. But it pleased Him to give His Word through "holy men" who spoke and wrote as they were moved by the Holy Ghost (2. Peter 1: 21). Thus it is God Who chose certain men, whom He knew before He created them (Jer. 1:5; cf. Isa. 6:8ff. and Ezek. 2: 1ff.), to be His prophets at a certain time and to certain people. It is God Who for that purpose sanctified (Jer. 1:5; Isa. 6:6f.) sinful men and put His Word into their heart and mouth (Isa. 6:7; Jer. 1:9; 15:16; Ezek. 2:8; 3:2f.). The fact that God dealt with each of the prophets in a different way shows that the personality, character, way of thinking and speaking of the individual man were not extinguished. It is God again Who gave the command to write (Ex. 17:14; Jer. 30:2; 36:2; Rev. 1:11; 14:13) and inspired the holy writers. But they retained their individuality and were not exempt from the labor, methods and responsibility of human authorship (Luke 1:1ff.; John 21:24; Acts 1:1; Rev. 1:11; Pauline epistles; Psalms). Thus the Bible has a truly human side. We therefore teach and confess that it pleased God to give us His Word under, or in the garb of, the human word of the Biblical writers.

10. As the Word of God, Holy Scripture is the perfect (Psalm 19:7), authoritative (John 10:35), sufficient (Gal. 1:f.; Rev. 22:10), and essentially clear (2. Peter 1:19; Psalm 19:7f.; Psalm 119,105) revelation of divine truth (John 17:7). As God's Word written by men and for men, Holy Scripture presents this truth in such a way that it can be appropriated by men. With the whole true Church of God we confess the Bible to be the inerrant Word of God. This inerrancy of the Holy Scriptures cannot be seen with human eyes, nor can it be proved to human reason; it is an article of faith, a belief in something that is hidden and not obvious. We believe that the Scriptures are the Word of God and therefore inerrant. The term "inerrancy" has no reference to the vari-

ant readings found in the extant textual sources because of copyists' errors or deliberate alterations; neither does it imply an absolute verbal accuracy in quotations and in parallel accounts, such absolute uniformity evidently not having been part of God's design. We believe that God used the holy writers as children of their time and that they retained the distinctive features of their personalities (language and terminology, literary methods, conditions of life, knowledge of nature and history as apart from direct revelation and prophecy). God made use of them in such a manner that even that which human reason might call a deficiency in Holy Scripture must serve the divine purpose. Furthermore, it pleased the Holy Ghost to employ authors possessing various gifts for writing on the same subject. How in such cases it is possible that differing accounts of the same event or the same saying are the true and inerrant report of one and the same fact cannot and need not always be shown by rational harmonization. We must believe it until "that which is in part shall be done away" and "that which is perfect is come" (1: Cor. 13:10). We reject the attempts of modern religious liberalism to make man the judge of the Word of God. None of the natural limitations which belong to the human mind even when under the inspiration of the Holy Ghost can impair the authority of the Bible or the inerrancy of the Word of God; for Holy Scripture is the book of divine truth which transcends everything called truth by the wise men of this world (1. Cor. 1:17ff., 27; Col. 2:8) and is therefore able to make us "wise unto salvation" (2. Tim. 3: 15).

*

IX
THE LUTHERAN CONFESSIONS

The discussions on the Attitude towards the Lutheran Confessions were initiated at the Joint Meeting of April 24th, 1952. On the basis of a statement submitted by Dr. Hamann and on the basis of theses drafted by Dr. Sasse, the following theses on the Lutheran Confessions were unanimously adopted at the Joint Meeting on September 25th, 1952.

1. With the fathers of the Lutheran Church in Australia, who came to this country as confessors of the Biblical truth expressed in the Lutheran Confessions, we solemnly reaffirm as our own confession the Confessional Writings of the Evangelical Lutheran Church as they are contained in the *Book of Concord*.

2. With the *Book of Concord* we teach that creeds and confessions are necessary for the Church as a means to

    (a) summarize the true doctrine of the Word of God ("compend and brief summary of all the Scriptures," *Large Catechism*, Preface 18, Trigl. p. 573; "sum of our Christian doctrine," Sol. Declaratio, De comp. regula 11, Trigl. p. 855);

    (b) express the common consent ("magnus conseusus," C.A.I, Trigl. p. 43) not only with the believers of today (Sol. Declar., De comp. regula 1 and 2), but also with the true Church of all ages from the time of the Apostles and the ancient creeds to the end of the world ("coram tota ecclesia," Sol. Declar., closing paragraph, Trigl. p. 1103);

(c) reject error and heresy (Preface to the *Book of Concord*, especially Trigl. p. 19; Epitome, De comp.regula 2 and 3, Trig!. p. 777) and thereby fight the...

Study Questions
1. When did Hermann Sasse first offer to help Herman Otten? ____
2. Sasse wrote that he was on Otten's side against ____ and ____.
3. What was the "volume of documents" Otten sent Sasse in 1959? ____
4. What has the Pope anathematized? ____
5. What is the only source of Christian doctrine? ____
6. Everything which Scripture says is ____.
7. Holy Scripture not only contains the Word of God but ____.
8. With the whole true Church of God we confess the Bible to be the ____ Word of God."
9. Holy Scripture is the book of divine truth which transcends everything called ____.

§

"COVER UP"

New Haven, Missouri
January 4, 1960

Professor Hermann Sasse, D. Th.
63 Clifton Street
Prospect, South Australia

Dear Professor Sasse:

Thank you for your kind letter of December 24.

As soon as possible I shall send you an essay in which Dr. Scharlemann mentions your position. When Dr. Scharlemann appeared before the N. Illinois District Pastoral Conference of our Church, he again attempted to quote you as being in support of his position. One of my friends is mimeographing the minutes I took at this conference and I will send you a copy.

Thank you for enclosing the *Theses on Scripture and Inspiration.* I will return the other material you mention in your letter.

Enclosed are a few extra photostats of some articles I've had in my files. I have written to Dr. Pelikan but he never answers any questions.

16

I doubt whether it would do much good for you to write to Dr. Behnken in regard to my case. He agrees with the Board of Control, insisting on the peculiar *per se* principle and that Matthew 18 applies in all cases regardless how public the matter is. We have spoken at great length about the doctrinal confusion in our Church. So far no official action has been taken and every effort is being made to "cover up."

The "hearing" has been set for January 20. I have competent counselors but we would appreciate your prayers. May the Lord preserve our Church.

With kindest regards,
Sincerely,
Herman Otten

(Ed. The counselors were Dr. Siegbert Becker of Concordia Teacher's College, River Forest, Illinois, Pastor Kurt Marquart, Weatherford, Texas, and Pastor Walter Niewald, New Haven, Missouri)

Study Questions
1. Otten sent Sasse an essay by ____.
2. Who never answered Otten's questions? ____
3. Otten told Sasse that every effort was being made to ____.

§

ST. LOUIS SEMINARY
STILL SELLING SASSE'S LETTER

Jan. 22, 1960
Box 192
Concordia Seminary
801 DeMun Ave.
St. Louis 5, Mo.

Prof. Dr. Theol. Hermann Sasse
41 Buxton Street
North Adelaide, S. Australia

Esteemed Dr. Sasse,

We view your recent publication, *This is My Body,* as a great contribution to Lutheran theology and to all who are interested in the true exposition of Scripture. We appreciate especially the solid manner of presentation whereby the important issues are always in the forefront, and the appealing style of writing. Most of all we appreciate the conviction expressed concerning the truth of the Scriptures as God's infallible

17

Word to man.

Possibly you will recall your "Letter Number 14" of June 1950, in which you stated your position on the inerrancy of Scripture in the negative. We know from your book and from your excellent statement at San Francisco in June of 1959 that the Spirit has led you in the opposite direction. For this we thank God.

Nevertheless we have cause for concern about that letter. It is still being printed and disseminated. At the present time it is available in the Seminary Print Shop for thirty cents, under the title, *De Scriptura Sacra: The Doctrine of the Written Word,* translated by R. Gehrke.

This presents serious concerns for us and for you as well. First, there are those who are not aware of the fact that you no longer hold this previous view of Scripture, and who therefore quote you as an authority for a position you no longer hold. Second, the whole area of revelation as you presented it has been taken over by several religious leaders in this country.

We sincerely desire and request, therefore, that you prepare another letter answering the arguments you yourself have posed in the former letter. Such a document would not only vindicate you, but would also be of great help to the brethren here and everywhere, and would further the cause of the true doctrine expressed in the *Brief Statement.*

This is a large task, but it would not be without good fruits. We are led to the conviction that you are in a special position to offer convincing statements in this matter, since you yourself have struggled through the entire question. Furthermore, the extreme joy among many of our clergy over your book will give you a hearty reception from most readers. Finally, we feel that your acquaintance with the German mode of thought, and especially that of J.C.K. von Hofmann, will enable you to meet the issues squarely, fairly, and victoriously.

To that end may the brilliant light of truth from our Epiphany Lord shine brightly to guide your work.

Very Respectfully,
Kenneth K. Miller
Karl Lutz

Study Questions
1. Kenneth Miller and Karl Lutz informed Sasse that his essay ____ was being sold at the print shop of Concordia Seminary, St. Louis.
2. Miller and Lutz asked Sasse to prepare ____.

§

SASSE'S CONCERN FOR
ST. LOUIS SEMINARY

Ed. Both Missouri Synod liberals and conservatives claim Dr. Hermann Sasse supports their position. When we were involved in the Concordia Seminary-Otten case almost 10 years age, we wrote to Dr. Sasse for a theological opinion on the use of Matthew 18 and some advice which we could use when we argued our case before the Board of Appeals of the Lutheran Church-Missouri Synod.

In 1958 we told Dr. John W. Behnken, then president of the Missouri Synod, and a few others that there were professors at Concordia Seminary teaching that the Bible contains errors and various other doctrines contrary to Holy Scripture. Concordia Seminary argued that we had violated Matthew 18 because we did not have a private conversation with every professor we mentioned in our conversation with Dr. Behnken. Concordia Seminary argued that it was always sinful under all circumstances to repeat disturbing public matter without first conducting a private conversation. Dr. Sasse's reply shows that already nine years ago he was greatly concerned about the theology being taught at Concordia Seminary.

* * *

65 Clifton Street
Prospect, South Australia
April 18, 1960

Mr. Herman Otten
New Haven, Missouri

Dear Mr. Otten:
Thank you for your letter of April 5 and for the confidence you show me. I do not want to interfere in any way in matters concerning the faculty of St. Louis. On the other hand, it is my principle never to refuse any theological advice for which I have been asked from where ever the request may come. So I want to answer briefly your question. But will you kindly allow me to send a copy of this letter to one of the members of the faculty whom I know personally and who, as I am convinced, is certainly most concerned about the whole case. For such a serious disagreement between a student and his faculty is most regrettable.

I am surprised that just in this case such measures have been taken. If you have spoken to a pastor of your Church about what you regarded as false doctrine, you have done what many of your fellow-students have done. As a matter of fact, everywhere in the Lutheran world the situation at Concordia Seminary has been and is being discussed. I have heard from so many quarters comments on what many people regard as a hopeful situation, scil. That the old theology of Missouri as represented by the *Brief Statement*, is dying out The names of professors with whom you had difficulties are quoted everywhere. As far as I know there are even publications at your seminary (*The Seminarian* or what is the title, I have not seen it) in which theological views are discussed and defended which are supposed to be contradictory to the traditional theology of your Church. So I wonder why just you have been accused of what, as far as I know from other Churches, has been done by other students or former students. You have at least spoken to one of your pastors, others have publicized their opinions in wider and different circles. I cannot know why just your case has become so important.

As to your questions, Matt. 18 does not in itself refer to false doctrine, e.g. if a person has given grave offence in the Church by spreading false doctrine. Matt. 18 refers to the local Church, not a community like the community of teachers and students in the seminary. For there is not equality, but a relationship of subordination. Your professor is not only your brother – this he is definitely not in his capacity of teacher – but your "father" in the sense of Luther's explanation of the Fourth Commandment in the *Large Catechism* (par. 1141). It applies also to the teacher in his relationship to the student (see also Paul's usage of "pater" and "teknon") what Luther says: "Hence also they are called fathers in the Scriptures, as those who in their government perform the functions of a father, and should have a paternal heart toward their subordinates" (141, Trigl. 621). The ethical question seems to me to be: Have you kept the Fourth Commandment towards your professors, and have they fulfilled the duties of spiritual fathers? For there is a reciprocity of duties, as you know. The secular ruler loses his divinely given authority if he does not fulfill his duties towards his subordinates. It is this question which has to be discussed. You are not their equals. They can destroy your academic career, you cannot destroy theirs. I do not know what discussions have preceded your talk to your pastors. I presume that some lively discussions have taken place in the classroom and outside. This would, as far as I can see, suffice for a professor to know what the attitude of a student is. In any case a student should let his professor know that and why he rejects certain views taught. If that has been done, nothing more can be required. If this has not been done, it is a grave omission, but not necessarily a violation of the law of love. For everything a professor says in the classroom is said in public, just as everything a pastor says from his pulpit. It may happen . . . and it take the responsibility for such deviation. In his study he may think what he wants. In his lectures he may present the problems in all sincerity. What he publishes he must be prepared to answer. If he has not a final answer, he must refrain from publicly teaching such matters, but rather frankly confess that he has no solution.

Your case seems to be an outcome of the situation of your faculty. Everybody knows that some of your professors have publicly taught things which are not reconcilable with the Lutheran Confessions. They have done so bona fide in a situation in which certain doctrinal issues must be discussed again. I am convinced that they themselves will see their mistakes. The Mariology e.g. put forward by Dr. Piepkorn even in Germany or in a German translation is untenable. So is the prayer for

20

the dead. Also what has been circulated throughout the world by another man concerning the Bible is untenable, as the author himself will probably see himself if he continues his studies. It should never have happened that the satisfactio vicaria or the truths about the soul and its destiny after death could be rejected or the Lutheran idea of the Church be abandoned. Of course, it was and is necessary to rethink some of the most outstanding doctrines as presented by Pieper and the *Brief Statement*. But as the situation appears from what you have sent me, the old fight between modernism (Heidelberg) and fundamentalism is now going on in St. Louis, the same fight which has been going on during the last generation in other Churches. The worst which can come out of such controversies are disciplinary matters. Nothing is settled by disciplining students for the failure of the Church and the facility to settle great doctrinal issues in the proper way and in time before a bellum omnium contra omnes starts.

I do not know whether my reply can be of any help. I am very much concerned about Concordia Seminary which is and ought to remain the last stronghold of confessional Lutheran theology. The eyes of the world are directed to St. Louis. The enemies of the Lutheran Church hope that this fortress will fall. There must be found a solution to the personal as well as to the theological questions. Without a Christian solution of such a case as yours I cannot see any way out of the great emergency of which it is a symptom.

With all good wishes for your future and kind regards,
Yours Sincerely,
H. Sasse

Don't be discouraged dear brother. I am sending a copy to my friend Franzmann. He will keep it confidentially and also any action you take. The great mistake is to make men like Piepkorn and Scharlemann professors before they have got a sufficient hearing.

Study Questions
1. The St. Louis seminary maintained that it was always under all circumstances a sin to repeat a disturbing public matter without first having a ____.
2. Sasse sent a copy of his response to Otten to ____.
3. According to Sasse, if a student has publicly challenged the position of a professor nothing more should be ____.
4. Sasse wrote that many were aware that some St. Louis professors were publicly teaching things not reconcilable with ____.
5. Sasse insisted that the Mariology put forth by Dr. Piepkorn is ____.
6. According to Sasse, the material Otten sent him showed that the old fight between modernism and fundamentalist was going on at ____.
7. Sasse wrote that the enemies of the Lutheran Church hoped that ____ would fall as a fortress of confessional Lutheranism

EVEN THE BEST CONSERVATIVES
HESITATE TO TESTIFY VS. COLLEAGUES

New Haven, Missouri
April 22, 1960

Dr. Hermann Sasse
63 Clifton Street
South Australia

Dear Dr. Sasse:

Many thanks for your kind letter of April 18. I am particularly pleased that you sent a copy of it to Professor Franzmann. Kurt Marquart hopes to persuade Professor Franzmann to testify at our hearings in May with regard to the positions of Drs. Scharlemann and Hummel. It seems as if even our best conservative men hesitate to publicly state that they cannot agree with their colleagues. Unfortunately, Professor Franzmann and I have not been able to agree whether the steps prescribed by our Lord in Mt. 18 must be followed in every case of public false doctrine, but Professor Franzmann has definitely rejected some of the views proposed by Drs. Scharlemann and Hummel.

By this time you have probably heard that our Home Mission Division has joined the Home Mission Division of the National Council of Churches (NCC). This action has been hailed by other Lutherans as a significant "crack" in the seawall "which has traditionally separated the Missouri Synod Lutherans from other Church bodies in the ocean of world Protestantism" (*Lutheran Herald,* December 29, 1959, p. 16). Our congregation here in New Haven has petitioned our District to ask Synod to reconsider this step. A few days ago I received a copy of a letter which was sent to all 600 lay delegates present at the San Francisco Convention. The letter commended them on the *Brief Statement* resolution but informed them about certain matters that have happened since then.

Thanks again for taking time out from your busy schedule.

With kindest regards,
Sincerely,
Herman Otten

P.S. I assume you will not object if I send your letter to Kurt Marquart, one of my counselors. You also met him this summer in S.F.

Study Questions

1. Even the best conservative men hesitate to testify against ____.
2. The LCMS's Home Mission Division joined ____.

§

LUTHERANS FORFEITING THEIR HERITAGE

by Hermann Sasse

(The following is an editorial from *Lutheran News*, November 11, 1965, "Are We Forfeiting Our Heritage?" By Dr. Hermann Sasse in the October 22, 1965 *Christianity Today*. Dr. Sasse teaches at Immanuel Theological Seminary in Adelaide, Australia. He was formerly professor of Church history at the University of Erlangen and active in the World Conference on Faith and Order.)

In Germany, where this humanism is organizing itself as "the Third Church" (besides Catholicism and Protestantism), the situation is similar. The Lutheran ministry is undermined by the theology of Bultmann and his disciples, the moderates among them being the most dangerous because their nihilism is hidden behind some orthodox phrases and pietistic sentiments. It happens again and again that they will not seek ordination. As one of these honest men declared to his bishop (this happened in the Church from which Bultmann comes), "I could perhaps preach on an ordinary Sunday. But how could I preach at Christmas or Easter? I cannot preach on myths." He is right. The gaps are filled with girls who crowd theological lecture halls. Some of the bishops, pious and conscientious Lutherans, refuse to ordain them. But most of them have no objections, especially since the new hermeneutics (is not that the art of making the Bible say what we want to hear?) and the "evangelical" understanding of the New Testament "which makes obedience to Christ's commandments "legalism" support them, to say nothing of the great authority of Karl Barth, also on their side.

Thus the Church of the Reformation perishes in the old Lutheran countries. Ranke, the great historian of the Reformation, once said: "The German nation has one great love, and this was Luther." It has been stated that today no one loves Luther any more. We could perhaps add: with the possible exception of some Catholics who have just discovered him. But who loves Luther in Germany, in the Scandinavian countries, and in the Lutheran Churches of America, where they do not even understand him?

Will we forfeit the heritage of the Reformation? We Lutherans are rapidly doing so.

Study Questions

1. The Lutheran Ministry is being undermined by ____.
2. The gaps are filled with ____.
3. The Church of the Reformation perishes in ____.

23

§

CONVERSATIONS WITH ROME

By Dr. Hermann Sasse, 1950 Translated by M.C. Harrison

Christian News, August 14, 2000

We had come as far as that fifty years ago, and should already then have known how mistaken it was to return in our theology to the words of God given in Holy Scripture for the Church and her theology, here given in a way not dependent on human opinions, and not having to be first discovered by some "scientific methodology." Liberalism lives on as ever it did, and when was it ever otherwise? In Liberalism we have the return of Erasmian Humanism and of the Enthusiasts of whom Luther says in the Smalcald Articles, "Enthusiasm lurks in Adam and his children from the beginning to the end of the world. This poison, implanted by the old dragon, is the source, strength and power of all heresy, also of the papacy and Muhammedism." (III, 8, 9)

If this is indeed the way things always go, then it would be most extraordinary if this were not also the case with the greatest and most dangerous of all heresies with which the Church of the gospel has had to contend: Roman Catholicism. Out of the struggle with this the Lutheran Church was born. As long as the Gospel and Roman Catholicism confront each other, this struggle cannot cease, then that would be a sure indication that the Lutheran Church was no longer Church of the Gospel. It may perhaps come to that. Perhaps it has already come to that in part of what was once Lutheran Christianity. As long as the Church of the Reformation continues, the struggle with Rome will go on. Neither party has the option to end the struggle. Each knows what the other is, or believes that it knows. In certain circumstances Rome can be very tolerant toward Protestantism. There can be very friendly conversations with the Evangelicals. Rome can show itself willing to learn. This in in fact happening in our day as is evidenced by the Catholic Bible movement. Rome has taken to herself evangelical chorales including the festival of hymns of Luther. All this we can also see happening in Germany today. With some forceful persuasion Johann Sebastian Bach can also be converted. Does it not indeed belong to the nature of the Roman Catholic Church to be so comprehensive as to have a place for all partial truths, and be able to include them into that Church where the whole of catholic truth is to be found?

The test case is Martin Luther. There is evidence of his being understood to a certain extent, and in our day to a quite astonishing extent.

24

But it is impossible to approve, accept, or to assimilate Luther. For Catholics, and even for the piously ecumenical, Luther is the heretic. The condemnation of 1520 still stands. This is the dogmatic judgement and the foundation of post-Tridentine Catholicism. This remains irreformabilis; it cannot be revised. For the pope, and with him then every Roman Catholic this judgement stands to the end of the world.

Then the Roman Catholic Church will stand with this judgement seat of Christ, and will be judged by him. What also still stands is the judgement which Luther gave when he burnt the papal bull and the Roman Canon Law. This was still a part of his solemn confession at the end of his life. It was not some fit of anger that prompted him to name the pope as the Antichrist. At that time there were faithful Catholics who did the same. Luther was fully aware that his judgement would have to be answered for before the judgement seat of God. For him it was a part of doctrine, of the Christian doctrine of the Church. He knew well "what lies ahead for me to answer for in the final judgement of the Lord Jesus Christ." He was aware of what he time and again said to himself. "If this is wrong, then you are guilty of so many souls going to hell." To affirm that the pope is the Antichrist, and everything that follows from that, is indeed something that Luther will have to answer for before the judgement seat of Christ, and with him the Lutheran Church which either makes this affirmation its own, or at least tolerates it, and has not struck it from the Smalcald Articles. If it is indeed the case that the pope is there in the place of Christ, then what a failure to grasp the truth, indeed what a sin in Luther's judgement, a judgement it must be said that does not strike the individual pope as a man but his office. Also upon this, God will give his judgement at the Final Judgement.

What a truly tragic situation for Christianity! Is the pope the Vicar of Christ on earth or is he the Antichrist? That is the question that it is finally all about in the discussions between Evangelicals and Catholics that have gone on for centuries. Upon all that has been said God will give the final judgement at the Final Judgement.

Study Questions
1. According to Sasse, ____ is the most dangerous and greatest of all heresies.
2. As long as the Lutheran Reformation continues, the struggle with ____ will go on.
3. For Catholics, Luther is ____.
4. Luther insisted that the pope was the ____.

§

THE CHURCH DIES FROM APOSTASY, NOT MARTYRDOM

From Cyberbrethren, A Lutheran Blog
October 8, 2013

"The blood of the martyrs is the seed of the Church" so the ancient saying goes. In this excerpt from a letter Hermann Sasse wrote to Lutheran pastors around the world, in 1954, he puts his finger precisely on the source of the Church's great struggle and greatest danger: apostasy from the Christian faith. We have seen this apostasy growing ever stronger throughout liberal mainline Protestantism of all stripes.

"The Church is not dying from martyrdom, but apostasy. How did it happen, that a small booklet, which appeared in 1848 under *The Communist Manifesto* [1948], has gained such a power over minds? It began in the Christian countries. Karl Marx [1818-1883] was the son of the baptized Jew, but his closest collaborator, Friedrich Engels [1920-1895], came from a pietistic factory family in Wuppertal, one of the many pious families which have always been such loyal supporters of missions. And they found their followers among Europe's workers, Catholic and Protestant. And now, this small book, which became the catechism of Europe's workers, has become the confession of uncounted millions throughout the entire world, perhaps the most-used textbook in contemporary humanity, the contents of which even illiterates learn. What does this mean? Does it indicate that the power of the Christian faith has been extinguished, or that the Christian missionaries and the Islamic missionaries in Africa, and you will be shocked, even if you consider that the figures aren't comparable. Consider Islam's power. Consider that our mission had its great successes among the primitive people, but that there has not yet been a break-through into one of the main high religions of Asia. We do not want to minimize in any way the rich harvest which God has, despite everything, still granted to our mission work. With nothing but thankfulness can we consider the sometimes superhuman work which our missionaries, and not only the Lutheran ones, perform under conditions of unspeakable difficulty. But the big question can't be silenced, whether Christendom as a whole hasn't lost something. It is not only the changed world situation, the awakening of various people-groups who now continue the nationalism of our nineteenth century and thence steer straight into communism, which makes our work so difficult. It must be a deep sickness, which has taken from Christendom of all denominations the power which it once had. Such a sickness once destroyed the Churches of Africa and Asia, save for a small remnant, as many Christians could hardly wait until they became Muslims and could thereby escape the special tax which they had to pay. A similar sickness is passing through Europe's Churches today. It is useless to close one's eyes to it. It doesn't help, if [we renovate] the altar [and make it] higher and prettier, or if more and more clergymen march out in pompous robes. We have nothing against a good liturgy and a liturgical movement. But if that is supposed to be a substitute for the absent congregation and for the lost confession, then that is a sign that the Church is terminally ill. It won't help, either, if theology becomes more and more subtle, and whenever possible uses a language which an ordinary mortal can no longer understand. Even that can't be a substitute for that from which the Church lives. That is the theology which can be prayed, like the great theology of the Middle Ages and of old Lutheranism. That is the theology like the Nicene Creed [A.D. 385] or the Augsburg Confession [1530]. That is the theology which even children can already learn, like the *Small Catechism* [1529]. If we had such a theology, then the Church would be helped in many respects. One need only to consider the repulsive vanity and glory-seeking of modern theologians of all denominations in order to remark that something here is wrong, that the secularization of the spiritual life is located in exactly that place from which the cure should come."

Sasse, *Letters to Lutheran Pastors* #35, September 1954

Study Questions
1. The blood of the martyrs is the ____ of the Church.
2. The Church is dying from ____.
3. Karl Marx was the son of a ____.
4. It doesn't help if we make altars ___ and clergymen march in ____.
5. Good liturgy is not a substitute for ____.

§

ALC LUTHERANS CLASH ON INERRANCY OF THE BIBLE
Lutherans Alert Charge that Some ALC Leaders Defend Theological Liberalism
Christian News, December 26, 1966

A controversy on the inerrancy of the Bible continues to trouble the American Lutheran Church, (ALC) one of the three major Lutheran bodies in this country. An editorial in the December, 1966 *Lutherans Alert*, a theological journal published by conservative Lutherans in the ALC, claims that "there seems to be a concerted effort on the part of the leadership of Synod (ALC, ed.) to foist on the membership a new theological liberalism with regard to the Scriptures which will in turn allow all sorts of theological peculiarities."

Rev. David Moke, a contributing editor of *Lutherans Alert*, writes in the December issue that "the hierarchy of the ALC is vehement in its aim to destroy the Truth of Scripture. It is very sad when President Schiotz in his essay, 'The Church's Confessional Stand Relative to the Scriptures' emphasizes a false and liberal view of Scripture which is not Lutheran

27

nor Scriptural. Forcing contradictions on Scripture passages which are not there (p. 2) and then claiming that, 'One could go on in this manner' shows his lack of humility before God's Word."

Rev. Mikkel Lono, another contributing editor of *Lutherans Alert*, states in the December issue of the publication: "Among printed material mailed to ALC pastors by Augsburg Publishing House is a pamphlet entitled, 'The Church's Confessional Stand Relative to the Scriptures.' This is a reprint of an address by Dr. Schiotz delivered to two district conventions in 1966. It purports to set forth the stand of the American Lutheran Church concerning the inspiration of the Scriptures, which, he said, is that the inerrancy claimed in the confession of the Church refers not to the text but to the truths revealed in the text."

Lono claims that "IN THIS ADDRESS THE AUTHOR CLAIMS THAT THERE ARE CONTRADICTIONS IN THE BIBLE, and if it contradicts itself it cannot be inerrant. . . Three instances are given in the address, suggesting that many more could be given."

After explaining the "contradictions" Schiotz lists as being found in the Bible, Lono writes: "Dr. Schiotz said: 'ALC holds that the inerrancy referred to here (namely, in the constitution) does not apply to the text but to the truths revealed for our faith, doctrine and life.' Dr. Schiotz holds this, but not ALC. Even should Dr. Schiotz prevail upon a convention of the Church to so declare it would not be the official position of ALC. That is declared in the UNALTERABLE words of the fourth article of the constitution which states very clearly: 'The American Lutheran Church accepts all the canonical books of the Old and New Testaments as a whole and in all their parts as the divinely inspired, revealed and inerrant Word of God, and submits to this as the only infallible authority in all matters of faith and life.'"

Sasse on Schiotz

The December *Lutherans Alert* also contains excerpts from a letter written by Dr. Hermann Sasse, a prominent Australian Lutheran theologian quoted by Schiotz in his "The Church's Confessional Stand Relative to the Scriptures." Sasse wrote to Rev. Raymond Larson, Vice-president of *Lutherans Alert*, that Schiotz's "quotations from my articles are correct, but taken out of their context and therefore apt to misunderstandings." A *Lutherans Alert* editorial, entitled "A Word of Testimony from Dr. Hermann Sasse," concludes:

"Will you, dear readers, give the widest possible exposure to this issue so that as many as possible of those who read Dr. Schiotz's article might have this correction made in their thinking?

"Dr. Sasse does not espouse liberal theology! He does hold the INERRANCY of the TEXT of Scripture! For his testimony we thank God!"

Lutheran News and Schiotz

Lutheran News has had some correspondence on inerrancy with Dr. Schiotz, who is president of both the ALC and the Lutheran World Federation, during the past few months.

The June 28, 1966 *Lutheran Standard* said in a report titled, "Inerrancy of Bible Applies to Truth, Not Text, Schiotz Tells North Pacific District": "In interpreting the ALC Constitution, which speaks of the Bible as 'Inerrant,' Dr. Schiotz said that inerrancy does not apply to the text but to the truth revealed for our faith and life. He cited Luther to back up his contention that the authority of the Bible is not to be based on textual inerrancy."

Lutheran News wrote to the ALC president on July 1, 1966: "Could you kindly tell us whether the report 'Inerrancy of Bible Applies to Truth, Not Text Schiotz Tells North Pacific District' in the June 28, 1966 *Lutheran Standard* is accurate?

"The *Lutheran Standard* report appears to indicate that you believe the Bible contains errors of fact. Do you believe The Lutheran Church-Missouri Synod's definition of inerrancy is correct as it is found in paragraph one of *A Brief Statement*: 'Since the Holy Scriptures are the Word of God, it goes without saying that they contain no errors or contradictions but that they are in all their parts and words the infallible truth, also in those parts which treat of historical, geographical, and other secular matters John 10:-35?'"

Dr. Schiotz replied on July 15: "Your letter of July 1 awaited me as I returned from the annual meeting of the Church Council of the American Lutheran Church. In this meeting the Church Council asked that I make available to our congregations the address made at the North Pacific Convention of the ALC. This will probably be sometime in the fall. At that time you will have to draw your own conclusions."

The October 31, 1966 *Lutheran News* reported:

Schiotz on Inerrancy

Dr. Schiotz received 758 votes out of a total vote of 873 on the first ballot for nomination of ALC president. He was declared president of the ALC after receiving 813 out of a total of 903 ballots cast on the second ballot.

Dr. Schiotz is also president of the Lutheran World Federation (LWF) and serves on the Central Committee of the World Council of Churches.

In a sermon at the communion service opening the General Convention of the ALC, Dr. Schiotz emphasized the all-inclusiveness of the Communion table. He called upon Church members to support the efforts of those working against discrimination. President Schiotz has been criticized by some in the Church for his statements on civil rights issues. This past summer he urged Lutherans to back the program of Dr. Martin Luther King.

Some ALC conservatives have been critical of Dr. Schiotz's stand on the inerrancy of the Bible. Dr. Schiotz states in "The Church's Confessional Stand Relative to the Scriptures," an address distributed at the General Convention here: 'Let us turn to the American Lutheran Church and its teaching regarding the Scripture. The constitution states, 'The American Lutheran Church accepts all the canonical books of the Old and New Testament as a whole and in all their parts as the divinely inspired, revealed, and inerrant Word of God, and submits to this as the only infallible authority in all matters of life.' The ALC holds that the inerrancy referred to here does not apply to the text but to the truths revealed for our faith, doctrine and life. The ALC has not voted this statement in a general convention. I base this interpretation on a number of factors."

Dr. Schiotz then lists his reasons for claiming that the ALC does not hold to the inerrancy of the original text of the Bible.

He says that "First of all, the four antecedent Churches did not use the word 'inerrancy' in their constitutional statements although the former ALC had a footnote wherein this was used. The UNITED TESTIMONY does not use the word 'inerrancy' in the absolute sense, but calls the Bible 'the only inerrant and completely adequate source and norm or Christian doctrine and life.'"

In his arguments against the inerrancy of the Bible, the ALC president is not merely saying that various manuscripts contain copyist errors.

Propaganda

On November 14 Dr. Schiotz wrote *Lutheran News* in connection with some correspondence concerning Pastor Richard Wurmbrand. "Your October 31st issue of *Lutheran News* and its report on *my* address to the North Pacific and Southeastern Minnesota District conventions of the ALC is an excellent illustration that you are more concerned about propaganda than truthful reporting."

Lutheran News replied:

"We would also appreciate if you could let us know how we misrepresented your address to the North Pacific and Southeastern Minnesota District conventions of the ALC. We want to be entirely truthful. Perhaps you could tell us whether you agree with the *Brief Statement of the Doctrinal Position of the Missouri Synod* when it says: 'Since the Holy Scriptures are the Word of God, it goes without saying that they contain no errors or contradictions but that they are in all their parts and words the infallible truth, also in those parts which treat of historical, geographical, and other secular matters, John 10:35.'"

The ALC president answered on November 21: "You inquire for an illustration of how you misrepresented my address to the North Pacific and the Southeastern Minnesota District conventions of the ALC. On page two in columns one and two of the *Lutheran News* for October 21, 1966, you state: 'Dr. Schiotz then lists his reasons for claiming that the ALC does not hold to the inerrancy of the original text of the Bible.' By inserting the words, 'the original text of the Bible,' you have completely misrepresented what I said."

The editor of *Lutheran News* replied on November 23:

"When you say in the essay we quoted in our October 31 issue that 'The ALC holds that the inerrancy referred to here does not apply to the text,' are you merely referring to the text which we have today? In your opinion does the ALC insist on the inerrancy of the original text of the

Holy Scriptures in all matters, including historical, geographical, and other matters? It appears to me that the entire context of your statement concerning 'inerrancy' indicates that you are not just referring to some relatively minor copyist errors.

"Permit me to ask again whether you agree that 'Since the Holy Scriptures are the Word of God it goes without saying that they contain no errors or contradictions, but that they are in all their parts and words the infallible truth, also in those parts which treat of historical, geographical, and other secular matters. John 10:35.'

"Perhaps the best way for us to straighten out this entire matter would be to reproduce your address on 'The Church's Stand Relative to the Scriptures' in *Lutheran News*. May we have your permission to do this?"

Dr. Schiotz answered in December:

1: "You and I have access to the same scriptural text, a text that is based on thousands of fragmentary manuscripts. I could not, therefore, in my essay speak of anything other than the text that is known today. Your interpolation in your October 31 issue of *Lutheran News* of the phrase, 'the original text,' is, in my judgment, misrepresentation.

"No, I cannot give my permission for you to print the *Church's Confessional Stand Relative to the Scriptures*. This is an address that was given to official district conventions of the American Lutheran Church and was printed by request of the Church Council for distribution to ALC pastors."

According to the October 26, 1966 *Minneapolis Star*, the 1966 General Convention of the American Lutheran Church "took no action on a petition from ALC congregations in Kenyon, Minn., and Tacoma, Wash., disputing an essay by the Dr. Fredrik A. Schiotz, Minneapolis, ALC president, on whether the Bible is without error.

"Dr. Schiotz' essay, given to two district conventions during the past summer, had maintained the ALC does not hold that the Bible text is without errors. It holds, however, that the truths of the Bible are not affected by any possible errors, he said.

"The requests had urged a two-year study of Dr. Schiotz' essay claiming it was contrary to the Church's traditional understanding."

"The appeal failed to reach the convention floor since all requests must come from districts or the ALC Church Council."

Study Questions
1. ALC President Schiotz claimed that the inerrancy referred to in the confession of the Church did not refer to the ____ of the Bible but to the ____.
2. Dr. Schiotz was also president of ___ and served on the ____ of the ____.
3. Schiotz urged Lutherans to back the program of ____.
4. Did Schiotz give *Christian News* permission to reprint his "The Churches Confessional Stand Relative to the Scriptures?" ____

31

§

SASSE – SCHIOTZ – INERRANCY

Bleckmar, Germany
December 19, 1966
(Home Address:
6 Wellington Square
North Adelaide
South Australia)

Editor, *Lutheran News*
New Haven, Mo.

Dear Brother Otten:
Your letter of November 23 was forwarded to me from Australia. As
to the address by Dr. Schiotz, "The Church's Confessional Stand Relative
to the Scriptures," I am not very happy about it. The good doctor does me
the great honour of quoting from articles of mine. I cannot quite understand what my personal views have to do with the official teaching of the
American Lutheran Church as it is presented by texts quoted pp. 6ff.
Even there it does not become clearer what is official teaching of the
Church and what private views of individuals or suggestions made by a
committee. It seems to me that the American Lutheran Church has at
present no clear and unambiguous stand concerning the doctrine of Holy
Scripture. It has a heritage, expressed in the Constitution and in the
United Testimony and it is striving for a new formulation which, how-
ever, has not been reached yet. It is certainly the right of any Lutheran
Church to redefine its doctrine in such matters if the circumstances demand that, provided that the confession of the Church is not altered
thereby.

It may be assumed from the wide circulation of the address that it
wants to point to a future solution of the problem. If this is so, it deserves
thorough examination. Its author would probably be the last to resent a
critical discussion, provided such criticism is competent and dictated by
a deep concern for the maintenance of the pure scriptural and confessional truth. If you should publish a critical article it should be clear that
such concern and nothing else in your motive.

If I may say a word in reply to your request I should like to point out
that I am not quite happy about the way Dr. Schiotz has selected passages from my articles. Taken out of their context they might suggest
that I reject the inerrancy of the Scriptures. The contrary is true. What
I try to do is to show how the inerrancy of Scripture must be understood

in view of what our human reason might regard as error. To evaluate these articles they must be read in toto. Since they have been written in connection with the union negotiations by the Australian Lutheran Churches it would have been advisable to quote our Theses of Agreement concerning this doctrine in which we have reached full agreement as the basis for our new Lutheran Church of Australia. These theses which are easily accessible to everyone have much more authority than any private publication.

Dr. Schiotz's article suffers, if I may add this, from oversimplifications, and not only in his conclusions from the passages quoted from the articles mentioned. The decision of the Ancient Church concerning the Biblical canon was much more complicated than the article suggests. Many synods in East and West had to busy themselves with the problem. The issue was not what "we believe", but rather which writings had to be made practically unanimously. That guided democracy Church has become a feature of Modern Protestant synods was unknown to the early Church. Unknown to the early Church as to the Church of all ages before modern rationalism began to influence Christendom was the conviction expressed by some of Dr. Schiotz's theologians that the believer's "best efforts to formulate a theology in terms of propositions and statements will fall short. To assume that the Church can arrive at human concepts or expressions that are in every respect correct is as much a symptom of pride as to assume that the Church or its members can achieve sinlessness in their daily lives" (p. 9). Although on the same page "the disdainful use of such terms as orthodoxy, neo-orthodoxy, liberalism, nationalism, pietism, fundamentalism, modernism" is forbidden, we dare to call this rationalistic and pietistic nonsense. In so doing we are in the good company of Martin Luther, who in his great discussion with Erasmus' rejection of firm and clear dogmatic statements, showed that this dogmatic way of thinking and speaking belongs to the very nature of Christianity: "Tolle assertiones, et Christianismum tulisti." "Take away the firm dogmatic statements, and you have taken away Christianity" (Weimar Edition 18, 603). One must read the first pages of *De servo arbitrio* to understand that the denial and possibility and necessity of firm dogmatic statements was to Luther the end of the Christian faith. We refuse to believe that this is the conviction of the American Lutheran Church as long as this Church confesses the Apostles' and the Nicene Creed in its services and sings joyfully the *Te Deum* with its assertions.

This may suffice to show the direction in which a fraternal admonition addressed to the American Lutheran Church has to move. We can only hope that this Church with venerable tradition of true Lutheran theology will come to a truly Christian and Lutheran solution of the great problem of a re-definition of the doctrine of Holy Scripture, with which all Churches are confronted today.

You will allow me to send a copy of this letter to Dr. Schiotz.

Yours very sincerely,

Hermann Sasse

x x x

Dear Brother Otten,

This is my reply. I am sorry for the delay. I am at present in Germany and hope to be in St. Louis and Springfield in the midst of January on my way back from Australia.

With best wishes and the greetings of this holy season.

H. Sasse

I leave it to you if you want to publish it.

Study Questions
1. Sasse was not happy that Schiotz had ____.
2. Luther said take away firm assertions and you take away ____.

§

RESPONSE TO SCHIOTZ ADDRESS SASSE AFFIRMS INERRANCY

Christian News, January 6, 1967

Dr. Hermann Sasse, world famous Lutheran theologian, has informed *Lutheran News* that, contrary to some reports, he affirms the inerrancy of Holy Scripture. *Lutheran News* had asked Dr. Sasse to comment on the use Dr. Fredrik Schiotz, president of the American Lutheran Church and Lutheran World Federation, had made of some of his articles on the inerrancy of the Bible.

Dr. Schiotz had quoted the theologian to support his position on the inerrancy of the Bible during an address he delivered to two district conventions of the American Lutheran Church during 1966. Dr. Schiotz denied *Lutheran News* permission to reprint the address.

Dr. Sasse wrote *Lutheran News* from Bleckmar, Germany, on December 19: "If I may say a word in reply to your request I should like to point out that I am not quite happy about the way Dr. Schiotz has selected from my articles. Taken out of their context they might suggest that I reject the inerrancy of the Scriptures. The contrary is true." Dr. Sasse's entire letter is on p. 16.

Lutheran News wrote Dr. Schiotz on December 23: "We will be glad to publish any response you may care to send to the letter by Dr. Sasse or the December 26 *Lutheran News*. Since you have refused us permission to reprint your essay on 'The Church's Confessional Stand Relative to the Scriptures, could you kindly tell us where we may direct interested readers to write for copies of your essay? We are particularly concerned that

34

officials of the Missouri Synod study your essay."

Dr. Sasse was called to the chair of Church History, History of Doctrine, and Symbolics at Erlangen University, Germany, in 1933, where he taught until 1949. Since 1949 he has served on the faculty at Immanuel Theological Seminary in North Adelaide, Australia. He has been a guest professor at Concordia Seminary, Springfield, Illinois, and is the author of several books and more than 300 major articles.

§

SASSE – SHIOTZ INERRANCY ARTICLES

January 8, 1967
Dear Herman,

A reading yesterday of the Sasse-Schiotz inerrancy articles in the current Lutherans Alert suggested the thought that you might like to have an excerpt from the ELCA Queensland Pastoral Conference Minutes of Aug. 15-17 (Toowoomba) for background information. I am also sending a copy to Kent Spaulding.

The other materials enclosed are of varying interest.

A blessed new year in our Savior!

Cordially,

Harold Romoser

Has Scharlemann said much more than this?

x x x

Dr. Sasse opened the discussion on inspiration and inerrancy by expounding on the Theses of Agreements on Scripture and Inspiration. Examples of Bible difficulties were cited, such as the time of the crucifixion and the different accounts of the raising of Jairus' daughter. Attempts have been made to harmonize these things, but we don't have to harmonize them to satisfy our reason: "We still accept the inerrancy of Scripture," he said.

Dr. Sasse claimed that Genesis 1-3 are not real history. The real history begins with the calling of Abraham. We cannot imagine how things were before man. Genesis 1 describes things beyond our imagination and therefore they cannot be described literally in human words, hence these things must be taken as pictures or symbols, as in the book of Revelation. Augustine tried three times to interpret Genesis 1 literally without success. He stated that no one can say what a day is in Genesis 1. Where does a day begin or end? What is meant by the seventh day? Can we really believe that the stars and the vast universe were created only after the earth? For these questions we have no answers. That is why the Church has never dogmatized on the days. A literal interpretation of Genesis 1 is impossible, he said.

Dr. Sasse questioned the statement in the Declaration and Plea that there can be no contradictions in Scripture. There are contradictions to our human reason. There are contradictions in God for example when He told Hezekiah that he would die, and then added fifteen years to his life, also God's wrath and His love are contradictions.

Pastor Marquart asked Dr. Sasse for a definition of "inerrancy". He defined it as the absence of errors, that there are no false statements in the Bible. Yet the O.T. writers follow ancient methods of historiography, e.g. numbers were not meant statistically but rather as round figures of adjectives: "big", "very big", etc. The number of an army was always exaggerated in ancient times. This was not regarded by them as a lie. So the O.T. writers wrote for their times and had no intention of telling a lie. According to our standards these things could not correspond to fact. We should not apply our categories of historiography to the ancient writers of Scripture. The 18,000 carpenters working on the temple was probably not meant as an accurate figure. Luther said he could not imagine so many working on the temple, Dr. Sasse said.

Pastor M. Grieger asked Dr. Sasse to define truth. Dr. Sasse claimed that the absence of falsehood is a philosophical concept of truth, a theological concept of truth includes more, also steadfastness and faithfulness. The truth of the Exodus story remains truth even though mathematically the numbers (600,000) may not have been correct. Dr. Sasse holds that in Genesis 1 God simply wants to tell us that He, through his mighty Word, created the world, and that the creatures were created in sequence. The creation story presupposes that the earth is older than the stars and the galaxies because they speak to simple people like us and Moses. "My grave concern is that the Church makes the same mistake as in the time of Galileo", said Dr. Sasse.

In a paper on "Sacred Scripture and the Holy Spirit" Hamann, Jr., writes: "The orthodox presentation of this mystery (inspiration) in all likelihood is historically surveyed a variation of ancient heathen views of inspired writings. Dr. Sasse has produced a convincing array of evidence for this in an essay of his entitled: *Sacra Scriptura: Bemerkugen zur Inspirations lehre Augustins,* where the following summary sentence is found:

"Es gehoert ze den grossen Tragoedien der Kirchengeschichte, dass die Christenheit unter den Autoritaet des groessten der Kirchenvaeter eine Theorie durch die Jahrhunderte zu schleppen hatte, die nur muehsam verchristlichte Gestalt einer heidnischen Lehre von inspirierten Schriften ist."

Study Questions
1. According to the ELCA Queensland Pastoral Conference Minutes, Sasse claimed that Genesis 1-3 is not ____.
2. No one can say what a ____ is.
3. Marquart asked Sasse for a definition of ____.

SASSE SEEKS MEETING WITH OTTEN

St. Louis, Jan. 14, 1967
Dear Brother Otten.
I am here at Concordia for a few days. On Tuesday I shall proceed to Concordia, Springfield until Saturday, 21st. On the 22nd I am to see Dr. Schiotz in Chicago before leaving for home. I would like to see you, but cannot see how this is possible. Any message reaches me at Concordia, Springfield.

    With kind regards,
    Yours sincerely,
    H. Sasse

§

CONCORDIA SEMINARY SPRINGFIELD HONORS SASSE WITH D.D.

The degree of Divinity was bestowed upon Professor D. Hermann Sasse, Th.D., during a special convocation-chapel service held in Immanuel Lutheran Church. Springfield, earlier this year. Dr. Sasse was presented by Dr. J.A.O. Preus, president of Concordia Theological Seminary, Springfield. The degree was conferred by Dr. Fred Kramer, academic dean.

Dr. Sasse's convocation lecture was on "Rome and the Reformation: *Sola Scriptura*". Dr. Sasse delivered two additional lectures while he was on the campus. One lecture was on "Thoughts on the Eve of the Reformation Jubilee of 1967", followed by a lecture on "Rome and the Reformation: The Doctrine of Sin."

Dr. Sasse is being honored by Concordia Seminary, Springfield, in recognition of his work as a confessional theologian and modern day professor of the truth. His commitment to the Lutheran Confessions, inspired by his devotion to sound Biblical theology, is coupled with a genuine ecumenical concern. Dr. Sasse played a major role in the negotiations which led to Lutheran Union in Australia.

Dr. Sasse's lectures on the campus of Concordia Seminary, Springfield, are the first of a series of special academic and religious events which will commemorate the 450th anniversary of the Reformation. On October

31, a special lecture will be delivered by Dr. Jaroslav Pelikan of Yale University, followed by lectures on Luther and Justification, and Luther and the Church. The latter will be delivered by members of the seminary faculty.

Lutheran Journal (Australia)
LJ Spring 1967

§

SASSE RESPONDS
TO UNAUTHORIZED PUBLICATION

(We are publishing these letters because Concordia Seminary, St. Louis, had been selling an essay "Letter 14," on Holy Scripture by Dr. Hermann Sasse after he had made it clear that he no longer defended the position he took in this essay on the doctrine of the inerrancy of the Bible. It appears to us that certain liberals within the Lutheran Church-Missouri Synod have been quoting from this essay in order to make it appear that Dr. Sasse supports their anti-scriptural notions. Dr. Sasse's "Letter 14" was again referred to at the New York convention by a liberal Missouri Synod professor, who argued that if Dr. Sasse would not affirm the doctrine of the Inerrancy of the Bible neither should the Missouri Synod. Ed.)

(Dr. Sasse was Professor of Church History at Erlangen, Germany from 1833 to 1949, when he moved to Adelaide, Australia. He teaches there at Luther Theological Seminary, and maintains active contact with Church developments in Europe and America both in study and travel. "Holy Church Or Holy Writ? The Meaning of the *Sola Scriptura* of the Reformation," one of his latest studies, is available from the Intervarsity Christian Fellowship; 1519 North Estor Street, Chicago 10, Illinois, $.45. Ed.)

6 Wellington Square
North Adelaide; South Australia

June 17, 1967
The Rev. Herman Otten
New Haven, Missouri

Dear Brother Otten:
Thank you very much for your letter of May 11 which reached me these days (please notice the change of address). Many thanks for the copy of my "Letter 14" which you purchased on May 10 at the bookshop at Concordia St. Louis. I am shocked by this matter. Some years ago I wrote to

38

the students responsible for the unauthorized publication, and simultaneously to Dr. Fuerbringer strictly forbidding further duplication and sale of it. I called the attention of the students to the fact that their act was not only an infringement of the law, but also a grave violation to the Seventh Commandment to say nothing of the human side of the affair. I forbade any further circulation of this document. I received an apology from the students who promised they would obtain from further publication. From Dr. Fuerbringer I received a reply to the effect that boys are boys. I must try that I can still find this correspondence. I had called the attention of Dr. Fuerbringer to the bad consequences which such practice must have on the human and theological education of future pastors. They had to learn to respect the law and to respect also the human rights of theological authors.

There has been a discussion going on in Australia and elsewhere of the questions I raised in that letter, written in 1950. We all have learnt a lot meanwhile. I have corrected certain statements in the subsequent letters and have written a lot on the problem. I was always sorry that our American brethren were of no great help to us when we in Australia had to seek a solution to the great problem of the doctrine "De sacra scriptura." So this whole affair was and is of certain importance for our Church here.

I simply cannot understand how after my correspondence with St. Louis this misuse of my letter could arise again. I have been at St. Louis twice during these years, for one term I was lecturing traveling from Springfield where I was a guest lecturer and I stayed a few days at Concordia this year. I have not discussed the matter with Dr. Fuerbringer or anybody else, nor have I been in the student's book store. It seems to me that a new generation of students who did not know of what had been going on had been encouraged, I do not know by whom, to take up the duplication and sale of the paper again. They seem to have not even contacted Dr. Gehrke. He would have been upset, especially since he knows that I gave to Dr. Jungkuntz a revised version which was to be published together with other papers of mine. I know that neither these nor other friends of mine in America would have approved of this action of the students at St. Louis. I shall ask for their help. Unfortunately, the academic year is now over. But I shall announce to those responsible that I would have to take legal action. I shall demand that the sale be stopped and the unsold copies be destroyed.

I ask myself where else such a dirty business could happen, printing and selling without authorization the works of an author. If this is indicative of any trend in that Church which we all have loved and honored, then one might despair of its future. But I cannot think that this is the case.

I send a copy of this to Drs. Gehrke and Jungkuntz. Once more I thank you for your thoughtful action in writing to me and sending the copy.

With fraternal greetings,

Yours sincerely,

Hermann Sasse

x x x

6 Wellington Square
North Adelaide,
South Australia.
29th June, 1967

Student Bookstore,
Concordia Theol. Seminary,
St. Louis, Missouri, U.S.A.

A friend of mine sent me, these days, a duplicated copy of an article of mine which I had written in 1950, in the translation of my friend, Dr. Ralph Gehrke. He had just purchased it at your store. Several years ago this article was published by your bookstore without my permission. This was regrettable as the essay, written during our Australian discussion of the doctrine of Holy Scripture contained formulations which I could not maintain. It was one of my letters to Lutheran pastors. Immediately after this I corrected what had to be corrected in the subsequent letters and made a thorough investigation of the Patristic material. No one seems to have taken cognizance of these corrections although the publications came into the same hands as the first article. In the following years I have published several more articles which are available in your library. But just the first letter was reprinted again and again by your store. I wrote to Dr. Fuerbringer as well as to the manager of your store. I called his attention to the fact that such an unauthorized publication which went on for years was a grave violation of the international Law of Copyright, apart from the moral aspect of the matter. Your store promised that it would not occur again.

Now the production has been taken up again. Had I known of this I should have spoken to your President, as well as to you on the occasion of later visits to St. Louis. Now you seem to compel me to take legal action against you to protect my rights as author. Before I do this, I ask you firstly to inform me at whose request you have resumed the production and sale of the 17-year-old article? Secondly, why after my correspondence you have not contacted me or Dr. Gehrke? The latter knows that the article has been revised and that the revised text is in St. Louis ready to be printed. Thirdly, I demand from you that the sale of this paper is immediately discontinued and that the stencils as well as the still existing copies are immediately destroyed. Fourthly, that you inform me that my requests have been complied with.

I must frankly confess that I am at a loss to understand how this could happen at Concordia Seminary, St. Louis. I have always found the students of your seminary friendly, helpful, and co-operative. I have meanwhile lectured to a large class for a whole quarter and was impressed by the seriousness of these Christian young theologians. I assume you have been misused by powers outside your institutions.

A copy of this letter is being sent to your president, to the dean of stu-

40

dents, to Dr. Harms, and to some other men who know me and who will be shocked by this sad affair.

Sincerely,
Hermann Sasse

§

WITHDRAWN SASSE ESSAY - STILL FOR SALE AT ST. LOUIS SEMINARY

July 7, 1967
Dr. Hermann Sasse
6 Wellington Square
North Adelaide, South Australia

Dear Dr. Sasse:

Many thanks for your letter of June 17.

May we have permission to use your letter in order to publicize the fact that the sale and distribution of your August, 1950 "Letter No. 14" does not have approval?

A friend of mine noted on June 22 that it was still for sale at the St. Louis seminary bookstore. There really doesn't seem to be much that can be done to stop the liberals from distributing this letter. Several years ago Dr. Alfred Fuerbringer promised Dr. Harms that Dr. Martin Scharlemann's essay The Bible as Record, Medium, and Witness would not be sold at the seminary. However, I purchased copies of this "withdrawn" essay at the seminary after Dr. Fuerbringer had made his promise to Dr. Harms.

Fraternally,
Herman Otten
*

Hermann Sasse
6 Wellington Square
South Australia, 5006
15th July, 1967

Rev. Herman Otten,
The Editor
Lutheran News
Box 168
New Haven, Missouri, U.S.A

Dear Brother Otten,

Thank you for your letter of July 2. You may make use of what I wrote concerning the sale of my "Letter No. 14". I enclose a copy of a letter I wrote to the Student Bookstore at Concordia, St. Louis. You may make it short but so that the readers understand that this duplication was unlawful and that I had protested in vain against it. I have had no reply from St. Louis. It may well be that the same people who were interested in distributing Scharlemann's essay are behind the publication of my letter. But this is only personal suspicion of mine.

With greatest interest I read the copy concerning the appeal of your congregation. I showed it to Dr. Hoopmann, who has just visiting me. We both were, as you know, never happy about the former decision of Missouri. We are glad that now the decision has been reversed. I cannot see what the consequences may be for you and for your congregation. I have repeatedly written in this matter to Dr. Behnken and I know that also he was far from happy about the whole affair. I can, of course, give no advice as to what should be done. You must leave it to Missouri to take the first step.

I assure you once more of my deep sympathy. We are looking forward to hear about the results of the Synodical Convention which must be over by now. We were expecting that the great decisions concerning LWF and ALC may have been postponed to the next Convention. We are just discussing, in Australia, our future relationship to the overseas Churches. The trouble is that our Churches today are like ships rapidly moving and constantly changing their course. The principle of Church fellowship as practiced in the past were based on the assumption that the Churches were more or less stationary. Who would ever have anticipated that even the Roman Catholic Church could go through such revolutionary changes as we are experiencing today.

Should you see Pastor Noack, the Honorary President of our Queensland District, give my regards to him. I shall try to answer his letter as soon as possible. At present I am having some heart trouble and cannot write as much as I should like to do.

May God give you wisdom and guide you and your congregation in the decisions you have to make. With kindest regards and every good wish.

Yours Sincerely,
Hermann Sasse

P.S. I shall send you, for review, a little book *Holy Church or Holy Writ - The Sola Scriptura of the Reformation*. It may be ordered from the Inter-Varsity Christian Fellowship, 1519 North Estor Street, Chicago 10.

Study Questions
1. Sasse was glad that ____ had been reversed.
2. "The trouble is that our Churches today are like ships ____."

§

HOLY CHURCH OR HOLY WRIT?

The Meaning of the *Sola Scriptura* of the Reformation
By Hermann Sasse
The 1967 IVF Lecture in Queensland

THE AUTHOR

Dr. Hermann Sasse, trained in theology and classics at Berlin, was, after years of active service in the ministry of the Lutheran Church in Germany, Professor of Church History at Erlangen from 1933 to 1949 when he moved to Adelaide. He teaches there at Luther Theology Seminary, and maintains active contact with Church developments in Europe and America both in study and travel. In numerous books and articles published over the past forty years he concerned himself especially with the ecumenical movements of the time and their theological implications. The present study arises from the decision the authority of Scripture made at the Second Vatican Council.

I

HOLY WRIT or Holy Church. The Crisis of the Protestant Reformation is the title of an important book which the well-known French-American Catholic theologian George H. Tavard published in 1959[1]. Father Tavard belongs to a school of theological thought in the Roman Church which had given up the traditional view that Scripture and Tradition are two different sources of revelation and tried to replace it by the assumption that there is only one source of revelation, namely Holy Scripture, while tradition is the interpretation of Scripture by the authoritative teaching office of the Church. Tavard's book, well written and based on a new study of the sources, mainly those of the Middle Ages and of the English Reformation, helped to pave the way for the sweeping victory which this new school of thought won right at the beginning of the Council when the 'schema' on the 'Sources of Revelation' (De fontibus revelationis) was rejected by the majority of the bishops. Carefully prepared by a number of conservative theologians this draft of a dogmatic constitution dealt elaborately in five chapters with the following problems:

  1. The Double Source of Revelation. 2. The Inspiration, Inerrancy and Literary Form of Scripture. 3. The Old Testament. 4. The New Testament. 5. The Holy Scripture in the Church.

The document was presented by Cardinal Ottaviani, the head of the Preparatory Theological Commission.

In the ensuing debate which began on 14 November, 1962, one Cardinal after another arose to reject the scheme. Said Cardinal Lienart (Lille):

  This schema is not adequate to the matter it purports to deal with, namely Scripture and Tradition. There are not and never have been two sources of revelation. There is only one source of revelation-the Word of God, the good news announced by the prophets and revealed by Christ. The Word of God is the unique source of revelation. This schema is a cold and scholastic formula, while revelation is a supreme gift of God-God

43

speaking directly to us. We should be thinking more along the lines of our separated brothers who have such a love and veneration for the Word of God. Our duty now is to cultivate the faith of our people and cease to condemn.[2]

Liénart was followed by Frings (Cologne):

The primary purpose of a Council is to provide for the pastoral needs of the day, to teach the truth, to stimulate its preaching in such wise that it will be received.

Comparing the schema with texts presented to the First Vatican Council of 1870 which had been criticized for their scholastic approach, the Cardinal continued:

What is even worse than the manner of presentation is the doctrine itself. Why speak of two sources of revelation? This is not traditional and only in recent centuries, as a result of false historicism, have certain theologians tried to explain the matter thus.

Frings continued:

What is said here of inspiration and inerrancy is at once offensive to our separated brothers in Christ and harmful to the proper liberty required in any scientific procedure.

While Cardinal Ruffini supported the schema and Ottaviani's defense of it, and while others, like the Archbishop of Genoa and the Cardinal Archbishop of Compostella, declared it to be a sufficient basis for the discussion of the great problem, quite a number of outstanding bishops and members of the College of Cardinals took the side of Lienart and Frings. Cardinal Bea recognized in a fair and balanced verdict the merits of the great work put into the schema but found that the whole direction of this work had been wrong. It did not correspond to the purpose of the Council. 'What then did the Pope have in mind?' when he summoned the Council. He desired

that the faith of the Church be presented in all its integrity and purity, but in such manner that it will be received today with benevolence, for we are shepherds[3].

The debate went on for almost a week. Then came one of the most dramatic moments of the Council and perhaps in the history of the Roman Catholic Church. A vote was taken on the question whether the schema should be retained as the basis of the discussion. Out of the 2,209 fathers present 1368 voted for the interruption of the discussion of the schema, while 822 wanted the discussion to be continued. However, as the standing rules required for a decision of this nature a two-thirds majority (which would have been a majority of 1473) the conservative majority had won. This might have led to a deadlock the whole work of the Council had not Pope John intervened. Making use of the power of the pope over the Council he ordered the schema to be withdrawn. A special committee under the joint chairmanship of Cardinals Ottaviani and Bea was to be appointed to prepare another document. The result of their work is the 'Dogmatic Constitution on Divine Revelation' (*Dei verbum*). The first draft of the new document was ready in 1963 for the Second Session. It underwent further improvements before it was discussed by the Council briefly at the Third and finally at the Fourth Session. The definitive vote was not taken until November, 1965, shortly before the end of the Council. It was adopted almost unanimously and promulgated by Pope Paul on 18 November.

II

THE DRAMATIC story of this document shows how important the problem it tries to solve was and is to the Roman Church, and not only to this Church. The question of the nature and the authority of the Word of God is today, along with the question of the Church, its nature its authority, its unity, foremost in the mind of all Christians on earth. It is one of the great discoveries of Christendom in this century of revolutionary changes that in spite of all divisions and separations the Christians and the Churches of whatever denomination are bound together by the strange solidarity of common history. They experience the same joys and disappointments, successes and failures, opportunities and frustrations.

Great spiritual movements, healthy or unhealthy, spread through the whole of Christendom irrespective of denominational borders. It is by no means so as it was believed forty years ago that the fall of one Church means the rise of another. They are all confronted with the same enemies the same emergencies Together they rise, together they fall.

It was the Eastern Orthodox Church which had to learn this in the Russian Revolution of 1917 and in the extinction of the earliest Christian Churches by the Turks in Asia Minor a few years later. In vain the Ecumenical Patriarchate of Constantinople issued, in January, 1920, its touching encyclical, 'Unto all the Churches of Christ wherever they be', trying to bring home to the Churches of the West this truth and to persuade them to form a 'League of Churches'[4]. Today we all know of this common destiny that binds us together. Even the great theological issues are everywhere the same. To many it was a great surprise that the Second Vatican Council had to deal with exactly the same problems, ecclesiastical and theological, that are on the agendas of our synods and conferences. This is no surprise to the Church historian. For he knows that this has always been so. What is new is that the Churches have begun to draw their conclusions from these facts; unfortunately, as the sad history of the Ecumenical Movement shows, often wrong conclusions.

If we look at the reasons given by the majority of the bishops for their rejection of the schema proposed by Ottaviani's Commission, three recur all the time. First, the document did not correspond to the purpose of the Council, which was meant to be a pastoral Council rather than a Council summoned to define theological doctrines. Secondly, it would not serve the ecumenical aim of the Council to bring about a rapprochement with the separated brethren on either side. Thirdly, it was said to contain, a false doctrine in the unquestioned assumption, expressed already in the title, that there are two sources of revelation, namely Scripture and Tradition. In these three reasons, which are closely interconnected, the great change which has taken place in Roman Catholicism during the last decades finds expression. This change had become noticeable in the 'new theology' which in Western and Central Europe arose during the pontif-

45

icates of Pius XI (1922-39) and Pius XII (1939-58) and which slowly gained ground, especially in the years after the Second World War, in Rome also. Under Pius XII, who was fully aware of the situation, Rome stood at the cross-roads.

The accession of John XXIII marks the turning point. The Roman Church as we knew it, the Church of the Syllabus, of the First Vatican Council, the Church which was always at loggerheads with the modern world, had come to its end. A new era began of which no one can know where it will end. The exciting debates, the passionate controversies, the obvious breakdown of a centuries-old discipline within Roman Catholicism, the revolutionary excesses in the Catholic Churches in America and the Netherlands, are indicative of a deep spiritual crisis within the largest Church of Christendom which may well end in the breakdown of its organization, in the disintegration of the vast body of the Roman Church.

Even the Roman Catholic Christian who firmly believes in the divine institution of the papacy cannot completely rule out the possibility that in future centuries the Pope, the Patriarch of the West, may share the destiny of the patriarchs of Alexandria, Antioch, or Constantinople without, of course, ceasing to be for the faithful remnant of the Roman Church the successor of Peter and the Vicar of Christ with all the prerogatives of the primacy.

We modern Protestants, who are used to getting our information about the history of the Church in our time either from the sensational reports of *Time* magazine or, what is still worse, from our official Church papers which are always inclined to glorify their own denomination, should refrain from all malicious self-complacency, as if our poor and weak Church bodies obviously had the power to survive such a catastrophe. It could be a catastrophe for all Christendom. Nor should we think that this crisis of the Roman Church will lead to a wonderful ecumenical Church in which every Christian and every community which calls itself Church could find a proper place after the terrible dogmatic attitudes of former centuries had finally been overcome. Such a 'Church', as certain ecumenical enthusiasts envisage it, the great future Re-united Church, based on a minimum of Christian faith and on a maximum of ecclesiastical and secular politics, would most certainly not be the Church of Christ, but the kingdom of Antichrist, while the true Church of Christ, as the little flock to which our Lord has promised the Kingdom (Luke 12:32), would pray in its catacombs the 'Maranatha' (I Cor. 16:22) of the first Church, 'Amen, Come, Lord Jesus', in firm belief in his promise: 'Surely, I am coming soon' (Rev. 22: 21) .

III

ONE MUST keep in mind the situation of the Roman Church at the beginning of the Council in 1962 if one wants to understand the reception which the schema *De fontibus revelationis* found and the document which was finally accepted in 1965. One of the great tasks of the Council was to finalize the unfinished business of the First Vaticanum and to settle certain problems that had arisen from the decisions of this Council which had never finished its work. It had to be adjourned sine die after the Italian army had conquered Rome in September, 1870, and the Papal State had ceased to exist. Since it had never been formally closed it was an open question whether a new council, as it had already been envisaged by the predecessors of Pope John, would have to be regarded as a new session of Vatican I. John XXIII decided that the Council of 1869/70 had to be regarded as closed since none of its members was still alive.

That Council had finalized two dogmatic constitutions, the 'Constitutio Dogmatica de Fide Catholica' and the 'Constitutio Prima de Ecclesia Christi'. The former dealt with the problems of the divine revelation, the acceptance of this revelation, the nature of faith, faith and reason. In dealing with the divine revelation it affirms the doctrines of Trent on Scripture and Tradition and the sole right of the magisterium of the Church to interpret the Scriptures authoritatively. It goes beyond Trent by defining the dogma of the inspiration of Scripture. Immediately after the Council the great debate in the Roman Church on the doctrine of the inspiration of Scripture and its consequences began. The Modernist controversies gave to these problems a great urgency. The great Bible encyclicals from 1893 to 1943 tried to develop the doctrine. It was unavoidable that the new Council had to make a solemn declaration on this issue which had become one of the most vital questions of the Roman Church and of all Christendom.

Not less urgent was another legacy of Vatican I, the unfinished dogma of the Church. The elaborate schema of a dogmatic constitution 'De Ecclesia Christi' which was put before the Council could not be debated. Only one chapter of it, the dogma of the papacy, was finalized as the famous 'Constitutio Prima de Ecclesia Christi'. Everyone knew that a coming council would have to take up the matter. A great amount of theological work was done by Catholic scholars to prepare a later solution of this problem. The encyclical *Mystici Corporis* issued by Pius XII in 1943, was generally regarded as a forerunner of a 'Constitutio Secunda de Ecclesia Christi' to be expected from another council.

It is beyond the scope of this essay to discuss what has been proclaimed by the Second Vaticanum as a 'Dogmatic Constitution on the Church'. It gives a most important doctrine on the Church and tries to overcome the one-sidedness of the constitution of 1870 by adding the doctrine of the College of Bishops as the successor of the College of the Apostles, while it re-affirms the doctrine of the bishop of Rome as successor of Peter and Vicar of Christ. Through it is de facto the supplement to the constitution of 1870 it is not called 'Constitutio Dogmatica Secunda de Eoclesia Christi'. *Lumen mundi*, as it is called after the first words, is a dogmatic constitution, as *Pastor aeternus* of 1870 was and also the new document on Revelation (*Dei verbum*) is a dogmatic constitution. Its doctrinal content must be accepted by all Catholics. However, we find in the dogmatic constitutions of the Second Vaticanum a new way of proclaiming doctrine.

What this new way is becomes dear from the objections raised against

47

the schema proposed by the Theological Commission in the historic discussion of 1962. We remember especially the words we have quoted from the speech made by Cardinal Bea. The Pope's intention in summoning the Council was

> that the faith of the Church be presented in all its integrity and purity but in such manner that it will be received today with benevolence. *For we are shepherds.*

This council was to be a pastoral council. How it was meant to deal with doctrinal matters and the question of truth and error had been stated in the famous words spoken by Pope John when he opened the Council on 11 October, 1962:

> At the outset of the Second Vatican Council, it is evident, as always, that the truth of the Lord will remain forever. We see in fact, as one age succeeds another, that the opinions of men follow on another and exclude each other. And often errors vanish as quickly as they arise, like fog before the sun. The Church has always opposed these errors. Frequently she has condemned them with the greatest severity. Nowadays, however, the Spouse of Christ prefers to make use of the medicine of mercy rather than that of seventy she considers that she meets the needs of the present day by demonstrating the validity of her teaching rather than by condemnations.

This is certainly a healthy reaction to the excessive use of canones in former councils where everyone who had doubts concerning a newly proclaimed doctrine was liberally threatened with eternal hell-fire. But such leniency may sometimes be exaggerated. Neither the prophets, nor the apostles, nor even our Lord himself could do without some very strict censures. The Bride of Christ seems already to be having serious trouble with some naughty children who capitalize on her good heart. We do not doubt that someday the right balance will be restored. There are errors which do not vanish like fog before the sun because behind them is the superman power of God's adversary. In his opening address John XXIIII said: 'The substance of the ancient doctrine of the deposit of faith is one thing, and the way in which it is presented is another.' It is just this in itself lawful distinction which the old evil foe has used to destroy the doctrinal substance in many Protestant Churches. Every heretic has claimed that his false doctrine is only 'a new way to teach the old truth.' We can only ask our Catholic brethren to learn from our experience and to be on their guard.

The pastoral character of the two dogmatic constitutions proclaimed by Vatican II on the Church and on Revelation (besides these there are a 'Constitution on the Sacred Liturgy' and a 'Pastoral Constitution on the Church in the Modern World'; the rest of the documents comprises nine 'Decrees' and three 'Declarations') finds its expression in their language. They do not speak the language of former constitutions, the language of theological definitions and documents, but the language of a pastoral letter, of spiritual admonition and even, especially in the doctrine on the Church, of Biblical theology. This corresponds to the change in the image of the Church which is symbolized by the fact that the Pope no longer wears the tiara of the Supreme Pontiff, with its medieval-imperialistic implications, but the mitre of a bishop, and that he signs the documents: 'I, Paul, Bishop of the Catholic Church.' The new form of presenting doctrine might indicate that the era of the Roman Church in which one dogma after another has been proclaimed has come to an end. The Catholic Church of the future will make dogmatic decisions more sparingly. None of the dogmas once proclaimed can be retracted, but they will be interpreted more in their practical and liturgical meaning, as is done in the last chapter of the 'Constitution on the Church', 'The role of the Blessed Virgin Mary, Mother of God, in the Mystery of Christ and the Church.'

IV

THIS CHANGE in the formulation of doctrine is of greatest importance for the relationship of Rome with the 'separated brethren'; for nothing has contributed more to the estrangement between the Christian Churches than the constant proclamation of new dogmas which are unacceptable to non-Roman Christians. Between Rome and Eastern Orthodoxy there stand no longer only the issues which were at stake at the Councils of Lyons in 1274 and Florence in 1439, but also the dogmas proclaimed at Trent and at the First Vatican Council and the Mariological dogmas of 1854 and 1950. The Eastern Church also celebrates the feasts on the 8th of December and the 15th of August, but it can never accept the *dogmas* of the Immaculate Conception and the Assumption of Mary. What in the Roman Church has been defined as an irreformable doctrine to be accepted by all members of the Church Catholic has remained in the East in the sphere of the liturgy and of pious opinions and mystical speculations. Hence the connection between the 'pastoral' and the 'ecumenical' character of Vatican II, as is also emphasized by the critics of the schema on the 'Sources of Revelation'. The Roman Church has at the recent Council fully accepted, without giving up any of its claims, the idea of a 're-union' of all Christians, individuals as well as communities, in one visible, truly Catholic Church on earth.

This entry of Rome into the Ecumenical Movement of our time has completely changed the ecumenical situation. We are all now no longer confronted only with the Anglican concept of a future Re-united Church, based on that minimum of doctrine which East and West, Catholicism and Protestantism have in common, and with the concept of Church unity that underlies the World Council of Churches. These concepts presuppose that Rome would eventually give up her claims and cease to be Roman. We are now confronted with a plan for reunion in an ecumenical Church in which all Churches, without giving up any of the treasures each of them possesses, but spiritually and theologically renewed and enriched by what they can mutually accept, would come together under the renewed office of the supreme shepherd of all Christians who would rule the Church Universal together with the universal college of bishops.

The advantage of the Roman plan over those of Canterbury-Lambeth and Geneva is its feasibility. It would include Rome in the process of reunion which could never reach its goal as long as the largest Church of

49

Christendom remained outside. If it were really God's will that all Christians should be united in one visible ecclesiastical organization, if this were the meaning of Christ's 'ut omnes unum sint', then Rome's ecumenical programme would be the only realistic one, and it could hardly be understood why it should not be adopted by the non-Roman Churches within the Ecumenical Movement. It could be that with the Second Vatican Council Rome has taken over the leadership of this movement. At any rate this Church is determined to do all in its power to carry out its great plan, not from lust for ecclesiastical power, but from its deepest convictions concerning the Church, its catholicity and unity. It will mobilize all its man-power, all its resources, material, spiritual, theological, ecclesiastical, in the interest of the great ecumenical idea of a reunited Church. It will shrink back from no work, nor from any sacrifice which it can possibly make without abandoning what it must regard as the irreformable truth of the Gospel. It will proceed on the road of ecumenism trod at the Second Vaticanum wherever this road may lead. There is no way back to the Church as we knew it even at the time of Pius XII.

In this context the third of the objections raised against the original draft must be understood. The traditional understanding of Scripture and Tradition as two sources of revelation of equal rank must make any union with Protestant Churches, including the Anglicans, impossible. Just as Rome can never accept the *Sola Scriptura*, so the Churches of the Reformation can never accept Holy Tradition as a second source of Christian doctrine beside Holy Scripture. This is the result of the great theological 'dialogue' which has been going on since the sixteenth century between the major branches of Western Christendom, both in polemical controversies and in the irenical attempts at union or at least at peaceful co-existence. For all great theology in the Western world has been a constant dialogue between Catholics, Lutherans, Anglicans and the various Reformed groups, as their learned theological works show.

To overcome the deadlock the 'new theology' in the Roman Church, encouraged and supported by the discussions within the ecumenical organizations of our time, has proposed a new theory which was taken for granted by the bishops who rejected the original draft; there is only one source of revelation, Holy Scripture. Tradition is the authoritative interpretation of Scripture by the Church. Since the doctrine of two sources had its basis in the decree of the Fourth Session of Trent (April, 1546) on the Holy Scriptures and the Traditions of the Apostles, a new interpretation of this decree was necessary. Trent does not speak expressly of two sources or of one source of revelation. The word fons ('source'), appears only in the statement that the Gospel is the source of all saving truth and of discipline of conduct. This truth and this discipline, it continues 'are contained in written books and in unwritten traditions' ('in libris scriptis et sine scripto traditionibus'). Both the Scriptures and the Traditions must be accepted 'with equal pious affection and reverence' ('pari pietatis affectu ac reverentia'). It is quite clear that the dogma of the Church, the content of the divine revelation, is to be found neither in Scripture alone nor in the Traditions alone. If the meaning of such a text is to be found in the text itself and not elsewhere, it is quite clear that the two-sources theory is the doctrine of Trent, and it is quite astonishing that the defenders of the one-source theory could read their view into that clear text, maintaining that the doctrine of the two equally authoritative sources was an arbitrary interpretation by the theologians of the counter-Reformation period.

That 'systematic' theologians like Hans Küng could commit such a blunder might be understandable, but that they were supported by historians of the rank of Geiselmann and even Jedin the historian who is writing the standard work on the Council of Trent, can be understood only from the fact that Catholic historians have learnt to interpret history from a dogmatic point of view. One is reminded of Archbishop (later Cardinal) Manning's word addressed to the historians who like Doellinger, could not accept certain historical statements of Vatican I on the papacy: 'one must overcome history with the dogma'. These historians have tried to find a basis for their interpretation by asking not so much what the fathers of Trent actually said, but what they intended to say. They have indeed rejected the statement of the first draft that the Gospel is contained *partly* ('partim') in written books, and *partly* (partim) in unwritten traditions. But this had to be done because it would have provoked the unanswerable question, Which part belongs to the Scripture and, which to the Traditions? Even the present text has not prevented this question from becoming a testing ground for the acumen of the professors of Fundamental Theology. Still the present constitution gives one answer in which all theological schools had agreed: 'Through, the same Tradition the Church's full canon of the sacred books is known' (Article 8). The real issue was the statement that Scriptures and Traditions must be received with equal pious affection and reverence. It was against this phrase that a minority of the Council of Trent fought a losing battle, recommending that something like 'similar' be said instead of 'equal'.

It is to be expected that the new constitution will put an end to the attempts of the 'new theology' to interpret Trent in the sense of the one-source theory. It repeats expressly the decision of Trent with the characteristic inversion: 'Therefore both the sacred *Tradition* and sacred *Scripture* are to be accepted with the same sense of devotion and reverence' (Art 9). This sentence is preceded by another which, according to Karl Rahner, was inserted in the text of the constitution at a later stage at the special request of Pope Paul VI: It is not from Scripture alone that the Church draws her certainty about everything which has been revealed'. This sentence is a rejection of the *Sola Scriptura* of the Reformation even if it speaks only of the *certainty* about the content of revelation and not of the *content* itself. For the certainty can in this context not be separated from the content. It is not only in this sentence that the document breathes a spirit of compromise and ambiguity which seems to be inseparable from modern ecumenism. Is Rome going to become a second Geneva?

V

BUT IT is time to turn the constitution itself. Its title is the 'Dogmatic Constitution on Divine Revelation'. The first words, by which it will also be known, are *Dei verbum* ("Hearing the Word of God"). It is a short document, compromising 26 articles, divided into the Preface (art. 1) and six chapters:

I. Revelation itself (2-6). II. The transmission of the divine Revelation (7-10). III. The divine Inspiration and the Interpretation of Sacred Scripture (11-13). IV. The Old Testament (14-16). V. The New Testament (17-20). VI. Sacred Scripture in the Life of the Church (21-26).

The Preface defines the object. Starting from John I : 2f the Council announces its intention to set forth, following in the footsteps of the Councils of Trent and of Vatican I,

authentic teaching about divine revelation and about how it is handed on, so that by hearing the message of salvation the whole world may believe, by believing it may hope, and by hoping it may love.

Chapter I states the fact of Revelation.

In His goodness and wisdom, God chose to reveal Himself and to make known to us the hidden purpose of His will. The invisible God speaks through Christ, the Word made flesh, to men calling them into fellowship with Himself.

This revelation is realized by deeds and words, Christ being the mediator and the fullness of it. After a short reference to the natural revelation of God in the works of creation the chapter speaks of the supernatural revelation in which God acts and speaks to men from the first promise of salvation (Gen. 3: 15) through the patriarchs, Moses and the prophets of Jesus Christ.

The Christian dispensation as the new and definitive covenant will never pass away, and we now await no further new public revelation before the glorious manifestation of our Lord Jesus Christ.

This revelation is to be accepted by men through 'the obedience of faith'. This obedience is now no longer regarded, as in the 'Constitution of the Catholic Faith' of Vatican I, as mainly intellectual assent, but as a personal commitment in which 'man entrusts his whole self freely to God' (Art. 5). This obedience of faith is a gift of the grace of God. The chapter ends with a re-affirmation of the doctrine of Vatican I that God, the beginning and end of all things, can be known with certainty from created reality by the light of human reason.

Chapter II on the 'Transmission of Divine Revelation' contains the decision of the crucial issue of the source or the sources of Divine Revelation. The question as it had been formulated on either side was not taken up. The new starting point permitted a different way of solving the problem. Art. 7 speaks of God's will that what he had revealed for the salvation of man should be handed on to all generations 'Therefore Christ the Lord, in whom the full revelation . . . is brought to completion, commissioned the apostles to preach the gospel to all men.' The commission was fulfilled in their oral preaching and 'by those apostles and apostolic men who under the inspiration of the . . . Holy Spirit committed the message

52

of salvation to writing.' To keep the gospel whole and alive, the apostles 'left bishops as their successors, handing over their own teaching role' to them.

> This sacred tradition, therefore, and sacred Scripture of both the Old and New Testament are like a mirror in which the pilgrim Church on earth looks at God . . . until she is brought finally to see Him as He is, face to face (Art. 7).

One wonders why, in this context, nothing is said about the nature of the Old Testament and its meaning for Jesus, the apostles and the Church of the Apostolic age. We have to come back to this.

In this way Scripture and Tradition belong always together. 'Sacred tradition and sacred Scripture form one sacred deposit of the Word of God, which is committed to the Church'. This is the main thesis put forward in the following articles of the chapter from which we have already quoted the sentence about the *Sola Scriptura* and the re-affirmation of the Tridentine sentence on the equal devotion and reverence which we owe to Scripture and Tradition.

> The task of authentically interpreting the Word of God, whether written or handed on, has been entrusted exclusively to the living teaching office of the Church (Art. 10).

This office

> is not above the Word of God, but serves it by explaining it faithfully with the help of the Holy Spirit; it draws from this one deposit of faith everything which it presents for belief as divinely revealed.

So a third factor in the transmission of the revelation comes in:

> It is clear therefore, that sacred *tradition*, sacred *Scripture* and the teaching authority of the *Church* . . . are *so linked together that one cannot stand without the others*, and that all together and each in its own way under the action of the one Holy Spirit contribute effectively to the salvation of souls.

The short Chapter III deals in three articles with "The divine Inspiration and the Interpretation of Sacred Scripture". The doctrine of Vatican I on Inspiration is re-affirmed, the doctrine of its inerrancy which was so strongly maintained in the Bible Encyclicals of the modern popes from 1893 to 1943, and therefore regarded as something which could not be denied by any Catholic, is weakened to the vague and noncommittal formula that

> the books of Scripture must be acknowledged as teaching . . . without error *that truth which God wanted put into the sacred writings for the sake of our salvation* (Art 11).

Everyone asks: What is this truth? What does belong to it, what does not? Art. 12 deals with the tasks of the exegete to clarify by scholarly research the meaning of Holy Scripture 'so that through preparatory study the judgment of the Church may mature.' In any case the final judgment on what the Scripture teaches lies with the Church which carries out the ministry of guarding and interpreting the Word of God. The chapter ends with a short art. 13 on Chrysostom's doctrine of the condescension of God when he speaks to us in Holy Scripture and with the comparison of God's speaking in human language to the Incarnation.

Chapter IV deals with 'The Old Testament' in three small articles. Again the history of salvation is alluded to.

> The principal purpose to which the plan of the Old Covenant was directed was to prepare both for the coming of the Christ . . . and to the messianic kingdom, to announce its coming by prophecy . . . and to indicate its meaning through various types (Art. 15).

'*Now* the books of the Old Testament reveal to all men the knowledge of God and of men.' They contain teachings about God, sound wisdom about human life and a wonderful treasury of prayers. In these books 'the mystery of our salvation is present in a hidden way. Christians should receive them with reverence'. The last article speaks briefly about the relationship between the Old and the New Testament. God is 'inspirer and author of both'. The New Testament is 'hidden in the Old, the Old made manifest in the New'. The books of the Old Covenant acquire their full meaning in the New Testament and in turn shed light on it and explain it. In chapter V, 'The New Testament', all emphasis is placed on the four Gospels and their trustworthiness:

> Holy Mother Church has firmly . . . held and continues to bold that the four Gospels . . . whose historical character the Church unhesitatingly asserts, band on what Jesus Christ . . . really did and taught.

> The sacred authors wrote the four Gospels, *selecting* some things from the many which had been handed on . . . *reducing* some of them to a synthesis, *explicating* ('expanantes') some things in view of the *situation of their Churches*, and preserving the *form of proclamation* but always in such fashion that they told us the *honest truth about Jesus* (Art. 19).

One notices a certain anxiety in view of the dangers of a new Modernism which stands at the door of the Roman Church.

The last Chapter, 'Sacred Scripture in the Life of the Church', deals with the need of the Church for the use and the study of the Scriptures.

> For, inspired by God . . . they impart the Word of God Himself ... and make the voice of the Holy Spirit resound in the words of the prophets and apostles.

> All the *preaching* of the Church must be nourished and ruled by sacred Scripture. For in the sacred books the Father who is in heaven meets His children and speaks with them (Art. 21).

'Easy access to sacred Scripture should be provided for all the Christian faithful.' The Church with maternal concern sees to it that suitable and correct translations are made into different languages, especially from the original texts of the sacred books. And even 'co-operation with the separated brethren' might be possible in producing new translations (Art. 22). The Church should further the scholarly exploration and exposition of the sacred books.

> This sacred Synod *encourages* the sons of the Church who are *biblical scholars* to continue energetically with the work they have so well begun, with a constant renewal of vigor and with *loyalty to the mind of the Church* (Art. 23).

Art. 24 reminds the faithful and the clergy that 'the study of the sacred page is, as it were, the soul of sacred theology.' The last articles underscore the importance of the Bible for the whole Church, the shepherds as well as the flock.

> Prayer should accompany the reading of sacred Scripture, so that God
> and man may talk together; for 'we speak to Him when we pray; we hear
> Him when we read the divine sayings' (Art. 25, quotation from Ambrose).

An interesting suggestion is made in the recommendation to prepare
'editions of the sacred Scriptures, provided with suitable comments, also
for the use of non-Christians and adapted to their situation.' The concluding article expresses the hope of a spiritual revival through the new
study of the Bible on all levels of the Church:

> Just as the life of the Church grows through persistent participation in
> the Eucharistic mystery, so we may hope for a new surge of spiritual vi-
> tality from intensified veneration for God's word, 'which lasts forever'
> (Is. 40:8; cf. I Peter 1:23-25).

VI

THE EVALUATION of the constitution *Dei verbum* may begin with
the last chapter. It reveals a process which is going on in the Roman
Catholic Church. In the passionate appeals of this chapter, as well as in
its practical proposals, which are based on experiences of the Catholic
Bible Movement that has now been going on for more than thirty years,
sounds the cry for the Bible which, though preserved and honoured in
the liturgy, had been lost to a large extent in the preaching and teaching
of the Church. A real hunger and thirst for the Word of God is awakening
in the Roman Church on all levels from the Roman curia to the parish
and the Catholic home, from the places of highest scholarship to the children in the parish schools.

This happens at a time, let us not forget that, when the Protestant
Churches of the world seem to have lost or to be losing the Bible. 'We
have lost the Word of God and cannot find it again.' With these words
the leader of a Protestant Theological College described the overall situation of his own Church and the Protestant Churches in general, after
he had returned from a long overseas trip where he had the opportunity
of investigating the situation in other parts of the world. I heard him saying that in the spirit of sadness and deep humility. He was not passing
judgment on others. And we, too, want to refrain this, when we have to
say a critical word about the present situation. Let me repeat what was
said before that Christians of all denominations are going through the
same experiences. The shame and glory of one Church is the shame and
glory of all Churches. We are all linked together by the same emergencies, needs, troubles and sins, as we are all linked together by the fact
that we all have the same Lord who is the judge and the savior of us all.
So let us rejoice with our separated brethren in the Roman

Church at the rediscovery of the Bible as the living and active (Heb. 4:
12) Word of God. Let us help them where they need our help. Let them
help us where we are in need of what they can teach us . Let everything
that has now to be said about the Constitution on Divine Revelation be
said and understood in this sense.

There is one thing we can learn from them. This is courage. The bishops assembled for the Second Vatican Council had courage. Think what it must have meant to them to give up the Latin liturgy and to take all the risks connected with such a change. All the great changes in theology, Church administration and discipline, of which no one can say where they will lead, have been made by men who had courage. What courage was needed to leave the ivory towers of the past, to face and to challenge the modern world from which the Church had been separated for generations. One can well understand the deep concern of Pope Paul when he sees the outgrowth of what is meant to be a renewal and what threatens to become a devastating revolution. But Churches that have no courage are doomed.

The Church of the Apostles was a courageous Church. Peter and Paul who fearlessly died as martyrs in the capital of the Roman Empire became the Romulus and Remus of a new Rome, as 'the shining army of the martyrs', of which the FS sings, has at all times conquered the world. The Reformers of the sixteenth century who opened a new era of the Church were men of courage. So were the confessors in England, Catholics and Protestants, who died with the same psalms on their lips because they dared to resist their royal tyrants with their acts of supremacy and conformity and have thus gained for the world that freedom of conscience which is now recognized everywhere as the presupposition of all healthy Christian life. The great founders of Christian missions from the old Irish and Syrian monks in Europe and Asia to the present day, the Pilgrim Fathers of many denominations who opened new chapters in the history of the Church in foreign continents, all testify to the truth that courage belongs to the nature of the true Church.

This courage is the fruit of faith; it is so also in the case of the Roman Church of our time which is not afraid to leave the safe fortress in which it had settled down, safe from the dangers of a hostile world, and to go 'to the land that I will show you', the unknown land of the third millenium of Christian history. She knows that her Lord will not let down his Church. She believes firmly in his promises. It is refreshing to see in this age of doubt, uncertainty and despair at least one Church which still dares to believe.

Having said this, we have to say something on the doctrine contained in this 'Dogmatic Constitution.' It is, as we have seen, an attempt to overcome one of the crucial issues, the great contrast between, on the one hand the Churches that confess the *Sola Scriptura* of the Reformation and, on the other, Rome, which is bound to the doctrine of Trent and the two Vatican Councils that the Word of God comes to us in sacred Scripture and sacred tradition, which must both be accepted with equal piety and reverence because they cannot be separated. These - so we are told in the new constitution- and the teaching office of the Church which has to interpret Scripture and tradition authoritatively and infallibly 'are so linked and joined together that one cannot stand without the others.' Can we accept this? This is the question which the constitution addresses to us.

VII

OUR ANSWER begins with a question we have to put to our Catholic friends and brethren. How is it to be explained that the Roman Church has so little understanding of the Old Testament as the Word of God given to the Church? K. Rahner and H. Vorgrimler, in their German edition of the texts of the Councils, say concerning the fourth chapter of *Dei verbum*:

> One should not silently pass over the shortcomings of this chapter which hardly does justice to the facts that the Old Testament was the Holy Writ of Jesus and the Primitive Church and that it contains a much longer experience of mankind in its relationship with God than does the New Testament.

Similar observations can be made concerning Catholic books on the Bible, even of Karl Rahner's 'Inspiration in the Bible'[6]. Holy Scripture proper is for the Church the Old Testament, as Luther always maintained. The Church could, according to him, perhaps exist without a written New Testament, as she indeed did in the first generations, but not without the Old. What the Old Testament in the three parts of the Hebrew canon (see Luke 24:27, 32 and 44) meant to Jesus everybody knows. One has only to think of the answer he gave to the tempter (Matt. 4:4), 'It is *written*, Man shall not live by bread alone, but by every *word that proceedeth out of the mouth of God*.' The most frequently quoted Bible passage in the Church of the first centuries is, as far as I can see, Isaiah 53. The proclamation of the apostles and of the entire first Church is the glad tidings that Is. 53 and certain psalms which were understood to prophesy the resurrection of the Messiah have been fulfilled, 'whereof we are all Witnesses' (Acts 2:32). 'According to the Scriptures' (I Cor. 15: 3 and 4) means even in the Nicene Creed 'according to the Old Testament', though the clause of the same Creed on the Holy Spirit, 'Who spake by the prophets' was soon understood as referring to the whole Bible, including the New Testament (see Epiphanius and the Armenian form of the Creed).

We understand what it means to us all if our Catholic brethren have now learnt that not only some Messianic prophecies, but the whole Old Testament in the history of salvation points to the coming of the Messiah and the Messianic Kingdom, even the chapters and passages that deal with creation. But the mutual interdependence of creation and salvation, so important to the Old and the New Testament and to the early Church, must be fully evaluated. The creator is certainly the redeemer, but the redeemer is also the creator. Hence it must be seen that the Old Testament looks not only into the depths of history, but also into the depths of the universe. With its traditions which go back into the oldest history of mankind and look even beyond that into 'the beginning' it is indeed, as it were, as the Greek synagogue understood it, 'the oldest book in the world'. At the same time it looks into the depths of nature (certain psalms, Job, Proverbs 8: 22ff., and other passages on the divine 'Wisdom'), as also does the New Testament (e.g. Rom. 8: 19ff.; Hebrews 1).

The meaning of the statement that the entire Bible is God's Word (and therefore God's revelation, for we should never forget that both Church and Bible know the equation 'revelatio sive locutio Dei', and that it is most dangerous to try to separate these two) and that the Old Testament is God's Word in no lesser degree than the New Testament, we all, Catholics and Protestants, would understand better if we had a better understanding of the Inspiration of Holy Scripture. The doctrine that the Scriptures are sacred and canonical, 'because they, having been written under the inspiration of the Holy Spirit, have God for their author and are as such given to the Church', as the First Vaticanum puts it[7], is not a theory of certain theological schools, but is a dogma of the entire Church, expressed already in the clause of the Nicene Creed on the Holy Spirit, 'Who spake by the prophets' ('qui locutus est per prophetas'), and based on numerous passages of the New Testament. However, how inspiration must be understood, how the equation of the human words of the Bible with the Word of God is to be understood, on this the Church has never spoken.

It belongs to the tragedy of the Church in the centuries of the dissolution of the Roman Empire and the disintegration of the ancient civilization in West and East that the doctrine of the Holy Spirit was never finalized. Certain questions remained open and have been differently answered by the theologians of the East and the West. The most famous case, though by no means the only one, is the question of the Filioque, the question whether the Holy Spirit proceeds from the Father or from the Father and the Son, one of the great differences between the Eastern and the Western Church.

The history of the liturgy also shows that the problem of the Holy Spirit has never been fully solved. The liturgy knows no solemn oration addressed to the Holy Spirit who with the Father and the Son lives and reigns forever one God world without end, the only exception being the *Adsumus* at an ecumenical council. Even at Pentecost the oration is addressed to the Father. In the old Latin liturgies we find invocations of the Holy Spirit, especially the 'Veni Sancte Spiritus' of Pentecost, but even Pentecost is liturgically speaking not a feast of the Holy Spirit, but the last day of Paschaltide. Often one has the impression that in the Catholic Churches Eastern and Western the Mother of God has taken the place which properly belongs to the Holy Spirit, at least in popular piety. In this context it must be realized that Inspiration also as the work of the Holy Spirit has not been properly understood.

When in the Sistine Chapel in Rome the Nicene Creed is sung with its 'Qui locutus est per prophetas' many eyes may look to the ceiling with Michelangelo's overwhelming paintings of the prophets and sibyls. What have the pagan sibyls to do with Isaiah and Jeremiah? They have also prophesied. They have even prophesied the coming of a saviour. Vergil, who describes in the sixth book of the *Aeneid* the holy ecstasis of the Sibyl of Cumae when the spirit of her god fills her, in the fourth eclogue gives the prophecy by the same sibyl of a child who will soon be born and who, when he has grown up, will bring back the golden age of peace to a wartorn world. Constantine made use of this poem in his famous speech at the Council of Nicea. The medieval juxtaposition of prophets and sibyls which still resounds in the 'teste David cum Sibylla' of the *Dies irae* in the Requiem Mass goes back to St. Augustine. But what has Vergil's and his sibyl's political saviour to do with the Immanuel of the First and the Servant and Lamb of God of the Second Isaiah?

This confusion shows what is bound to happen if the inspiration of Scripture is understood in terms of a psychological process. This is what happened in the ancient Church when the Latin Fathers Augustine and Jerome in the dying Roman Empire around A.D. 400 and Gregory the Great in the dark ages around 600 tried to describe with the means of ancient psychology the process that goes on in the soul of a man who is writing with paper and ink a divine book, every word of which must be regarded as God's Word. The result of these efforts was that theory which was handed on throughout the Middle Ages, survived even the Reformation and celebrated its triumph in the orthodox theology of Roman Catholicism, Anglicanism, Calvinism and even Lutheranism in the seventeenth century until it broke down in the era of Enlightenment and historical scholarship.

God gives the 'impulse to write'. He provides ('suggests' or 'dictates', which can, but must not, be understood in the sense in which we speak of 'dictation') the content and the fitting words. The result is a flawless, perfect book without error or contradiction. The personality of the individual writer is supposed to have been preserved. This should explain certain differences in the style and manner of presentation. In this way the absence of any mistake or 'error' is safeguarded. If contradictions, inaccuracies or mistakes should be found, they must be explained by way of harmonization or by the assumption that a copyist may have made an error. For the original copies have been lost. What a pity, one can only say.

So we have a Bible of which, in spite of this theory of inspiration, we can never say with absolute certainty: This is most certainly the unadulterated Word of God. For we never can know whether or not perhaps very early copyists' errors have crept into this or that text. One has only to think of what it means that for the Church of the first centuries the Septuagint was its Bible-it took some time until Augustine was reconciled with Jerome's venture of a Latin Bible translated from the Hebrew-and that this is still the case in the entire Eastern Church. The problem begins already with the Old Testament quotations in the New Testament.

Modern Protestantism has tried to solve the problem of an antiquated, untenable theory of the inspiration of the Bible by ignoring not only this theory, but also the dogma of Inspiration itself. The result is that the Word of God has been lost altogether. Is the Roman Catholic Church now going the same way? Sometimes it looks like that. The constitution under discussion also seems to point in that direction. But we cannot believe that Rome can never abandon the dogma, so clearly reaffirmed at the First Vaticanum. So we ask our Catholic brethren why they do not try to reinterpret the dogma of Inspiration, following the example set by the encyclical *Divino afflante Spiritu* of 1943 in which the life-work of the great Bible scholar Augustine Bea has found a wonderful climax. The shortcomings of *Dei verbum* are largely due to the neglect of this task.

<h1 style="text-align:center">VIII</h1>

ONE SHOULD have expected that at the time of the Reformation the question would have been raised whether the old form of the doctrine had to be abandoned. But the time for that had not yet come, mainly because the historical problems involved were not yet understood by the Reformers and by their adversaries. Thus Christendom had to carry the burden of a tradition which was taken for granted. This was pathetic in the case of the Protestant Churches. Despite their serious appeal to the Scriptures in all matters of faith and despite the amazing progress which the exegesis of Scripture was making they failed to ask whether the doctrinal formulations of the dogma of inspiration were really biblical. It is perhaps the greatest tragedy of the Churches of the Reformation, the Churches of the *Sola Scriptura*, that the doctrine 'De sacra Scriptura' with which their great works on dogmatics began was not the doctrine of Scripture itself, but a venerable Patristic tradition. Our Churches had to pay heavily for that. Some have died of this error and others are today dying of it.

Rome, on the other hand, was not much better off. It developed in contrast to the *Sola Scriptura* the Tridentine doctrine of Scripture and Tradition, both of which have the same authority. This is not only the doctrine of the post-Tridentine theology. It is the doctrine of Trent itself, as we have seen. It is a myth that the 'two sources' theory has replaced an older doctrine which regarded the Scriptures as the only source of doctrine and tradition as the authoritative interpretation of the Bible by the teaching office of the Church. There had never been in the Church a unified doctrine in this matter, as there had also never been, in spite of all more or less authoritative lists of the biblical books, any unanimity concerning the borders of the canon. There were always men who treated our 'apocrypha' as Jerome and Luther have treated them. Luther's view that the epistle of James is no apostolic book and should, therefore, not be regarded as canonical was shared by his great adversary, the learned Thomist Cardinal Cajetan. It was the decree of Trent which put an end to the centuries-old discussions.

How fluid the borders between the Bible and the Fathers were appears from the enumeration of the sacred Scriptures by schoolmen like Hugo of St. Victor. The 'Apostolic Canons', the old Church rules attributed to the apostles, are still today in the canon of certain Oriental Churches. Even at Trent it could happen that their inclusion in the canon was suggested[8]. It is strange to see the very arbitrary and opportunistic reasons for the acceptance of a certain book, e.g. II Maccabees, with its support of the prayer and sacrifice for the dead (12:4311.). A strict doctrine of traditions (the plural is still used in the decree of Trent) seems to have been developed in reaction to the Reformation by the new theology that grew mainly in Louvain and which wanted a reform of the Church[9].

Since medieval theology always considered Holy Writ as the proper source of doctrine, the master or doctor of theology was doctor of sacred

Scripture. His duty was to interpret the Scriptures according to the sense held by the Church whose task it was to interpret the Bible with authority. Where the borders of the Scriptures were and whether there was a second source of doctrine remained, in the Middle Ages, an open question. The authority of the Fathers was respected and identified with the authority of the Church. But during the centuries after the breakdown of the unquestioned authority of the papacy around A.D. 1300, the trend towards a *Sola Scriptura* is noticeable. It is not yet the *Sola Scriptura* of the Reformation, but that of Wyclif, Hus, the medieval sects and of late scholasticism. If at Wittenberg, under the leadership of Luther, a new centre of biblical studies arose nothing could be said against the *Sola Scriptura* as at least a possibility within Catholic theology. The same is true of the *Sola Fide*. Both 'solas' were only declared heresies at the Council of Trent.

IX

THIS BRINGS us to the final and decisive question: Is the new constitution acceptable to the Churches of the Reformation today, or can it at least be regarded as a step in the direction towards a solution of the old controversy? Our answer must be: It presents a good starting point for a serious dialogue between Rome and the evangelical Churches, but not more. It helps to clarify the issues, to formulate the real status controversiae. What is the point at issue? We do not deny the existence of a living tradition in the Church. The doctrine is not simply passed on by passing on a book. As the prophetic and apostolic writings have grown out of the oral proclamation of the prophets and apostles, so they are passed on not only as written or printed books, but as the basis of the preaching and teaching of the Church. Such tradition must have existed already in the time of the Old Testament. When the people fled to Egypt or were deported to Babylonia they did not have in their pockets a Bible or parts of the Bible. The content of the sacred writings lived on in their memory, the books, as far as they existed, were kept in their synagogues and restored and copied, read aloud—even private reading was done aloud (Acts 8:3)- and meditated on, taught by the fathers and memorized by the children in the house, constantly meditated on by pious people (Deut. 6: 6ff.).

When we speak of tradition we should not only think of the apostolic tradition in the New Testament, but also of this tradition which kept the written Word of God alive in the centuries before Christ. There are, of course, traditions of various natures. There were in Jerusalem the traditions of the Sadducees who regarded only the *Torah* as God's word and had very strong liturgical interests. There was the tradition of the Pharisees, and again among them several schools of thought. There was the tradition kept in the Rabbinic schools. There were the simple people in whom the faith and the hope of the fathers lived. Mary and Joseph, Zacharias and Elisabeth, Simeon and Hannah may be found among them. In these circles the *Benedictus*, the *Magnificat* and the *Nunc dimittis* were sung. They were the first to recognize the Messiah while the

61

Guardians of Jewish orthodoxy put him to death.

Tradition stood against tradition. The psalms, the prophets were interpreted differently by the different traditions, just as later the Petrine texts of the Gospels were differently interpreted by the traditions of the East and the West. It is the same with the oral preaching of the prophets. Jeremiah proclaimed the destruction of Jerusalem. He was denounced as a false prophet. Had not Isaiah prophesied just the opposite and been vindicated by the events? Jeremiah regarded the prophets of a happy end at his time as false prophets. The people at Jerusalem were confused. Where was the divinely appointed infallible teaching office to decide this issue with authority? Who was to decide in the earthly days of our Lord whether his claim was right or wrong? If a clear decision might have been expected anywhere, then it was in the Sanhedrin where the learned doctors of Scripture and the most eminent religious leaders of God's people constituted the highest spiritual authority which existed in the world at that time. Their decision was wrong.

But there must be, we are told, an infallible teaching office to explain the Scriptures. If God wanted to reveal himself to men he would not give them only a book which can be and is being interpreted in various ways. It is a logical conclusion that he must have provided a living teaching authority, whatever it may be, a council or a pope or a theological faculty or some Church committee. What is the use of a revelation which every individual can understand at his pleasure? This was the argument of Erasmus also in his great contention with Luther. Why did this great leader of European culture and scholarship, this master-mind of his time, refuse to accept the Reformation? The encounter between the Reformer and the great Humanist was an event of the first magnitude in the history of European culture. For it foreshadowed what was going to happen in the subsequent centuries until the present time.

In his *De libero arbitrio diatribe,* Erasmus defended in the free will of man, what was to him the dignity of man. This was threatened by Luther's doctrine that man is a poor miserable sinner who can do nothing for his salvation. That man is weak, imperfect and inclined to all sorts of sin, Erasmus would admit. He was very realistic in his view of man after all his experience as the son of a priest. But it was the 'sola gratia', by grace only, which he rejected. And he defended God against Luther, God who is good and not a tyrant who condemns people who can do nothing but sin. God is light and not darkness, as his disciple Zwingli a few years later maintained against the Reformer of Wittenberg. And he attacked Luther's treatment of Scripture. The *Sola Scriptura* is closely linked with the *Sola Gratia.* To understand Scripture we need scholarship, the knowledge of the interpretation by the Fathers and the guidance of the Church. We should be careful with our own judgment. Luther, he feels, is too dogmatic. Scripture is full of mysteries. We should abstain from those 'firm assertions' in which Luther indulges. Over against Luther's dogmatism he confesses that he would rather side with the sceptics. In all these points Erasmus speaks on behalf of modern man who, though knowing of man's weakness, has not given up his belief in man; who believes in grace, though not in grace alone; who wants the Bible, but not the Bible only; who wants to retain Christianity, but an undogmatic Christianity; who believes in God, in Christ, but whose faith is always intermingled with a certain amount of scepticism.

What is Luther's answer? There is no Christian faith which is not based on the Word of God, and the Word of God we find in the Scriptures, and in Scripture only. The Fathers can err. Traditions are human. Whether they convey to me the truth, I cannot know unless I see that their content is confirmed by the Scriptures. To the objection that the Scriptures are sometimes dark, contradicting each other and therefore in need of an authoritative interpretation, Luther replies with his doctrine of the *claritas sacrae Scripturae*, the clarity of the Scriptures. As a biblical scholar, Luther knew of course of the problems of exegesis. During his whole life he remained the humble student of the Bible, constantly improving not only his translation, but also his exegesis. The clarity of the Scriptures is not the clarity of a text-book on mathematics or of a historical work written according to the rules of modern historiography. Their clarity lies rather in their content. This content, the content of the entire Bible (Luke 24:44, cf. Acts 10:43: 'To him give all the prophets witness, that through his name whosoever believeth in him shall receive remission of sins') is Christ. 'Tolle Christum e scripturis, quid amplius invenies?' ('Take away Christ from the Scriptures, what else will you find?')[10]

Christ is the content of the Scriptures not in the sense that he would be the object of a theological work on Christology. He is the content of the Bible because he is present in the Bible. It is not the human author who reminds us of him by speaking of him. It is God the Holy Spirit who makes him present through his divine witness. For this is the work of the Paraclete who brings to the remembrance of the disciples what Jesus has taught them (John 14:26), who bears witness to him and supplements the testimony of the eyewitnesses (15:26; 16: 12f.) and glorifies him. For the Spirit and Christ belong always together, our two 'Paracletes' (cf. John 14: 16 with I John 2 : 1) whose mutual relationship belongs to the mystery of the Blessed Trinity (see also what St. Paul says about the understanding of the Old Testament by the Jews, II Cor. 3: 14-18). This real presence of the Triune God in the Scriptures distinguishes the Bible from all other books in the world and makes it divine revelation.

This revelation of the Triune God is accepted by faith. By that faith which the Holy Spirit creates 'where and when it pleases God'[11] in those who hear the Gospel. According to Luther and Calvin it is this 'testimonium Spiritus Sancti internum' which makes us understand the testimony which the Holy Spirit gives in the Scriptures to Christ. The great truths about Christ which the Church confesses in the Creeds are not human opinions, they are divine truth: the true humanity of Christ in which he is 'of one substance with us', as the Chalcedonian formula puts it, our brother as the New Testament says (Heb. 2 : 17; Rom. 8: 29) ; his true divinity in which he is 'of one substance with the Father, i.e. 'God from God, light from light, very God from very God' (cf Heb. 1: 3); the unity of his divine-human person; his incarnation, suffering, and death 'for us', 'for us men and for our salvation'; his resurrection and ascension, his sitting on the right hand of the Father; his coming again with glory to judge both the living and the dead.

All these dogmatic statements are not human opinions and theories. They are the objective content of the divine revelation in Scripture, just as the content of the confession which Simon Peter made on behalf of the Twelve, 'Thou art the Christ', was more than a subjective opinion: 'Blessed art thou, Simon Bar-jona; for flesh and blood has not revealed it to you, but my father who is in heaven' (Matt. 16: 16f.). This is the origin of the dogma of the Church. It has not been invented by men. It is given in the divine revelation. This is the reason why Luther in De servo *arbitrio* takes exception to Erasmus' scepticism. 'The Holy Spirit is no sceptic', he says. 'Tolle assertiones et tulisti Christianismum'. 'Take away the dogmatic statements and you have taken away Christianity.'[12] Christianity is *per definitionem* a dogmatic, perhaps better, *the* dogmatic religion, based on the dogma 'Jesus is the Christ', which no man has invented. With the refutation of Erasmus Luther refutes the entire religious scepticism of the modern world whose spokesman Erasmus was. This includes the Christian scepticism which does not want a dogma, but only pious opinions and religious sentiments.

If this is the meaning of the *Sola Scriptura*, then it will be understandable why we cannot give it up. We have, like our fathers in the Reformation, the highest respect for the great heritage of the Church of all ages. The ancient creeds are our creeds. The Fathers of the ancient Church are our Fathers. We are in one Church with Ambrose and Augustine, with Athanasius and Chrysostom, with Anselm and Bernard. We make use of all the treasures of the Church in liturgy, Church order and pastoral wisdom of all centuries, in so far as we value the tradition of the Church very highly and preserve everything we can preserve. But not everything which comes to us from the past can be accepted. There are good and bad, true and false traditions. No Church would deny that. Every Church must have a rule and norm by which life and work, faith and order are measured. This is to us the Bible and nothing else. As far as the foundation of the faith is concerned and the preservation of the purity of the Gospel which was the concern of our fathers, even as it was of the Fathers of Trent, we can only say: 'Verbum solum habemus', 'we hold the Word alone'.

X

IF WE acted against this rule, what would be the consequence? We want our Catholic brethren to understand that we do not want to hurt them if we express our deep concern that the acceptance of anything else as the Word of God except the Bible and the proclamation of its content means *de facto* the acceptance of a human authority as equal to that of God. Even the *Constitutio*, as we have seen, makes it clear that sacred tradition, sacred Scripture and the teaching authority of the Church are so linked and joined together that one cannot stand without the others.

If this is so, then we are confronted with the alternative: 'Holy Church or Holy Writ?' Father Tavard in his book *Holy Writ or Holy Church* tries to show that both belong together, because Holy Writ cannot be understood without Holy Church. This is also the thesis of the constitution we have been considering But in the very moment in which we de facto subordinate the Scriptures to the authority of the Church, the Church becomes not only the judge, but also the source of doctrine.

What is the source of the doctrine of the dogma of the Immaculate Conception of 1854? Certainly not Holy Scripture. Nor is it an apostolic tradition. It is the Church, 'das Glaubensbewusstsein der Kirche' ('the Church's consciousness of belief). What is the source of the dogma of the Assumption of 1950? It is not based on Scripture in spite of the attempt to show by way of logical conclusions that it has a remote basis in the Bible. Nor does it belong to the apostolic tradition. From where does the modern Catholic Church know that the apostles knew what no one knew before certain legends of the fifth century were known? From where did the popes, who proclaimed these doctrines as 'revealed dogma' which must be believed by all Christians, obtain knowledge of such revelations? The Church has here become the source of the dogma.

It is not accidental that in the handbooks on dogmatics of the last generation in the Roman Church ecclesiology is not dealt with in connection with the doctrine of Christ or the doctrine of the Holy Spirit—where the article on the Church appears in the Creeds—but rather with the 'Fundamental Theology' which deals with the foundations of theology, and first of all with Revelation and the sources of the doctrine of the Church. In L. Lercher's *Institutiones Theologiae Dogmaticae*[13], the sequence is: Book I, On the True Religion; Book II, On the Church of Christ; Book III, On Tradition and Holy Scripture. In the *Sacrae Theologiae Summa* of the Spanish Jesuits, the first volume[14] deals in a similar way, with Tradition in the Treatise on the Church which is followed by the Treatise on Holy Scripture. The actual subordination of the Scriptures to the Church and the fact that the Church has become a source of doctrine cannot find a clearer expression.

The consequences are obvious. Who gives me the guarantee that a dogma whose only source is the Church, is divinely revealed by God? To point at some Scripture passages which may mystically hint at the doctrine and from whose mystical interpretation logical conclusions are drawn, is no substitute for a Scriptural proof. Whether the often beautiful but also fantastic typological interpretation of Holy Writ by the Greek Fathers is legitimate exegesis is more than doubtful. To develop out of the biblical doctrine of the first and the second Adam a doctrine of the first and the second Eve is not sound theology, as Fathers Tavard and de Lubac think. It is religious poetry, like the speculation on the tree of the cross and the tree in paradise. One should not forget that most of the exegeticed works of the Church Fathers are sermons preached and taken down in shorthand. To make them the pattern of a truly theological churchly exegesis for all times is impossible if we want to keep God's Word in its purity.

What happens if the Church becomes the source of revelation is shown by the development of the modern Catholic doctrine and cult of Mary. Man becomes the source of revelation. Four years after the dogma of the Immaculate Conception was proclaimed in 1854 the apparitions at Lourdes took place. Who was the Lady that Bernadette Soubirous saw and heard in a state of trance? 'I am the Immaculate Conception'. According to the Catholic doctrine this was a private revelation which cannot be the basis of dogma, since the public revelation on which the doctrine of the Church is built came to an end with the death of the last of the Apostles. No Catholic is compelled to believe the authenticity of the appiration of the Blessed Virgin at Lourdes. Nor is he entitled to deny it publicly. For the Church has recognized it by the canonization of Bernadette.

The same is to be said of the apparitions at Fatima which began on 13 May, 1917, on the very day when Eugenio Pacelli, the later Pope Pius XII, was consecrated in Rome Titular Archbishop of Sardes to take up his office as Nuncio at Munich. When during the coming months the 50th anniversary of the apparitions is celebrated in Portugal and in the entire Catholic world, we may ask the question as to what actually happened. I for one do not doubt that these children Bernadette and the three little visionaries in Portugal, had strange experiences. One should not doubt that strange phenomena occurred in places which obviously had a very old religious significance in past ages of paganism. But what we must doubt is that the lady (or ladies) of Lourdes and Fatima who spoke through a medium or several mediums in a state of trance was the Blessed Virgin.

I am not a Catholic, but a simple Lutheran who reads and meditates daily on the Bible and Luther's Catechism. As such I have so much love and respect for the mother of my Lord that I cannot believe that she, the humble handmaiden of the Lord who became the 'Theotokos', the Mother of God, could ever give such messages. The mouth who spoke the *Magnificat* could not say: 'I am the Immaculate Conception', to confirm the dogma of Pius IX. Still less could she say what the Madonna of Fatima said, referring to the punishments of God in World War I:

> In order to stop that I shall come to ask for the consecration of the world
> to my Immaculate Heart. . . . The outlook is gloomy. But there is a ray
> of hope: My immaculate heart will finally triumph.

One is reminded of the messages from beyond allegedly given through a spiritistic medium by great men of history whose mind seems to have deteriorated in the world of the spirits. Whatever that holy occultism of Lourdes and Fatima may mean—in both cases politics were involved, the politics of the Second Empire in France, and the politics of Portugal and the Pyrenaean Peninsula and even of European Catholicism as a whole since 1917[15]—in any case these revelations were not divine. Not the true and living God has spoken in these events, but human beings or, what is still worse, superhuman minds through the mouths of weak children.

Why do we mention this? Not to hurt in any way our Catholic brethren who seem not to have the freedom to discuss these things. Or may we except from the busy pen of Hans Küng a little book about Fatima? What we want is to show what happens if the Church becomes a source of revelation. We owe this testimony to our separated brethren, as we are gladly prepared to listen to their warning voice when they see us going astray in our theological thought and our spiritual life. In an age where we all have begun to realize that the Christians and the Churches of Christendom are rising and falling together we regard it as our ecumenical duty to confess again with the Church of the Reformation the 'articulus stantis et cadentis ecclesiae', the article with which the Church stands and falls:

Sola fide, sola gratia, sola scriptura, solus Christus.
By grace alone, by faith alone, Scripture alone, Christ alone.

Endnotes

1. London: Burns and Oates.
2. Quoted from Xavier Rynne, *Letters from Vatican City, First Session*, New York, 1963, p. 143.
3. Rynne, p. 148.
4. G.K.A. Bell, *Documents on Christian Unity, 1920-1930*, pp. 17-21.
5. Kleines *Konzilkompendium*, 1966, p. 364.
6. *Quaestiones Disputatae* I.
7. *Const. De fide Catholica*, Denzinger 1787, new edition 3006.
8. H. Jedin, *A History of the Council of Trent*, Vol. II, 1961, p. 57.
9. John L. Murphy, *The Notion of Tradition in John Driedo*, 1959.
10. *De Servo Arbitrio*, Weimar edition of Luther's Works, Vol 18, p. 606.
11. *Augsburg Confession*, V.
12. Weimar edition, Vol 18, p. 603.
13. Vol. I, fifth edition by Schlaginhaufen, 1951.
14. Madrid, 1958.
15. V. Montes de Oca, *More about Fatima*, Dublin, 1960, pp. 57f; T.T. Delaney, *A Woman Clothed with the Sun. Eight great appearances of Our Lady*, Image Book, New York, 1961, p. 194.

Study Questions

1. What is the only source of Revelation? _____
2. What was one of the most dramatic moments in the history of the Roman Catholic Church? _____
3. What had come to an end? _____
4. Official Church papers are always inclined to _____ .
5. The great future Re-united Church will not be _____ .
6. What had become one of the most vital questions of the Roman Catholic Church and all Christendom? _____
7. Every heretic has claimed that his false doctrine is only _____ .
8. What has completely changed the ecumenical situation? _____
9. Rome can never accept the Sola _____ .
10. What sentence requested by Pope Paul VI is a rejection of the *Sola Scriptura* of the Reformation? _____
11. What doctrine strongly affirmed by modern popes from 1893 to 1943 was weakened? _____
12. What stands at the door of the Roman Church? _____
13. The Protestant Churches throughout the world seem to have lost

_____ .

14. The Reformers of the sixteen century were men of _____ .
15. According to Luther, the Church could not exist without the _____ Testament.
16. What was so important to the New Testament, Old Testament and early Church?
17. The Redeemer is also the _____ .
18. What is the Filioque? _____
19. What have the pagan siblys in Michelangelo's Sistine Chapel have to do with Isaiah and Jeremiah? _____
20. The Bible does not contain any _____ .
21. What were Luther's views of the epistle of James? _____
22. What did the Council of Trent says about *Sola Scriptura* and *Sola Fide*? _____
23. Erasmus defended the _____ or man.
24. How does Erasmus speak on behalf of modern man? _____
25. Luther constantly improved his _____ .
26. Who is the content of Scripture? _____
27. What distinguishes the Bible from all other books in the world? _____
28. Who is present in the Bible? _____
29. How does Luther refute the entire religious skepticism of the modern world? _____
30. Not everything which comes from the past can be _____ .
31. Is the Church a source of doctrine? _____
32. What is the source of the dogma of the Assumption of 1950? _____
33. What took place four years after the dogma of the Immaculate Conception? _____
34. When did the public revelations on which the doctrine of the Church is built come to an end? _____
35. Who spoke the *Magnificat*? _____
36. What is the article by which the Church stands and falls? _____

§

GOEBEL'S STYLE PROPAGANDA IN CHURCH

6 Wellington Square
North Adelaide
South Australia 5006
1 December, 1968

Dear Brother Otten,

"Your question can hardly be properly answered because in came cases you do not know exactly what can be styled as an invitation. When Dr. Harms intimated to our President that he would appreciate an official invitation to our Convention he was informed that such an invitation could not be extended. We would then have to invite also other people and this would be impossible. Later we were informed that Dr. Harms would be in New Guinea for the celebration of your missions there. His departure from New Guinea to the U.S.A. would then coincide with our Convention at Albury, N.S.W. and the preceding General Pastors Conference. In what form his presence at our meetings was legalized, I do not know. Our synodical meetings, of course, are public. We simple pastors regarded this as a sort of friendly gate-crashing. Many of us felt that this was a case of great tactlessness. Dr. Harms knew, and he admitted that, that the declaration of Church fellowship with Missouri of the ALC would smash our union. Nevertheless he made use of this opportunity to address several meetings as if he was invited. He was supported by Professor Boumann, St. Louis, who had been flown out for this purpose. Many of us were surprised that the President of Missouri resorted to such methods to sell us his fellowship with the ALC and to plead for future fellowship with Missouri. I do not think that he did a great service to his own Church.

"There are, of course, different opinions within our Church concerning the confessional status of Missouri. Old ties of fellowship, the happy remembrance of many of our older pastors who had either studied at St. Louis or were deeply influenced by the theology of old Concordia play a role. In our own ranks we have men who desire wider fellowship with other Lutherans. In fact we all do. We do not want to isolate ourselves. It is our heart's desire that the Lutheran Church in your country may recover from the tremendous inroad Modernism has made almost everywhere. We feel that this cannot be stopped either by the constant assurance that all is well. Nor can it be stopped by a simple return to the theology of the *Brief Statement*. What you need, or rather what we all need, is that Holy Scripture and the confessions of our Church are regained as the living truth which our time needs. What can be done in the present situation before Denver I do not know. If Missouri joins the ALC, which is bound to the definite ecumenical course of our time, the cause of the Lutheran Church in America may be lost.

"I had a sleepless night when I read the last issue of the *Reporter* from which you quote. This is Goebel's style propaganda in the Church. I have the deep confidence that your people will reject this if the theologians are not protesting what should be the sacred duty of all pastors and professors."

x x x

Thus far, dear Brother, my answer. You may quote from it, but without

69

mentioning my name. Had I time I would write an article. But this is at present not possible. You should have assistance in editing your paper to help you to avoid unnecessary mistakes. I would not attack a confessional Reformed theologian like Klaas Runia. He is fighting a good fight for the authority of Scripture and against the ecumenical dangers which have been threatening also the conservative reformed. You know that the "Reformed Ecumenical Synod" has rejected the WCC this year.

With all good wishes for the holy season of Advent and Christmas,
Yours fraternally,
According to what we have been told,
Hermann Sasse

§

CONCENTRATE ON ECUMENICAL ISSUE

H. Sasse
6 Wellington Square
North Adelaide, South Australia
6 Dec. 1968
Dear Brother Otten:
The other day I replied to your question whether or not Harms had been invited. I can give no other answer. But I want to ask you when you refer this not to mention my name and to leave out the words "His Master's Theological Voice" which I use for Bouman. Both men have done a tremendous damage to our Church through the tactless way in which they advertised their fellowship with the ALC and encouraged indirectly all those in our former UELCA who have still a longing for the flesh-pots of the Lutheran World Federation (LWF). They took so much of our time which was needed for our own business. In addition to them we had Repp here who finalized the doctor's examination for Janetzki. He conferred the D.D. on Pahl and made Church politics in a grand style. I tell you this, I shall write briefly to Wiederaenders. I hear encouraging things from Werning and A. Wagner (California). But I am deeply distressed, and so are most of us.

You will have a hard year. Be careful in all statements. Do by all means concentrate on the ecumenical issue. For on this matter all becomes clear, the whole apostasy from the Lutheran Church. God bless you in the new year and help us all to remain steadfast. Thank you for the *News.* I shall renew my subscription. All other periodicals I have cancelled. This will be my last year in office. On Jan. 1, 1970 I shall be retired.

With all good wishes for a blessed Christmas.

Yours in Christ,
Hermann Sasse

§

Brief Statement on Creation

6 Wellington Square
North Adelaide, South Australia
Good Friday 1969

Dear Brother Otten,

Thank you very much for you air-mail copy and the Badger cutting. I asked Dr. Preus to send you $2 to cover my subscription up to Denver. Then we must discontinue this subscription. It was the last paper I have subscribed to. I had to cancel all periodicals. By the end of the year I shall be retired – I am going to be 74 – and my salary will cease. I shall get a pension of $300 per annum. Up to that time I have to finish a book and other publications. This explains why I cannot do very much concerning the decision of Denver. I am sorry that you have to do your work as editor without more contributors. You may have been fighting a noble fight, though I feel sometimes you ought to have had the advice of older and more experienced men. My best wishes for your work and thanks for what you have done for us all. What a shame that we have not got periodical for conservative Lutheran theology with more contributors of the standard of Prof. Robert Preus. But this may come, if God will help us.

Today I want to write a few words on the *"Brief Statement"* which you mention. I have always objected against making this the document for which to fight. It is too weak, not a very careful work and open to criticism. I was present at the convention of San Francisco when it was reaffirmed. It was said that anyone who had objections against it should notify the proper authorities so that a re-examination was possible. None of the big professors who rejected it more or less publicly has the courage to come to the fore. This has created the ambiguous situation of Missouri. Theoretically your Church was upholding Pieper's theology while actually the contrary was taught at St. Louis. I always have regretted the state of untruthfulness which thus was created. This untruthfulness is the reason for the tragedy of St. Louis.

To show you the weakness of that document I take three examples. Unfortunately I have in hand not the full text, but only those articles which have been printed in a pamphlet containing the Common Confession and the parallels from the *Brief Statement*.

1. How can the sentence be justified that Adam before the fall was "en-

71

dowed with a truly scientific knowledge of nature"? What does scientific mean? No one denies that he had a profound understanding of nature. But this was in the realm of wisdom rather than in the realm of science. This idea is not scriptural, but goes back to certain Fathers of the 4th century who taught that Adam was the perfect philosopher, so perfect that he did not even need food. You would not regard such traditions as Christian faith.

2. Article 43 teaches that the prophecies of the Holy Scriptures concerning the Antichrist 2. Thess. 3:1. John 2, 18 have been fulfilled in the Pope of Rome and his dominion. Quite right. But is that enough? If this was the case, where was Antichrist in the first centuries when there was not yet a papacy? For Luther the papacy began after Gregory the Great. He found, as we know, Antichrist wherever man puts himself in the place which belongs to Christ alone. He saw Antichrist also in enthusiasts of his time, in Mohammed who dethroned Christ. Where is Antichrist today apart from the Roman papacy? Pieper found him in the Federal Council which is good Lutheran theology. Is he also in the WCC, perhaps in Missouri too? The mystery of Antichrist is destroyed if we say: He is in Rome, not here. Or with old Iowa: He belongs to the future, he is not here.

3. Article 27 Local Churches and local congregations. I am sorry that Mankato indulges in warming up the old controversy with Wisconsin – just at this critical time – whether only the local Church is Church. The whole concept of old Missouri is not tenable because according to the New Testament the ekklesia is the qahal of the Old Testament, the people of God, which can be there where two or three are gathered or a local Church or it can mean the people of God in whole provinces Acts 9, 31 where the Textus Receptus have Churches, but the better text is Church. It is really which decides the matter. (*Ed. Three sentences of this Sasse letter from the files of Christian News are not legible here*). His theory does justice to the fact that there was not one single form of Church institution in the earliest Church as we know from the newly uncovered texts from the 2nd century.

I could go on, but this is useless. The *Brief Statement* has no real authority. Who would die for it? It is obsolete. It cannot even be improved.

One word of warning I would like to say concerning the interpretation of Genesis. We had here, some years ago, old Professor Rehwinkel who lectured on such subjects and wrote a book on the age of the earth. He tried to improve Ussher's chronology without having any idea of Luther's Supputatio ummorum mundi, without knowing that this whole attempt goes back to the Church Fathers, East and West, who came to different results according to their various biblical texts (vulgate – Masoretic or LXX). Luther's and Ussher's results are based on the assumption that the world would last 6,000 years. This was regarded as prophecy of Elijah. Actually it comes from Talmud. This is the tragedy of a mere traditional theology. Rehwinkel declared: He who does not accept the biblical chronology (or what he regarded as such) has no savior. All his sources were Reformed apologists, Luther is not even mentioned. His book was recommended everywhere and highly praised. This is Fundamentalism, not Lutheranism. In the debates about this I was strongly reminded of a word I once heard at a convention of the Jehovah's Witnesses: "Lutherans make the best Jehovah's Witnesses". They have respect for the Scriptures, but many of them have been brought up in a wrong interpretation of Scripture.

I came across these days a passage from Luther where he speaks of the terrible judgement of the Flood. In this judgement not only the false Church of Cain perished, but also the true Church of Seth. For there must have been more than eight believers. The true Church perishing with the false Church – what a mystery. He concludes the statement with the words: Oh fear God and do not rely on the name "Church". "Fürchtet Gott und trotzet nicht auf den Namen der Kirche". This I had to remember when I read in your news the words of one of the presidents who stated that the Missouri Synod is the most orthodox Church on earth.

God bless you, dear brother, I send a copy of this to Bb. Werning.
With every good with and fraternal greetings,
Yours in Christ
H. Sasse

§

NEED FOR A 20TH CENTURY FORMULA OF CONCORD

April 14, 1969
Dear Dr. Sasse,
Many thanks for yours of April 4. We'll gladly send you *Christian News* free as long as you want it or we publish it. We've been hoping the silent conservative group within Missouri would start their own publication and we could then discontinue.

I never read that much into the sentence you quote from the BS regarding Adam's scientific knowledge, but basically I find myself in accord with several of the points you make. It appears to me that we still need some sort of Twentieth Century Formula of Concord by the time the LWF meets next year. Confessional Lutherans could gather around this Formula rather than the LWF. I wish such a Formula could be written by such men as you, Oesch, Montgomery, R. Preus, Marquart, Dannell, and Hardt.

M. Scharlemann is still arguing that the position he takes on Scripture is basically your position. He claims that he is familiar with the claim that you no longer defend everything you wrote years ago on the subject, but he wrote to us that Sasse only changed on a few "mickey mouse" matters. We're publishing his letter together with a statement you sent me a number of years ago on the St. Louis seminary. At the time I wanted to use your statement by presenting it to the Board of Appeals of the Missouri Synod, but such evidence was not allowed since there would be no opportunity to cross-examine. We're also publishing your entire letter on fellowship with the ALC. Parts of your letter have already appeared in BALANCE and it has been circulating among officials. I assume you're familiar with BALANCE.

In Christ,
Herman Otten

Study Questions
1. While the LCMS was theoretically defending Pieper's theology, St. Louis seminary was _____ .
2. "This _____ is the reason for the tragedy of St. Louis."
3. The mystery of the Antichrist is destroyed if _____ .
4. Otten suggested that a Twentieth Century Formula of Concord be written by _____ .

§

SASSE, SCHARLEMANN, AND INERRANCY

Christian News, April 14, 1969

Dr. Martin Scharlemann
1 Seminary Terrace North
St. Louis, Missouri 63105
Dear Dr . Scharlemaim:

May we have a copy of your answer to Mr. Ralph Lohrengel's letter to you of February 22, which we published in the March 10 *Christian News*. We understand that you have sent copies of your reply to Mr. Lohrengel to Dr. Theodore Nickel and President Edwin C. Weber. According to information we have received, you have written Mr. Lohrengel that "I have never denied the inerrancy of Scripture." Such a statement clearly implies that none of your essays, according to you, deny what you consider to be the doctrine of inerrancy. You still maintain that even the essays you withdrew at the 1962 Cleveland convention do not deny what you mean by the inerrancy of Holy Scripture. Since you have gone to considerable length pointing out what you consider to be errors in the Bible, evidently your view of inerrancy allows for the position that the Bible contains errors and even myths.

Since you still insist that the Bible contains errors, perhaps it would be well if you gave up the word inerrancy as your brother Robert does when he honestly writes in your *Lutheran Scholar*: "Unless one so defines 'error' that it does not really mean an error in the normal sense; or unless one holds to the word 'inerrancy' with a sort of blind dogmatism, the assertion that the Bible is inerrant, 'that is, contains no error, 'simply cannot be supported by the Biblical evidence itself."

According to Mr. Lohrengel's letter to you of March 17, which we intend to publish together with any reply you may send us, you still insist that your views on Holy Scripture are in accord with the Australian Theses of Agreement. When we mentioned this to Dr. Hermann Sasse, one of the chief authors of these Australian Theses, he wrote that your position on Scripture was "very superficial" "untenable" and "Anglican rather than Lutheran." Dr. Henry Hamann wrote in the September, 1961 *Australian Theological Review*: "If Dr. Scharlemann accepts these Theses on Scripture and Inspiration, and understands the term 'inerrancy' as we understand it, we shall rejoice and be glad. But he will have to leave behind, in that case, his essay, 'The Bible as Record, Witness, and Medium' (and others), his distinction between truth and fact, his theology of Word-deed. For there are in the 'Theses of Agreement' no gates and no sallyports through which such teachings could enter and find shelter."

Herman Otten

cc. Dr. Theodore Nickel

President Edwin Weber

Sasse, Scharlemann and the "Balance Boys"

How very interesting! So Dr. Sasse says that my essays present a superficial and Anglican view of Scripture! He must have said that with tongue in cheek, because almost all the points my essays make he himself gives in his letters that he used to send to his fellow Lutheran pastors in Germany.

I wonder if the "Balance" boys know this. They quote his work as though it were canonical. But they have never examined his views on scripture, as given in the letters I referred to.

Nor have they ever read his devastating essay on the *Brief Statement*. They could get a copy of that from the President of the Springfield Seminary. Dr. Sasse sent him a copy as a contribution toward a more profound Lutheranism.

Oh, yes, I know. Dr. Herman Harms used to say, "But Sasse has changed his position!" So I checked him (Sasse) out on that. I have his response. The change is about as important as shifting from the conviction that Matthew was written in 85 A.D. to the position that maybe it was composed in 69. In other words, it is a "mickey mouse" Item.

I've often wondered why you never reproduced that critique. Surely, you have a copy. Or are you slipping? Suppose your fans found out that there is some document of which you have no copy!

Let me repeat what I said to Mr. Lohrengel: I have never denied the inerrancy of Scripture - unless, of course, the Australian Lutherans (our brethren) did in 1956, when they accepted the THESES OF AGREEMENT! Do you think they did?

75

Martin H. Scharlemann
The Lutheran Academy For Scholarship
St. Louis, Missouri

March 27, 1969
Dr. Martin Scharlemann
Concordia Seminary
St. Louis, Missouri 63105
Dear Dr. Scharlemann:

Dr. Hermann Sasse was serious when he wrote us that your position on Scripture was "very superficial and untenable, Anglican rather than Lutheran."

I do not agree with everything that Dr. Sasse has written on Holy Scripture, but in fairness to Dr. Sasse it should be noted that he has retracted his "Letter No. 14", August, 1950. This is the letter you repeatedly refer to in support of your position. When you mentioned this "Letter No. 14" in your essay on "Revelation And inspiration" in Jefferson City on October 20-22, 1959, I tried to point out to the conference that Dr. Sasse no longer maintained the views you ascribed to him.

Dr. Sasse wrote to the student bookstore at Concordia Seminary on June 29, 1967: "A friend of mine sent me, these days, a duplicated copy of an article of mine which I had written in 1950 ("Letter No. 14"), in the translation of my friend. Dr. Ralph Gehrke. He had just purchased it at your store. Several years ago this article was published by your bookstore without my permission. This was regrettable as the essay, written during our Australian discussions of the doctrine of Holy Scripture contained formulations which I could not maintain. It was one of my letters to Lutheran pastors. Immediately after this I corrected what had to be corrected in the subsequent letters and made a thorough investigation of the Patristic material. No one seems to have taken cognizance of these corrections although the publications came into the same hands as the first article. In the following years I have published several more articles which are available in your library. But just the first letter was reprinted again and again by your store. I wrote to Dr. Fuerbringer as well as to the manager of your store. I called his attention to the fact that such an unauthorized publication which went on for years was a grave violation of the international Law of Copyright, apart from the moral aspect of the matter. Your store promised that it would not occur again. Now the production has been taken up again."

Our Australian brethren do not deny the doctrine of inerrancy of Scripture in their THESES OF AGREEMENT. However, as was noted in their *Australian Theological Review*, your essays on Scripture are not at all in harmony with these THESES.

Herman Otten

Ed. Both Missouri Synod liberals and conservatives claim Dr. Hermann Sasse supports their position. When we were involved in the Concordia Seminary-Otten case almost 10 years ago, we wrote to Dr. Sasse for a theological opinion on the use of Matthew 18 and some advice which we could use when we argued our case before the Board of Appeals of The Lutheran Church-Missouri Synod. In 1958 we told Dr. John W. Behnken, then president of the Missouri Synod, and a few others that there were professors at Concordia Seminary teaching that the Bible contains errors and various other doctrines contrary to Holy Scripture. Concordia Seminary argued that we had violated Matthew 18 because we did not have a private conversation with every professor we mentioned in our conversation with Dr. Behnken. Concordia Seminary argued that it was always sinful under all circumstances to repeat disturbing public matter without first conducting a private conversation. Dr. Sasse's reply shows that already nine years ago he was greatly concerned about the theology being taught at Concordia Seminary.

x x x

Christian News, **View of Inspiration Comes from Paganism**
March 29, 1969
Let me repeat to you as simply as I can, I checked out Dr. Sasse on the changes you and others refer to but never explain.

I wrote him a letter and asked him to tell me just where he had modified his position. Being an honorable man he replied. That letter I have before me right now. (Again, you don't have a copy; and I am beginning to wonder what your fans will think when they realize that here's another document you don't have a copy of. Surely, you will soon disappoint them!) He spelled out his modifications. They are of such insignificance is to deserve the label "mickey mouse matters".

The main points I have in my essays are treated in his letters; and he has not modified them in any significant way.

He is still convinced that the theory of inspiration propagated by your journal comes from paganism and not from Scripture. In fact, he calls it Reformed- Fundamentalist rather than Lutheran.

His gripe about our store making available his essay is a proper one. He wasn't asked. Just the way you never asked whether you could reproduce my essays. I share Dr. Sasse's belief that both are manifestations of very shabby ethics.

Incidentally, I have not yet seen a reference in your sheet to the apology your correspondent from Austin, Texas, sent me for misrepresenting my view of inerrancy. It didn't take him long to catch on to the degree to which you had misrepresented my position. And being an upright man, he apologized. You ought to print that letter, (Or, don't you have a copy of it? Tsk! Tsk! What will your readers think now?)

Martin H. Scharlemann,
Graduate Professor of
Exegetical Theology

April 1, 1969
Dr. Martin Scharlemann
Concordia Seminary

St Louis, Missouri

Dear Dr. Scharlemann:

If you will send us the statement from Dr. Hermann Sasse which shows that he modified his position only on certain "mickey mouse matters," we will publish it. We will also publish any document in which Dr. Sasse refers to our position on Holy Scripture as coming from paganism and that it is Reformed Fundamentalist rather than Lutheran.

We must frankly admit that we never received a copy of that apology you say our correspondent from Austin, Texas, sent you for misrepresenting your position. If you will send us a copy of this apology, we will immediately publish it.

The reprinting of an essay by Dr. Sasse, which he had retracted, cannot be compared to the reprinting of your essays. Dr. Sasse no longer defended the view of inspiration found in the essay reprinted by the Summary Bookstore and which you continue to use to support your position. On the other hand, you still defend the doctrinal content of your essays. When only various passages from your essays are quoted, you claim that you are quoted out of context. The State of the Church men were not guilty of any "shabby ethics" when they reprinted essays which you were vigorously defending. If you are so confident that your position is thoroughly Lutheran and scriptural, then why do you continue to refuse us permission to reprint your essay on *The Inerrancy of Scripture*?

Herman Otten

Ed. Dr. Scharlemann has not yet sent us the apology which he claims our correspondent sent to him. Our correspondent told us on April 5 that "I am of the same opinion still that, in essence, he said what I said he said at the Corpus Christi Convention, and you printed in Christian News.*" We still maintain that Dr. Scharlemann in his published un-retracted essays rejects the doctrine of the inerrancy of the Bible as defined in his church's* Brief Statement: *"Since the Holy Scriptures are the Word of God, it goes without saying that they contain no errors or contradictions, but that they are in all their parts and words the Infallible truth, also in those parts which we treat of historical, geographical, and other secular matters, John 10,35."*

Study Questions

1. Dr. Martin Scharlemann wrote that I have never denied the ____ of the Bible.
2. Sasse said that Scharlemann's view of the Bible was ____.
3. Scharlemann wrote that Sasse's change was a ____ item.
4. When Scharleman quoted Sasse's "Letter No. 14" in Jefferson City, Missouri, Otten told the conference that ____.
5. Concordia Seminary, St. Louis argued that it was always sinful to

   ____.
6. Scharlemann insisted that Sasse claimed that the theory of inspiration promoted by *Christian News* comes from ____.
7. Otten offered to publish the statement ____.
8. Scharlemann still defended ____.

A Word of Warning

Christian News, April 14, 1969

Dr. Hermann Sasse, the writer of this letter, is well known in world Christian circles. He was born and educated in Germany. In 1933 he was called to the chair of Church history and symbolics at Erlangen University, where be taught until 1949. In 1949 be moved to Australia, and since that time but served on the faculty at Immanuel Lutheran Theological Seminary in North Adelaide.

Dr. Sasse is the author or many books and hundreds or major articles. His early book, *Here We Stand*, was a major contribution toward defining Confessional Lutheranism against the encroachments of Barthianism and reformed theology. His great work, *This Is My Body*, is the definitive work of our century on the doctrine of the real presence of Christ's Body and Blood in the sacrament of the altar. A recent book, *In Statu Confessions*, comprises many of his finest articles.

Dr. Sasse is known as an authority on the ecumenical movement in which he was very active during its formative years in Europe before and after the war. He was a key figure in the merger of the sister Churches of the LCMS and ALC to Australia, where he was a member of the ALC sister-Church. Dr. Sasse has lectured for the Missouri Synod and had taught twice at Concordia Seminary, Springfield, Illinois.

This letter has been circulating in various circles within the LCMS.

(An Open Letter to the Lutheran Church-Missouri Synod)

It has happened several times in my life that I had to speak publicly a word of warning, a fraternal admonition to a wider circle of brethren in deep concern for the future of the Church. So I had in 1932, as editor of the "Kirchliches Jahrbuch fur die deutschen evangelischen Landeskirchen," to warn the German Churches against any compromise with the Nazi party and its hypocritical program. When in 1933 a "National Synod" met at Wittenberg to transform, at Hitler's command, the Federation of the German evangelical Churches into a unified "Deutsche Evangellsche Kirche," every member found on his desk my article "Die deutsche Union von 1933" which tried to show what the consequence for the Churches of the Reformation must be if they sacrificed their faith and confession to the alleged interest of the nation. This warning had to be repeated until the formation of the "Evangelische Kirche in Deutschland" in 1948 finalized the unification and de-confessionalisation of German Protestantism. When in 1947 the Lutheran World Convention was transformed into the Lutheran World Federation a letter addressed "To the brethren in the Lutheran Faith assembled at Lund" was read in the assembly by the late Professor Fred Mayer, St. Louis, warning against the new organization allowing to abandon the principles of Church fellowship contained in the Seventh Article of the Augsburg Confession. It was the result of the deliberations that had been made in a committee on "Church and Churches" appointed for the assembly of the Convention which had been scheduled for Philadelphia 1941.

If I again make use of my privilege as a public teacher of theology in the Lutheran Church and ask you to share this letter with those of your brethren who want to know my opinion concerning the great issue which your Church has to face at the forthcoming convention, this does not mean that I want to interfere with matters your Church has to decide. President Harms and Professor Bouman, who attended our recent convention, have made it an issue also for the Lutheran Church of Australia by explaining to us their plans to establish Church fellowship between Missouri and the ALC and by inviting us to establish Church fellowship with the Lutheran Church-Missouri Synod. Even if they had not done this, your problem would still be ours. It is in fact a problem for the entire Lutheran world. For what is at stake is nothing less than the right understanding of the great article of the Augsburg Confession on the unity of the Church. Because this is the case I am of the conviction that the three Lutheran Churches which belong to the Lutheran Council should not proceed with immediate fellowship negotiations, but rather postpone these decisions until during a synodical period of perhaps two years a thorough theological investigation of the pertinent issues is made on the highest theological level, which of course does not mean that the matter should be left to the professors and faculties. What I mean is that on all levels of the Churches certain basic problems with which all these Churches are confronted should be studied. This study should be done in a spirit of humble self-examination and in view of the ecumenical responsibility of the Lutheran Church.

Leaving aside for the moment the LCA, let us consider the present negotiations between Missouri and the ALC. They rest on the assumption that the two Churches are still what they were twenty or thirty years ago. It is true, both have the same confessions, though it should not be forgotten that even in this respect there is a fundamental difference. Missouri accepts the *Book of Concord* without qualifications, while the constitution of the ALC shows a remarkable lack of the clarity as to the authority of the various strata of the confessions. On the one hand the Formula of Concord has not the same authority as the Augsburg Confession, on the other hand it is declared that all confessions are received with the "Quia" of the confessional obligation. It must not be forgotten that the former ELC had never accepted the FC and that this was done in the merger as an act of courtesy rather than as an act of real confession. The old ALC had the FC, but it understood essential articles not in the sense of Missouri e.g., the article of predestination. But perhaps we all have moved away from the doctrinal standard of former generations. We accept the *Book of Concord* as the Anglican accepts the 39 Articles or as the liberal Presbyterians accept the Westminster Confession. This seems to be a process which is going on in all Christendom, even in Rome, as the new confession shows which Paul VI has recently published and which treats the doctrine of the Holy Spirit in the same gentlemanlike way as we treat the doctrine of predestination to say nothing of certain

80

doctrines of the Second Vatican Council which bluntly contradict the doctrine of Trent (e.g., the doctrine of sin). Should not we Lutherans examine honestly and seriously our real attitude to the confessions?

But not only the confessions must be examined but also the various theological statements with which Missouri and the ALC have tried to overcome their differences. We must be clear about the fact that our Churches are not firm buildings which invariably keep their place, but rather ships moving on a somewhat turbulent sea. As one who has followed the development of the Lutheran Churches in America since more than 40 years I can say that the theology which is being taught at Mount Airy, Philadelphia, is totally different from that which was taught 40 or 30 years ago. And the same is true of the seminaries of the ALC in Dubuque, Capital, and St. Paul. I know these seminaries since twenty years, as I at that time came to know also the seminaries or Missouri.

Now everybody would admit that faculties and seminaries must change, that there is a necessary and legitimate development of Christian theology. The great question, however, is whether the development was in every case legitimate. There may be and there have been developments which were not healthy, but rather indicative of a profound decay. When the impossible and superficial "Book of Confessions" with the new "Confession of 1967" was published by the Assembly of the United Presbyterian Church It was highly praised by the leading theologian of the local Lutheran faculty. This would have been unthinkable in 1947. The greatest and perhaps most tragic example of such a change is the development of Concordia, St. Louis. And this was not only a change of the generations, for it could happen that just older men suddenly underwent such a complete change of mind. It is no use if we close our eyes to these facts and that we issue to each other well meant testimonial orthodoxiae.

If we want to preserve to our children the Church of the Lutheran Reformation we must not shrink back from a thorough self-examination and from a real metanoia.

The most unsatisfactory means of discovering the real state of our Churches are conferences between pastors and laymen, discussions between local congregations of Missouri and the ALC to find out what amount or agreement exists between them and to conclude from such findings that Church fellowship is not only God-pleasing and necessary, but also demanded by the 7th Article of the Church of Australia (CA) because there is a consensus between us, greater than we had anticipated. Maybe that we agree on false opinions, in a weak faith and in a lack or theological understanding, it is a wrong Pietistic understanding of the great article on the true unity of the Church to assume that if a few Christians at a given moment find that they are in agreement they are entitled and even obliged to have Church fellowship. This is still worse if two pastors of different Churches come to this conclusion. Our congregations would do well to ask not only what their pastors teach, but also what their successors will teach. This they can find out when they know what kind of theology these young men are being taught. It seems to me that just the Lutheran Church - Missouri Synod has fallen an easy prey to this un-Lutheran, pietistic thinking on the Church and its unity. This is perhaps to be explained by the love of the Missourians for dogmatic discussions.

"Non in doctrina, sed in disputatione veritas amittitur" said Luther. Not in teaching, but in disputation truth is lost. This is especially true of the mission fields and young Churches which are trying to find new formulas of faith.

The ecumenical movement with its emphasis on new local confessions seems to have exercised a great influence on Missouri. An example is the formula of compromise which the Evangelical Lutheran Church in South India has reached in negotiations with the Church of South India. The Real Presence in the sense of the Catechism was negotiated away. The Lutheran doctrine is that in the Lord's Supper the consecrated bread IS the body, the consecrated wine IS the blood of Christ, which means that the body which was born of the Virgin, hung on the cross and was raised from the dead, and the blood which was shed for us. In virtue of Christ's words the consecrated elements are essentially the holy and substantially the blood of Christ though not qualitatively, quantitatively or locally present. The theses of India—I quote from the official German text contained in "Lehrgesprach uber das Heilige Abendmahl", edited by G. Niemeier, Munchen 1961, 337, teaches with the Arnoldsheim Theses of Germany the real personal presence of Christ (which is recognized by all Churches), and maintains that we receive in the sacrament the body and the blood of Christ in a spiritual manner ("spirituali modo" at FC. Form. Conc. VII is used, though not understood in the sense of the FC). It is expressly denied that we eat the material flesh of Jesus of Nazareth, which leaves the question open what the relationship between the body of Christ in the Sacrament and the crucified, risen and glorified body is. This is the modern version of Cryptocalvinism which seems to be accepted generally as a substitute for the doctrine of the Catechism. "It is the true body and blood of Christ". India is only one case in point. "Marburg Revisited" shows that this doctrine is now entering also the Lutheran Churches in America, partly as a consequence of modern Personalism and Existentialism in Christian theology. But even this sacrifice was without any result. For the Church of South India can according to its constitution and its confessional basic not accept any definite doctrine on the Lord's Supper. This doctrine is left to the individual and the individual congregation.

What are the deeper reasons for the crisis of Lutheran theology in America? The Lutheran Churches in America in all its branches was determined by its dogmatics. It has never developed a historical theology. By contrast, the Lutheran Churches or Europe had lost their dogma and replaced the dogma with history. A merely historical theology loses its ability to understand the great quest for truth. Historical relativism destroys the doctrinal content of the Church. But on the long run no Church can live by dogma alone. For the Christian revelation is a historical revelation and cannot fully be understood without a historic approach. The Christian faith rests on historical facts, the Bible is not only God's Word, but God's Word which has come to us in a long history. The European Churches were like ships whose propellers were working but compass and rudder did not work. The American Churches were like ships where compass and rudder were working, but the propeller was not working. So both types of Churches were drifting. When the American Churches began to understand their weakness they sent their young theologians to Europe to learn the historical trade. Many came back without the old doctrinal substance. Here lies the deepest cause for the crisis of the American Churches. What will be necessary is to translate historical theology into the dogmatics of the Lutheran Church? This will require a new training program for future professors. It is not possible that a young man comes back from Heidelberg or Tübingen and teaches what he has learned there and this is not very much since he had to spend most of his time on a specialized thesis to get the doctorate which in America is regarded as the sufficient training for a professor. Our American Churches will have to learn that only a post-doctoral training in real theology can furnish a man with the necessary qualifications for teaching on the seminary level. This post-doctoral training must include a process of spiritual delousing so that the terrific academic vanity, which is one of the curses of the European universities, is overcome.

These are some practical suggestions. It ought to be possible to delay the decision or the fellowship question. If a vote In Denver were taken there would be a substantial minority at least which could not accept it. This would probably mean that the question has to be put to the congregations. In any case such a question cannot be decided by a simple small majority. It would have to be an OVERWHELMING majority. If the decision can be delayed, the time should be used for a thorough overhaul of your entire Church. What Missouri needs is a new image. The present image is that of the right wing of the great American Lutheran Church which is always ten or twenty years behind the rest, but eventually accepts all decisions of the other Churches. What is the alternative? If you have two years, they should he spent, as I suggested, for a real self-examination in connection with a similar process in all Lutheran Churches. The greatest issue is the ecumenical problem. If you join the ALC, the joining of the LWF will automatically follow, the next step would be the WCC, the National Council and COCU. This is not worthy of a great Church, simply to follow all the rest only a few years later. Of course, we are told, fellowship with the ALC does not necessarily mean that we follow this Church wherever it goes. But why not? Why does Missouri not join the LWF, why not the other ecumenical organization? Is it not right for a confessional Lutheran Church to do that? If this is the reason, why has Missouri no objection against the membership of the ALC in these organizations? If you do not object against that, then there is no theological reason why Missouri does not join them. If you must leave the ALC the freedom to make this decision, then it cannot be wrong. Membership in these ecumenical organizations is then a MERELY PRACTICAL ISSUE. For practical reasons you remain outside, for practical reasons you may join in a few years' time.

Here the question arises whether participation in such organizations and movements is really an adiaphoron. In fact, this question leads into the depth of our understanding of the Church and its unity.

As to the LWF one could argue that a Federation of Lutheran Churches for co-operation in common tasks is possible. But here the question arises: What is understood by a Lutheran Church: The basis presupposes that the member Churches accept the Unaltered Augsburg Confession and Luther's Catechism, but why, then, is it possible that Churches which do not accept this doctrinal basis are full members? How is it possible that the Church of the Batak which has never accepted the Augsburg Confession and has not accepted the parts of Luther's Catechism which deal with the sacraments become a full member? And is it really enough to accept these Confessions only nominally? What about the member Churches which are de facto union Churches? That means Churches which grant the full rights of membership also to non-Lutherans or which themselves, as the Church of Pomerania a member of the "Church of the Union" in Germany.

The LWF has never adhered to its own constitution. What the moral aspect of this tact is, we do not want to discuss here. The deep reason for this broadmindedness is the simple fact, that also in many Churches who call themselves Lutheran the confession of the Church has disintegrated to such a degree that it ceases to mean more than a historical relic. Can a Church which claims to maintain the Lutheran Confession join such a federation? This would be tantamount to a denial of the Lutheran Confessions as the expression of the magnus consensus which is supposed to bind together the Churches of the Augsburg Confession. Missouri would cease to be a confessing Lutheran Church if it joined the present LWF, even in a qualified membership. Whatever the Church political advantages of such membership might be, these advantages cannot outweigh the loss of the real confession.

Furthermore, the LWF has become part and parcel of the Ecumenical movement as it is represented by the World Council of Churches. In fact, practically all member Churches of the LWF are also members of the WCC. Also a World Council of Christian Churches might be feasible, provided it is made clear what a Christian Church is. In Lausanne in 1927 we Lutherans together with Christians of other denominations proposed that the great Creeds of the Ancient Church, mainly the Nicene Creed, should be the common basis. But this was rejected and is constantly being rejected by "Churches" which reject the doctrine of the Trinity and the true divinity of Christ as binding dogma. How was it possible to accept as "Churches" those communities which reject the sacraments of Christ, even Baptism. And such a World Council claims to be the instrument of uniting all Christendom in a great ecumenical Church! The concept of Church and unity of the Church underlying the WCC is obviously irreconcilable with the doctrine confessed in the Seventh Article of the Augsburg Confession. It is a fact which is being recognized by a growing number of Christian Churches that the WCC has been instrumental in destroying the doctrinal substance of the Christian faith.

Let this be understood that what I am saying about the present ecumenical organizations is not the rash and irresponsible verdict of an unrepentant confessionalist who does not see the ecumenical problems. Since 1926 I have been active in the Faith-and-Order Movement. As a delegate to the World Conference at Lausanne, as member of its Continuation and its Executive Committees, as European Secretary of that Movement I have practically given the spare time, often years, of my life to the ecumenical cause. I was always deeply convinced that the situation of Christendom in this century requires a new order of the mutual relationship between the Churches, co-operation and doctrinal dialog. I have been working together with churchmen and theologians of various Churches, with men like Arseniew, Bulgakow and Glubokowsky of the Eastern Orthodox Church, with Anglicans like Bishop Gore, and Bishop Palmer of Bombay and the Bishop of Dornakal, with Lutherans like Olaf Moe of Norway, Wilhelm Zoellner of Germany, and with men like Frederick Knubel and Michael Reu in America. And I am still today co-operating with evangelical Anglican, with conservative Reformed, and even with Roman Catholic theologians. All these were men for whom the quest for unity was essentially the quest for the truth of God's revelation.

Our program, as presented by Elert at the first meeting of Lausanne, was to build Christian unity on the existing unities and not to organize existing unities to a utopian unity of a "future reunited Church." But all our endeavors were in vain. The big American denominations without real doctrinal basis, the Masonic belief in a "religion in which we all agree", and, last but not least, the Pietistic concept of undogmatic Christianity and of a chiliastic realization of the unity through the Spirit of God in the near future, as it was prevailing in the Christian youth organizations, made it impossible to base the ecumenical movement on a sound Biblical and doctrinal basis. Hence the movement ended not in unity, but in the disintegration of the existing Churches and that destruction of any dogmatic substance which has become manifest at Uppsala. The only achievement in the field of Church union was the Church of South India. But it is now generally recognized that this was a failure, not to be repeated. It was significant that the man who had done the most for it, William Temple, at the end of his life as Archbishop of Canterbury had to refuse the recognition of this Church and left it to his successor, the Free Mason Geoffrey Fisher to recognize it. Where this movement is bound to end is shown by the plans of COCU under the leadership of Dr. Blake and "Bishop" Pike to unite big Protestant bodies in America into a vast Church of forty or more millions without any doctrinal basis. I have never been able to understand why even a Church like the ALC can take seriously this enterprise, unless one must assume that also this Church is losing rapidly its doctrinal substance. If Missouri should go the same way or only approve of this ecumenical movement, the end of the Lutheran Churches in America would have come. Of the three great confessional Churches of the Reformation two have already lost their Reformation heritage, the Anglicans, and the United Presbyterians. If the Lutheran Church goes the same way, the road is open for a "reunion" of

Christendom under a decentralized and tolerant Roman papacy.

The *Sola Scriptura* and the *Sola Fide* are slowly dying in the world, in some parts of Christendom even not slowly, but rapidly. The Church of the future would certainly claim to be the Church of the Sola gratia, as even Rome does, but this would no longer be the sola gratia of Augustine and the Reformation, but the sola gratia of the universalism of Origen in which Rome and the Free Masons today seem to agree.

These are the thoughts I want to share with my American Brethren. Whatever your immediate decisions may be, you should know what is involved. We Lutherans are not interested in the preservation of the Lutheran Church as such. The Church which we confess in the Augsburg Confession is the Una Sancta perpetuo mansura. It is for the whole of Christendom that we want to maintain the pure preaching of the Gospel and the sacraments as Christ has instituted them. We owe this witness to our separated brethren in Rome as well as to the present Protestant world. We would betray our ecumenical mission if we joined a Church in which the basic doctrines of Holy Scripture deteriorates into non-committal theological opinions, each of which having the same right. This is what we should keep in mind if in the coming year or in a period of two years we have to set our house in order.

May I say in concluding a word as to the situation of the Lutheran Church-Missouri Synod as it appears to me as an observer and as a faithful friend of your Church. I was in America forty years ago when the great tragedy of the Presbyterian Church occurred. This Church broke asunder into a Modernist and a Fundamentalist wing. The witness of Calvin's Reformation was henceforth silenced, although either part, the modernist majority as well as the fundamentalist minority wanted to continue the heritage of the Fathers. The Social Gospel became the substitute for the Gospel of Christ on the one hand, a strict Biblicism replaced the old Reformed doctrine on the other. The five Fundamentals became the real confession of faith, but they did no longer confess the core of the Reformed doctrine and could be accepted by Baptists and other Protestants with little or no connection with the Reformation. The "Modernists" underwent a revival under the influence of Barth's theology. But the full Gospel was never really rediscovered, mainly due to the weakness of Barth's doctrine of the Word of God. The modern theology of young Missouri claims to be Lutheran, but the old Lutheran substance is weakening, as we all know. You have only to think of the heresies which were printed in "The American Lutheran" and which caught hold on the younger generation of professors and their students. Under this influence of modern German theology even the confessional consciousness was vanishing. Since this theology was no longer Confessional, also in Missouri the difference between Lutheran Churches and the Churches of the Union was vanishing. On the other hand, fundamentalism seems to be moving from the Reformed Churches into conservative Lutheranism. I often have wondered whether or not the *Brief Statement* was the first sign of a new confession. At least for many of the conservatives this was more important than the old confessions. This is a trend which we observe in the whole of Christendom including the Roman Church. They all want to have their "Barmen", even the youngest Church on the mission field. One of the reasons for this is the obvious fact that the old confession has become for many only a valuable, highly treasured inheritance from the fathers. Since you had not to fight for your confession as we had in Germany, the real existential importance of the confession was no longer fully recognized, it will be one of the great tasks of our Lutheran brethren in America to try to regain the full understanding of the nature of the Lutheran Confession as a confession which binds together not only the believers who at present believe, teach and confess the doctrine of the Gospel, but all generations of the true Church of Christ from the days of the apostles to the last day (comp. to the end of the Formula of Concord).

As I see it, it would be the one great task of the Lutheran Church - Missouri Synod to revive in American Lutheranism the genuine understanding of the Church according to Conf. Aug. VII and to draw the practical conclusion from this great article of the Lutheran faith. Missouri and the Churches in fellowship with her should have the courage which the recent "Reformed Ecumenical Synod" in Holland had (representing the Gereformeerde Kerk of Holland, the Christian Reformed Church in U.S.A. and the Reformed Church of Australia) to say a definite NO to the WCC in its present form, a NO to the ecumenical Church politics of the big Protestant Churches, including the Churches in the LWF. This would make your Church the center of those parts of Christendom which are not prepared to sacrifice the doctrine of the Reformation to the "ecumenism" of your time. It would be a great encouragement to all faithful Lutherans in the other bodies of the Lutheran Church in your country. For there are more faithful adherents to the Church of the Unaltered Augsburg Confession, also in the ALC and the LCA, than we are inclined to believe. One cannot judge the Lutheran Church from the official Church papers only, which do not represent the true opinions of the pastors and congregations, but rather represent the opinions of the administration and the leading Church politicians. In the present situation of our big Church bodies the voice of the "Stillen im Lande" can hardly be heard, and yet these are the people of whose faith and confession the future of the Lutheran Church depends. We should do what we can to keep close contacts with those in the various Lutheran bodies who are suffering from the state of the Lutheran Church, and cultivate such relations with them which are possible even in our divided state. Free conferences and forums not sponsored by the Church administrations, maybe one way of accelerating the day when the Lutheran Churches of America can practice that altar and pulpit fellowship which at all times since the days of the apostles has been the expression of the full unity of the Church, much more important than any declarations by synods and mergers of individual Church bodies.

These are some of the thoughts I wanted to share with my dear friends in the Lutheran Church – Missouri Synod on the eve of the greatest decision your Church had ever to make in modern times. I want to assure you that I belong to the many Christians throughout the world who pray that God the Holy Spirit may guide you all in your decisions so that Missouri may remain and become again what it was in the past: the Church where doctrine is still taken seriously and the substance of the Christian faith is not negotiated away.

With fraternal greetings,

Yours in Christ,

Hermann Sasse

Study Questions

1. Dr. Hermann Sasse taught at Erlangen University from____ to____.
2. This is My Body is the definitive work of the Twentieth Century on____.
3. What finalized the deconfessionalization of German Protestantism? ____
4. Missouri accepts the *Book of Concord* without____.
5. The greatest and most tragic example of change is the development of ____.
6. The Lutheran Church-Missouri Synod has fallen an easy prey to____.
7. The Church of South India cannot accept any basic doctrine of ____.
8. The Christian faith rests on____.
9. Young theologians who went to Europe came back with____.
10. What is necessary for teaching on a seminary level?____.
11. What is one of the curses of the European universities____.
12. Missouri needs a new____.
13. The LWF has never adhered to its ____ .
14. The WCC has been instrumental in destroying ____ .
15. Sasse gave years of his life to ____ .
16. What is slowly dying in the world?____ .
17. What was printed in the American Lutheran?____ .
18. The official Church papers do not represent ____ .

§

MISSOURI'S DECISION ON ALC FELLOWSHIP

DR. HERMANN SASSE
Christian News, May 12, 1969

THIS LETTER IS PRINTED AT THE REQUEST OF PARTICIPANTS AT THE LLL MILWAUKEE ZONE SEMINAR ON MARCH 2, 1969.

Dr. Hermann Sasse is the writer of the article, "The Decision of Denver." In 1933 he was called to the chair of Church history and symbolics at Erlangen University in Germany. In 1949 he moved to Australia, serving on the faculty of Immanuel Lutheran Theological Seminary in North Adelaide. Dr. Sasse is the author of many books and hundreds of major articles. His early book, *Here We Stand*, was a major contribution toward defining confessional Lutheranism against the encroachment of Barthianism and Reformed Theology. His great work, *This Is My Body*, is the definitive work of our century on the doctrine of the real presence of Christ's body and blood in the sacrament of the altar. Dr. Sasse is known as an authority on the ecumenical movement in which he was very active during its formative years in Europe before and after the war. He was a key figure in the merger of the sister Churches of the LCMS and the ALC in Australia, where he was a member of the ALC Sister-Church. Dr. Sasse has lectured for the Missouri Synod and has taught twice at Concordia Seminary, Springfield, Illinois.

Dr. Sasse wrote the following regarding the article that follows: "Dear Brother Werning: Yesterday I mailed to you a manuscript. You are free to publish it in any way you think fit. I wrote it as an historian, and mindful of the grave concerns which we all have. When I wrote this I was thinking of Dr. Behnken. Before each of the great synods and the crucial decisions he asked for my opinion, not to follow my advice, but to know what other conservative Lutherans were thinking. This is what I would have written to him in this case.

Yours in Christ,
Hermann Sasse."

THE DECISION OF DENVER

As the Lutheran Church - Missouri Synod at its Denver convention of 1969 decides whether or not it will establish Church fellowship with the ALC, an irrevocable decision will be made which will not only determine the entire future of Missouri, but will also be of vital importance to the whole of Lutheranism in the world. In the beginning of the 19th century, under the influence of the Pietistic and Rationalistic movements, the end of the Lutheran Church as a confessional Church seemed to have come. Entire Lutheran Churches, among them the largest (the Lutheran Church in the older provinces of Prussia), had accepted the union which wiped out the historic border-line between Lutheran and Reformed Churches.

Even in America, at that time still an appendix to Europe, the new General Synod was slowly moving in that direction. Then the great Awakening came, originally a sort of Pietistic revival, it turned 1830 into a rediscovery of Church and confession in many parts of Christendom. In many parts of Germany the Lutheran confession was rediscovered. Through migrations to America and, on a smaller scale, to Australia, the movement was transplanted into the New World.

The Lutheran synods in the Middle West of the U.S.A., consisting of German and Scandinavian immigrants, became a new stronghold of

Lutheranism in the world and the center of Lutheran confessionalism. Through the influence of Walther's *"Lutheraner"* the older type of American Lutheranism became again conscious of its confessional heritage. The rise of American Lutheranism was an historical event of the first magnitude. While European Lutheranism continued under the benefits, but also the disadvantages, of many centuries of a national establishment, the Lutherans in America were able to build up in freedom, relying entirely on the voluntary gifts of the faithful and strong Lutheran congregations unknown to the Old World. Their pastors, most of whom lacked the advantages of a high academic training in the old universities in Europe, proved that the faithful study of the Scriptures and the *Book of Concord* and available writings of Luther and some Lutheran fathers can give a theological education to make faithful witnesses to the Reformation message.

The great tragedy of confessional American Lutheranism was the split on matters of doctrine which occurred time and again and paralyzed its power. It began with the great dissent between Walther and Löehe on the question of Church and ministry. This led to the schism between Missouri and Iowa which extended later to other synods, especially when the "Gnadenwahlstreit," the controversy on predestination and election, broke out. It is pathetic to see in this last of the real theological controversies within the Lutheran Church, Walther and Missouri fighting alone for Luther's De servo arbitrio against their fellow Lutherans who were too deeply influenced by those remnants of synergism of which Pietism could never get rid. That all endeavors to solve these problems came to nothing may be regretted, but it should not lie forgotten, that even the European scholars were not able to help their American brethren.

The decision of Missouri at Denver will be the final end of these endeavors which in the negotiations of the past decades have been going on. But the various documents published reveal the fact that the real issues between Missouri and what has become in 1960 the American Lutheran Church are no longer the issues of former generations. New questions have arisen, the most important being the doctrine of Holy Scripture, its inspiration and inerrancy, and the problem of the confession of the Church, the nature of the dogma of the Church, its binding force and its application in the problems of modern Church life. Both Churches continue in their doctrinal statements the old doctrines of Scripture and confession, statements on which there was never a disagreement between the fathers of either Church. One often observed in the past that a pastor of the ALC preached as orthodox a sermon as his colleague from Missouri. It was on the whole a sound orthodox theology which was taught at Wartburg and at Capital some years ago. The students of that time did not differ very much from their fellow students of old St Louis. And yet something has happened which has created a totally different situation, it is a profound change in the attitude of the ALC towards Lutheran Confessionalism, while Missouri has maintained, at least in its official statements and its conventions, its confessional status, the ALC does no longer want to belong to the outspoken confessional

Churches in contrast to a mere nominal Lutheranism. Its aim is rather to be part and parcel of the great Lutheran Church of America which recognizes as of equal right all those who nominally (et de jure) accept the Lutheran Confessions. This underlies the decision of the Omaha convention which declared Church fellowship with the Lutheran Church in America and offers the same fellowship to Missouri, with this step the old confessional status of the ALC is given up. It is no longer the companion of Missouri in its fight for confessional Lutheranism. It puts Missouri into an impossible situation. For to declare fellowship with the ALC would now practically mean that Missouri accepts also fellowship with the LCA. Even if this were not declared on the highest level, how could this conclusion be avoided on the local level?

This new understanding of Church fellowship would leave far-reaching consequences for Missouri's attitude toward the LWF. If it is enough for the true unity of the Church that some confessional writings like the Augsburg Confession and Luther's Catechism are normally accepted, what prevents the Lutheran world Federation to declare itself, as Dr. C. Nelson suggests (*Luth. World*, vol. XV. No 4, 1968, p. 323), "to be the Lutheran Church on an international level?" When Dr. Nelson at Helsinki eloquently pointed out that it may be the will of God that the Lutheran Church, "obedient unto death" it should be prepared to die in order that the one holy, catholic and apostolic Church — whatever that may be— may live (Helsinki Report p. 95), one may imagine what the destiny of "the Lutheran Church on an international level" will be. To accept the offer made by the ALC to Missouri would mean that also Missouri ceases to be a Lutheran Church in the sense of the fathers, Church of the Unaltered Augsburg Confession in which the confession is not only a flag under which everybody can sail, but the expression of the great consensus in the pure doctrine of the Gospel and the right use of the Sacraments of Christ.

Hence the answer to the question with which Missouri finds itself confronted, only an unqualified No to the offer of the ALC and a definite end of all negotiations with the ALC in doctrinal matters. The question is whether Missouri is strong enough to give such a reply. It would presuppose that Missouri itself is aware of its own weaknesses. Too long has Missouri seen itself as the stronghold and guardian of Lutheran orthodoxy. We do not intend to discuss the false doctrines proclaimed by the theologians of the ALC. Such a discussion would immediately lead to the question whether not the same doctrines have been proclaimed in Missouri by men in St. Louis whose orthodoxy is being taken for granted (by some). One has only to read the incredibly naive theological "fashion" journal "*Dialog*" (Minneapolis) in order to understand the tragedy which is going on in all Lutheran Churches in America.

What is going on is a theological revolution which has its parallels in all Churches of the U.S.A., including the Roman Church. Behind this American tragedy becomes manifest a tragedy of the whole of Christendom, the loss of doctrinal substance. Are our brethren in Missouri able to see their own share in this tragic loss of the dogmatic substance without which the Church of Christ cannot exist? Hence the decision of Denver must not be a merely negative one. It must be a real "metanoia" in the sense of the New Testament, a going back, not into a repetition of the history of the past, but to the living Lord of the Church and His infallible Word. Let us all, whatever our outward Church connection may be, return to this authority and try to understand what today is required from Lutheran Christians.

The first thing we have to regain is a clear understanding of the Word of God which was for Luther always simultaneously the written word of the Bible and the faithful proclamation of this word in the preaching of the Church. They cannot be divided just as either is inseparable from the Word Incarnate. When we accept the Bible, we accept it as God's own word, given by the inspiration of the Holy Spirit and, consequently as truth, as the inerrant Word.

The second thing we have to learn again is the great dogmatic heritage of the Ancient Church in the great Creeds which we confess with the Church of all ages. Since the content of these creeds is thoroughly Biblical, as the Nicene Creed expressly claims, we do not allow a rejection of their contents, e.g., the Virgin Birth of our Lord and His bodily resurrection for alleged historical reasons. We reject expressly the error spread in our days that human language cannot express the truth of God sufficiently. The ALC has officially stated: "To assume that the Church can arrive at human concept or expressions that are in every respect correct is as much a symptom of pride as to assume that the Church or its members can achieve sinlessness in their daily lives. Both in living the faith and in knowing or expressing the faith, we all need daily forgiveness and amendment which the Holy Spirit alone can give" (Statement on Doctrinal Concerns, Exhibit G. Approved by the Church Council of the ALC in 1966.)

In his discussions with Erasmus as well as with King Henry VIII and on numerous other occasions Luther has made it plain that though our lives remain sinful, a statement of a clear Biblical doctrine is not sinful. Over against Erasmus' deprecation of firm dogmatic statements, Luther declares: "What Christian can endure the idea that we should deprecate assertions? That would be denying all religion and piety in one breath." "Take away assertions, and you take away Christianity" (De libero arbitrio WA 18,603: Packer-Johnston, *Bondage of the Will,* p. 67). Behind such deprecation stood, as Luther clearly saw, doubt of the truth of the Bible.

The third thing we have to learn again is the meaning of the confessions of the Lutheran Church. It is a most remarkable fact that the Church which in the 19th century became in many ways the confessional conscience of Lutheranism has not been able to develop the full Biblical and Lutheran understanding of the confession of the Church. This may partly be due to the error of Churches like Iowa which regarded as binding on the Church only such statements which were introduced in the confessions with a solemn formula such as "we believe, teach and confess," regarding all other questions as "open questions."

Missouri was afraid of subordinating the doctrine of the Scripture to the dogma of the Church. But this does not justify the failure to understand the full Biblical concept of the confession. Three times a solemn confession by Luther is quoted in the *Book of Concord*: his Large confession of 1528, his short or last confession of 1544 and the Smalcald Articles. In each case Luther confesses his faith in view of his death and the Last Judgment in which he will have to give account of his faith. This eschatological outlook belongs obviously to the nature of a Lutheran confession, as also the conclusion of the Formula of Concord indicates: "Therefore, in the presence of God and of all Christendom among both our contemporaries and our posterity, we wish to have testified that the present explanation of all the foregoing controverted articles here explained and none other is our teaching, belief and confession in which by God's grace we shall appear with intrepid hearts before the judgment seat of our Lord Jesus Christ and for which we shall give an account..." (*Book of Concord*, ed. Tappert, p. 636). This deadly seriousness of the Lutheran confession finds its expression also in the "Quia" with which we accept it in our ordination. We accept, of course, with this "Quia" the dogma of the virgin birth and of the second advent of Christ. But we can do it, and every Christian can do it, because "I believe in Him who was conceived by the Holy Spirit, born of the Virgin Mary," in Him who will come to judge the living and the dead.

The object of my faith is only indirectly the theological statement, directly it is He who demands my confession: "He who confesses me before men him will I confess before my Father who is in Heaven; and he who denies me before men, him will I deny before my Father who is in Heaven." It is certainly not accidental that in the language of the New Testament as in the language of the Church the "confession" means always at the same time "praise of God." Would it not be a great help to us Lutherans who want to keep up the Lutheran Church as truly confessing, faithful to the doctrinal content of the *Book of Concord*, if we better realized this profound Biblical understanding of the Lutheran confession? We would not give up one iota of its doctrinal content. But we would avoid the grave misunderstanding as if the confession were only a sum of statements which could easily be replaced by other statements.

How often have we been shocked during recent years by the suggestion made by orthodox Missourians, either to elevate the "*Brief Statement*" to the rank of a confession, or even to use it as a substitute for the old confession. It may even be assumed that not all members of the venerable Wisconsin Evangelical Lutheran Synod are quite happy with its new doctrinal statement, each sentence of which begins with "We believe that..." A great danger exists today on our mission fields. Each of the younger Churches wants to formulate its own confession under the pretext that the old confessions are "western," as if the doctrines of the Trinity and the Person of Christ had not been formulated by Asians, and our doctrine on original sin in Africa. If this process goes on, the Lutheran Church, which per definitionem is the Church of the Augsburg Confession, is bound to disintegrate into numerous denominations as happened with the Reformed Church.

What we said about the confession of the Church requires some remarks on Article VII of the Augsburg Confession. It should never be forgotten that this article, which is of so great importance for the Lutheran Church and its unity, does not speak of the Lutheran Church, but of the Una, sancta, catholica ecclesia perpetuo mansura. The unity of the Church it has in mind is, therefore, not only the unity of the Church of the Augsburg Confession. The consensus required for the true unity is, therefore, not the common subscription to certain confessional documents. A congregation, a district, a whole Church body do not become Church in the sense of this article by accenting legally and theologically certain documents, but by the fact that in their midst the gospel of the Sola fide is purely preached and the sacraments are celebrated according to the institution of the Lord (which includes also His understanding of the words of institution). This distinction between that which is essential for the Church and its unity and the mere adiaphora (the human traditions or rites and ceremonies instituted by men) becomes more and more important at a time like ours when our Churches are no longer the small groups of former generations, but big bodies, comprising thousands of congregations and pastors and millions of members.

The danger is that the administrative problems are solved by adopting the methods of the world. So the Churches in Europe are governed after the methods of the states, while in America they follow the example of the big business concerns. The central administration makes the decision. The task of the Church papers is to "sell" this decision to the people and to prepare the governing convention. All this is not ill will, it is the necessary consequence of a system whose primary victims are the Church administrators themselves. They are — or have been — Christian gentlemen, perhaps very good pastors themselves. But the system makes them "administrators" whose main task is to see to it that the policy is faithfully carried out as it has been determined by the governing body. Human traditions and decisions, then, constitute the unity of the Church. We have practically adopted the African and the Roman system. He is considered a good pastor who renders unquestioned canonical obedience to his superiors, whether he preaches the pure gospel and administers the sacraments as Christ has instituted them, this is a subordinate question, "we take that for granted," as the late Dr. Fry used to say. But can it be taken for granted in our Churches today?

How things have changed in our Churches, even in those which seriously want to remain orthodox, is shown by the great example of "Marburg Revisited." The Convention of the Lutheran Church-Missouri Synod of New York 1967 did not find any fault with the Lutheran-Reformed Discussions reported in "Marburg Revisited," although in these discussions the Lutheran doctrine of the true Body and Blood of Christ was negotiated away and replaced by a mere personal presence. The same happened in India, where under the leadership of Dr. Martin Kretzmann in a document which rightly has been incorporated into a collection of union documents of our time the doctrine of Luther's Catechism ("It is the true

94

body and blood of Christ") was abandoned. This happened in the year of the 450th anniversary of the Reformation. No one would have any serious objection against a Lutheran-Reformed dialog, as we all have to be prepared to give account of our faith and to learn whatever we have to learn from Christians of other denominations. But every serious dialog must be based on certain presuppositions. The participants must know what they are talking about. They must know what either party believes. At the time of the Reformation the colloquists had certain common beliefs. The resurrection and ascension of Christ were to them unquestioned facts of the divine revelation. This they are no longer today.

If we in conclusion may express a wish for the delegates at the Denver Convention, then it is that they all come well prepared to make a conscientious decision. This requires not only the thorough study of the convention papers, not only a critical perusal of the Church papers, but a clear concept of what they want Denver to be. Should it be the end of Missouri as a confessional Lutheran Church and the transformation of the old Missouri into one branch of a unified Lutheran Church which allows everybody individually to understand the Lutheran confessions as he likes? Or should it be the new beginning of a confessional Church, bound to the Scriptures and the *Book of Concord*, and therefore not in fellowship with the liberal and ecumenical Lutheranism of our time. By fellowship we mean what the theologians call "comunicatio in sacris," altar-fellowship. This would not mean that we refuse such cooperation as is possible with Christians of other convictions and especially those with whom we are connected through a great historic heritage. The old slogan, "Lutheran pulpits for Lutheran pastors, Lutheran altars for Lutheran communicants," may be a bad formulation, for neither a pulpit nor an altar can be Lutheran. But this old Acron-Galesbury Rule of our fathers expresses a role which has been valid in the Church at all times since 1. Cor. 10:16f. has made it clear that the communion of the sacramental body of Christ belongs together with the communio of the mystical body. None of us wants a repetition of the old strifes between Lutherans and Christians which so often have made the witness of the Church incredible. But we are deeply convinced that Christendom as a whole needs more than ever the unadulterated witness of the Gospel. The more we see around us the decay of the substance of the Christian faith, the less we are ashamed of giving a witness which no one else could give today. It would be the utmost lack of Christian love and true ecumenicity to refuse this witness.

This witness will be given at Denver, we are sure of that. May God give to those who have to speak that humility which helps to convince the erring brother more than anything else. Let your witness first of all be the confession of our own guilt, of our lack of courage perhaps to speak when clear speech was required. There is a time to be silent, and there is a time to speak. Sometimes there is a last opportunity to speak. It happened in a decisive hour in the Church history of Germany that a churchman of great authority was asked to speak a certain word He promised to do it. But he remained silent. Later he said: "I wanted to speak. I tried

95

to open my mouth. But I could not open it. It was as if a mighty power kept it shut." In such cases we need Him who loses our tongue with HIS mighty: "Ephphata."

May God bless the confessors of Denver and make this synod a "Ephphata", Convention.

Study Questions

1. What became a stronghold for Lutheranism in the world?_____ .
2. What happened through the influence of Walther's *Lutheraner*?____
3. What can produce faithful pastors?____
4. The great dissent between Walther and Loehe was on ____.
5. According to Sasse, the new question that has arisen is about_____ .
6. What was taught in former years at Wartburg and Capital? _____
7. The ALC no longer wants to belong to ____.
8. According to Sasse, *Dialog* is ____.
9. The first thing we have to regain is _____ .
10. What error about human language must be rejected? _____ .
11. Luther said take away assertions and you take away _____ .
12. What are "open questions?" _____ .
13. He is considered a good pastor who renders unquestioned _____ to his superiors.
14. The LCMS's 1967 convention in New York did not find any fault with ___.
15. What happened in India under the leadership of Dr. Martin Kretzmann?____ .
16. At the time of the Reformation the ascension and resurrection of Christ were_____ .

§

THE SACRAMENT OF THE ALTAR
Dr. Hermann Sasse
Reprinted from ENCOUNTER,
a youth magazine published in Australia.
Christian News, October 5, 1970

Why don't we hear more sermons on Holy Communion? I've heard only one sermon devoted to this subject and when I told my parents that, they, too could recall hearing only one. What do we teach and why?

These comments and others by young people prompted the Encounter staff to take up this subject.

We put our questions to Dr. Sasse.

What Is So Important About Holy Communion?

First of all let it be clear that our Church does not use the term "Holy Communion" in its confessions, even not in the Catechism, though unfortunately the word has now crept into our Liturgy, though not in the liturgical text itself. The Roman Church speaks of "First Communion" or "Last Communion". Here "communion" means the participation in the body of the Lord as in I Cor. 10:16f. But what Holy Communion means in modern Protestantism, no one knows. For many it is the fellowship which members of the congregation have and which is expressed by the common sacred meal. What makes this celebration different from a fellowship tea is its solemnity and the belief that Christ is in the midst of them according to His promise — Matthew 18:20, "Where two or three are gathered in my name, I am in the midst of them." But this is the case also where Christians gather around the Bible. Indeed, for the great majority of modern Protestant Christians there is no essential difference between these two forms of His presence or "Real Presence".

The Proper Name

The proper name of this sacrament in the Lutheran Confessions is the "Lord's Supper" or the "Sacrament of the Altar". We remember the definition in our Catechism. "What is the Sacrament of the Altar?" Answer: "It is the true body and blood of our Lord Jesus Christ, under the bread and wine given to us Christians to eat and to drink, instituted by Christ Himself."

Our Reformed friends are shocked. "Sacrament of the ALTAR?" Does that not sound like the Catholic Mass where body and blood of Christ are offered as a sacrifice for the living and the dead by the priest and the people?

No, the sacrament is not a sacrifice, but it is a sacrificial meal in which we receive what Christ has sacrificed for us, once and for all, at the Cross. If we want to know what this sacrament is, we have to turn to Christ. In the case of Baptism He has not given an explanation, but simply the command to baptize, i.e. to wash "in the name of the Father ... the Son ... the Holy Spirit". In the case of His Supper He has given an explanation in addition to the command: "Take, eat, this is my body, given for you. This do in remembrance of me".

The Whole Taken Literally

Now, it is not right to argue this way: "'Take eat' - yes, I can take that literally. 'This is my body'— no, that can't be taken literally, for I cannot understand it. 'Given for you'— yes, that can be taken literally. 'This do' – yes, that can be understood literally."

This is an impossible perversion of the text. We believe that the whole sacrament must be taken literally. St. Paul confirms that — I Cor. 10:16f. "The cup of blessing which we bless, is it not a participation (Greek: koinonia, Latin: communicatio) in the blood of Christ? The bread which we break, is it not a participation in the body of Christ? Because there is

97

one bread, we who are many are one body, for we all partake of the one bread." What makes us partake of the body and blood of Christ? Not our faith, as the Reformed Churches taught, but the bread and the wine. This is the commentary of St. Paul. In the following chapter he speaks of the unworthy eating of the sacrament. In this connection he makes it clear that that unbelief which makes us unworthy receivers includes also the failure to distinguish between the sacrament and ordinary food (v. 29).

Jesus Comes To His Church

This was the faith of the apostles. In this way the early Church celebrated the Lord's Supper every Sunday. The name of the Sunday was the Lord's Day. In the Old Testament the Lord's Day is the day of the Messiah, the day when He comes for judgment and redemption (Amos 5:18). The first Church prayed in the liturgy of each Sunday "Maranatha" (I Cor. 16:22), which means, "Our Lord, come". Compare Rev. 22:20. She was waiting for His second advent, and some lost their faith, because His coming was delayed (II Peter 3:3ff). But the Church could survive the disappointments and keep the faith, because already now each Sunday was a Lord's day, anticipating His second advent of glory. Jesus came to His Church in the sacrament and the Church sang what the angels sing in the presence of the Lord, the Sanctus (Is. 6:3; Rev.4:8).

Cannot Divide The God-Man

I trust it is now clear "what is so important about Holy Communion". Christianity is not only one of the many religions you can choose from. Christianity is, in its essence, belief in Christ as the Saviour of the world who is with us, not only in His divine, but also in His human nature, our Redeemer and our Brother. You cannot divide the God-man into a divine part which is here on earth and a human part which is in heaven. He is with us in His Word and in His Sacrament. Both means of grace belong together, just as the office of the keys, the power to forgive sins, which He has given to His Church and to the ministers of the Word, belongs together with Baptism and the Lord's Supper. The Reformed Churches with very few exceptions (e.g. the Anglican Church in the Book of Common Prayer) have lost it and replaced it by the exercise of Church discipline. We have kept it, even if only in remnants. But when we go to Church we should take confession and absolution very seriously. Hence, we should not regard the Sacrament of the Altar only as an appendix to the service.

Why Do We Have This Specific Teaching?

It is not necessary to go into the question now, why we Lutherans have this specific doctrine. The simple answer is: because it is Biblical. Strictly speaking, there is no specific Lutheran doctrine on the Lord's Supper. What Luther demanded from those whom he should recognize as orthodox in the doctrine of the Sacrament is only to accept the words of the institution as they sound: "This is my body". When his opponents said: "But I cannot do that, because I do not understand them", then his simple reply was always: "These words are to be BELIEVED. Who will understand the Virgin birth, the bodily resurrection of Christ, His exaltation and glorification, His second Advent?" When Zwingli made the point that eating and drinking cannot help the soul, Luther's answer was: "Leave that to God. He knows what we need". It is one of the most important aspects of our doctrine on the sacrament that God deals not only with our souls, our spirits, but with our bodies too. "Do you not know that your bodies are members of Christ?" (I Cor. 6:15). The redemption which Christ brought is the redemption not only of the soul, but of the whole man. This truth stands behind our belief of the resurrection of the body.

Where Do We Differ From Other Denominations?

It is quite clear, I think, where we differ from other denominations. We differ from the various Reformed bodies in the doctrine of the Real Presence of the body of Christ. We have in common with Rome the Real Presence, but we cannot accept for biblical reasons the idea of transubstantiation, which means the doctrine that the consecrated bread ceases to be bread. For Paul still calls also the consecrated bread "bread" (cf. I Cor. 11:28). Nor can we accept the idea of the sacrifice of the mass which is nowhere found in the New Testament. Jesus has never ordained His apostles sacrificial priests. The only passage Rome can adduce are the words: "Do this in remembrance of me". But nothing is said there of priests. The New Testament knows only, apart from Jewish priests, the priesthood in which all members of the true Church have a share.

A special case, especially in our country, is the Anglican Church. This Church has no longer a common doctrine on the Lord's Supper, but leaves it to the individual minister and layman either to retain the old reformed doctrine of the Thirty-nine Articles — which no longer have binding force – or to accept a catholic doctrine or no doctrine at all. The Methodists used to have the old Anglican doctrine. What the understanding of their "Holy Communion" will be now, no one knows, for this Church, together with the Congregational Church and the majority of the Presbyterians, will be absorbed by the coming "Uniting Church". We have to wait for their doctrinal formulas.

What Is "Close Communion"? Should We Practice It?

There are Churches which practice "open communion", which means, they invite to Communion all Christians. I remember a Methodist minister in America who told me proudly that even Jews had attended his communion service. Our Methodists would not be so open, and Jews would not attend our Protestant Churches. The Anglican Church invites-nowadays all baptized Christians to a Eucharist held by an Anglican priest. The Anglicans can be very broadminded. Thus, when the Salvation Army celebrated its centenary, the Anglican Cathedral of Adelaide was put at their disposal, although the "Army" rejects any sacrament. But perhaps this was regarded as a national affair ("Can what an Englishman believes ever be heresy?" is a famous saying by Bernard Shaw). Hardly any Church would be so open as to admit members of "The

Church of Jesus Christ of Latter-Day Saints" (Mormons), not even in Utah.

In The Ancient Church

The principle of the Ancient Church was that not only pagans and Jews, but also heretics were excluded from the sacrament. (Rom. 16:17f). They took that very seriously as the many warnings against heresies in the apostolic writings show.

Lutheran Practice

In the Lutheran Church the rule was kept that only those who accepted with the Christian faith the Lutheran doctrine of the Real Presence, could be admitted. This is still the rule in our Church in Australia, though in Europe and America, also in the Lutheran Churches the old Church order and discipline are breaking down. We maintain this "close communion" which actually is only the rule of the New Testament - for it would have been impossible in the Church of the Apostles to admit to the Lord's Supper those who did not desire to receive the true body of the Lord.

Not A Lack Of Love But A Witness

Our practice of "close communion" is not a lack of love, not isolation from people who may be better Christians than we are. It is not a judgment on other men for whom Christ died and who believe in Him as their Saviour. It means that we do not want them to receive the sacrament unworthily by taking offence at the doctrine which is embodied in the preaching, the liturgy and the hymns. At the same time it is a witness to the seriousness of the sacrament. If our Church watches over this rule it is not because we feel ourselves superior to other Churches, but because we owe to the whole of Christendom the witness to the sacrament as Christ has instituted it.

Proclaims Clearly The Gospel

My practical suggestion is that in this age when the doctrinal substance of the Christian Faith is diminishing everywhere, even in Lutheran Churches, we give more time to the deep study of the biblical sacrament. The Sacrament of the Altar is the clearest and most impressive proclamation of the Gospel (I Cor. 11:26). Where this sacrament fails the Gospel cannot remain in its purity.

• Meet Dr. Sasse, the man who answers our questions in these pages.

This year Dr. Sasse retired from full-time lecturing at Luther Seminary, Adelaide. But he has not retired from theological study and writing. In fact, he is busier than ever.

Dr. Sasse is not a narrow-minded Lutheran - one who knows and understands only one point of view. If his answers do not satisfy you, then read his book, "This Is My Body".

He has been studying sacramental theology and the history of the sacraments for about 40 years in close connection with theologians of various Churches, Eastern Orthodox, Roman Catholic, Anglican, Reformed and Presbyterian, among them the greatest experts of these Churches. He knows of the practical difficulties, e.g. if members of one and the same family cannot receive together the sacrament unless they want to defect from their Church. This is so not only in Australia. You find this tragic situation all over the world. As an active participant in ecumenical conferences for many years he has tried to do his share to overcome the distress of Christians who cannot participate in the one sacrament which Christ has given to His Church.

Study Questions
1. Do the confessions use the term "Holy Communion"? ____
2. For the great majority of Protestants there is no essential difference between what two forms of Christ's presence? ____
3. The proper name of this Sacrament in the Lutheran confessions is ____.
4. The sacrament is not a ____.
5. The whole sacrament must be taken ____.
6. The early Church celebrated the Lord's Supper every ____.
7. Christ is with us in His ____ and in His ____.
8. The Sacrament of the Altar should not be regarded as an ____ to the service.
9. What is transubstantiation? ____
10. Does the New Testament teach "close communion?" ____
11. Is Dr. Sasse a narrow minded Lutheran? ____

§

ABORTION STATEMENT
Commission on Theology, Lutheran Church of Australia
Christian News, December 28, 1970

The General Synod of the Lutheran Church of Australia issues the following as a guide to the members of the Lutheran Church of Australia, and as a statement to the public in the matter of legalizing abortion and of liberalizing existing legislation on abortion.

The Lutheran Church, with the Church of all ages, upholds the biblical view that the foetus in the mother's womb is human life created by God and, as such, this life is entitled to the care and preservation which God's command provides for all mankind. The foetus has the right to live and to be protected by the laws of the State. Abortion, in the sense of artificial or induced termination of pregnancy, is therefore not justified.

The Lutheran Church recognizes circumstances under which a termi-

101

nation of pregnancy may be considered, namely, when in competent medical opinion the life of the mother can be saved only by a termination of pregnancy. In such a case, it becomes a question, humanly speaking, of choosing between one human life and another and, consequently, a choice cannot be avoided. However, prior to the performing of an abortion, the mother, in addition to receiving medical advice should also, if possible, earnestly seek pastoral guidance.

Special cases, such as pregnancies which result from incest, rape, or any other perverted sexual relationship, and special problems experienced by members of the Church and the medical and nursing profession, must always be approached from the basic principle that the foetus is human life created by God; and the reasons advanced in favour of a termination of pregnancy in such instances must be evaluated in the light of this principle.

Members of the Church as well as medical and nursing personnel confronted with problems of conscience in connection with the performing of an abortion are advised and invited to consult the ministry of the Church concerning the Christian ethical aspects of these problems.

The Lutheran Church firmly believes that the conscientious objections of such personnel to the performing of abortions should be respected by the hospital authorities.

FEATURE ARTICLE
by Dr. H. Sasse.

Christian View of Abortion

At the First Ecumenical Council, Nicaea 325, it happened that a Bishop was present from one of those Christian communities which were not in fellowship with that body which called itself the "great" or the "Catholic" Church. He was Acesius, the Novatian Bishop of Byzantium which was soon to become "New Rome" or "Constantinople", the Eastern capital of the Roman Empire and the residence of Constantine himself. The Novatians were an orthodox Christian Church which varied from the Catholics in matters of Church discipline. Named after Novatianus, a learned Roman Presbyter who had been elected Bishop of Rome in 251 by a minority of the Church of Rome, they called themselves the "Katharoi", the "pure", who would not admit to the Holy Communion a person who had committed a grave sin, such as denial of Christ in the persecution, or adultery. The intention of the Emperor in inviting this Bishop as an "observer" or a "friendly visitor" to Nicaea, as we would call his position today, was obviously the healing of the schism in the future capital which from the very beginning was meant to be a Christian city. When all was over, he asked Acesius whether he accepted the great dogmatic decision. He emphatically affirmed: This is the apostolic faith which we always have confessed. What about the canons, the Church laws, especially concerning the celebration of Easter? Also this he accepted as the custom of the apostolic Church. Then, why do you not join us? Acesius replied by pointing out that the Church of Jesus Christ could never grant a "second penance" after baptism to those who had committed such grave sins. "Acesius", replied the Emperor, "take a ladder and go to heaven alone".

Problems of Church Discipline

This scene shows how seriously the early Church took the problems of Church discipline. It shows, furthermore, the great problem with which the Church of Jesus Christ was confronted. To belong to Christ, to be a member of Christ's body cannot be reconciled with fornication, as Paul makes it quite clear in I Corinthians 6. Every extra-marital sexual intercourse is according to the New Testament fornication and excludes from Holy Communion. On this the early Church was agreed. The disagreement began with the question whether there is a "paenitentia secunda", a second penance after the great penance of baptism. There was never any doubt that God in the Last Judgement could pardon any sin. We have touching examples of excommunicated Christians who did not lose their faith, but lived a life of penance hoping for God's final absolution. But it was a problem of pastoral care whether not here on earth already the Church could, after a long period of penance, readmit the penitent sinner to the Eucharist. The splits and schisms which have occurred over this issue show how seriously the problem was taken. While the rigorists at all times tried to maintain the old standards, great pastors, experienced bishops realized that the Church of Him who had come to seek and to save that which is lost would never become a club of pharisees.

The Unforgivable Sins

Apart from the sin of idolatry, which means denial of Christ there are in the early Church two sins which fall under the unforgivable sins; fornication and murder. We may assume that murder in the ordinary sense of the word did not occur in the Christian Church. In almost all cases where we hear of murder, abortion is meant. There is from the very beginning a really remarkable agreement within the Church that abortion in the sense of willful termination of pregnancy is murder. Didache 2 forbids to kill the unborn or the newly-born child or to expose it. The same rule we find in Barnabas 19:5. The Apologists confirm this. "Apud nos parricidium est", says Tertullian: "to us it is parricidium", the worst murder, the murder of a blood relative. Athenagoras is very outspoken in this matter and explains that even the embryo is already a human being and object of divine love and providence (Supplicatio 35). This principle contradicts the view expressed in the Roman Law: "Foetus pars viscerum matris". The embryo is still a part of the body of the mother. The human person begins to exist with birth, not with conception. On this principle the practice of abortion was based in the Roman world. Also in Rome we find resistance against this common practice. It is especially the Stoic philosophy which is opposed to abortion as a sin against nature. Laws against abortion were made by several emperors. But the wrong in abortion is not the wrong to the foetus, but rather to the mother or to the father of the unborn child.

The Embryo Is a Living Person

From where does the idea stem that the unborn embryo is already a human person whose life is to be regarded as sacred? Athenagoras refers to reason. "It would be inconsistent to maintain that the embryo is already a human being and to kill the child after he has been born and to forbid to expose a child, because such exposition would be equal to killing him. But we (Christians) are in every regard and in all things very consistent. For we are servants of reason and not perverters of it." The emphasis is here on consistency, on rational thinking. This might suggest that behind the whole idea there is a sort of Stoic thinking of a lex naturae. But this cannot be the root of the Christian view of abortion. Christian apologetics as Christian theology is also in this point the continuation of Jewish thought and its Biblical background. It is the firm conviction of the Old Testament that the embryo in his mother's womb is a living person. One may think of Jacob and Esau in Rebecca's womb, or of Jeremiah 1: "Before I formed you in the womb I knew you, and before you were born I consecrated you; I appointed you a prophet to the nations". According to the Jewish rabbis even the embryos in their mother's womb joined in the hymn of praise after the passage through the Red Sea. The Hellenistic Jews like Philo have the same idea that already the embryo is a human person (De specialibus legibus II, 318-220). It is the Christian view, underlying the pertinent passages of the New Testament, and of greatest importance for the understanding of the Incarnation of the Son of God. It may have originally been the view of the most ancient cultures, as texts like the oath of Hippocrates shows whose content goes back to times immemorial. In the medieval Church this view was darkened by the reception of Aristotle's view of the beginning of the animated life of the embryo.

He taught "that the future child was endowed at conception with the principle of only vegetable life, which was exchanged after a few days for an animal soul, and was not succeeded by a rational soul till later, as his followers thought, on the fortieth day for a male, and the eightieth for a female child" (Cath. Enc. Vol. I, 46f.).

The Sanctity of the Life of an Unborn Child

One of the great contributions of Christianity to human civilization was among others the restoration of the Biblical concept of the sanctity of the life of an unborn child who is already an object not only of God's providence, but also of God's grace. Christianity came into a world which did not recognize this sanctity and, therefore, did not hesitate to destroy such life when this was desired for whatever reasons. The legislation of the Christian nations followed this Christian understanding of pregnancy. If in wide parts of our Western world, the legislation of the State is being changed so as to correspond with the views held by the majority of the people who no longer understand the Christian principle, it is up to the Church to educate its own members and to uphold in its midst the eternal law of God. This is what the ancient Church did. She never gave up the conviction that the destruction of an embryo is equal to killing a human being. All members of the Church knew this as the oldest catechetical documents, such as the "doctrine of the Twelve Apostles" show. This belonged probably also to the instruction of the proselytes to the synagogue. Also the Christian women knew this. This knowledge gave their married lives a sanctity which was absent even in the happiest of pagan marriages. Since also the Christians are sinners it happened that also this divine commandment was broken. Such violation of the divine commandment led to the excommunication of the sinner, which was either, as in the early times, a permanent state of penance until death, or it was a temporary one which was terminated with a solemn act of reconciliation and readmission to the Lord's Supper, usually in Holy Week. The fact that the synods of the 4th and later centuries had to repeat the rules time and again shows that cases of abortion occurred at all times even if in the early centuries much less frequently than in the post-Constantinian era.

An Example from Real Life

I give an example from real life which may illustrate the problem how the law of the State and the law of the Church may be in an insoluble conflict. In the beginning of the third century Callistus, Bishop of Rome, allowed marriages in the Church between persons who could not enter a full marriage according to the laws of the Roman Empire. There was no "connubium" between persons from senatorial or equestrial rank and persons of the lower casts such as slaves and persons freed from slavery. Since in the Church there were more women than men of the higher classes, a Christian woman could not easily find a husband if she wanted to marry within the Church. Callistus declared that such marriages were possible within the Church because no law of God forbade them. It is a similar situation to that in which we found ourselves as pastors in Germany when the laws of Hitler prohibited marriages between persons, one of whom was not of the descent which was supposed to be the only one qualifying for citizenship and legal marriage. When a couple came to us asking us to marry them, we pastors in the "Confessing Church" could not refuse to do that if both were baptized Christians. We had to tell them, however, that their marriage was not valid in the sense of the law and that they, as well as the pastor who had married them, were liable to grave punishment. Such a marriage was valid "in foro interno tantum", only before God and their consciences. Before the world the relationship was an unlawful concubinage. Callistus was right when he found that the Law of the State and the Law of the Church may disagree. What was the consequence of this permission in the reality of life? Hippolyt, the adversary of Callistus, in these matters as in others, counter-bishop to Callist until after the death of Callist he became his lawful successor, describes in a rather polemical, but probably not quite unjustified way what happened in Rome. He reports: "Callistus permitted females, if they were unwedded, and burned with passion ... or if they were not disposed to overturn their own dignity through a legal marriage, that they might

105

have whomsoever they would choose as a bedfellow, whether a slave or free, and that a woman, though not legally married, might consider such a companion as a husband.

Whence women, reputed believers, began to resort to drugs for producing sterility and to gird themselves round, so to expel what was being conceived on account of their not wishing to have a child either by a slave, or by any paltry fellow for the sake of their family and excessive wealth. Behold in what impiety that lawless one has proceeded, by inculcating adultery and murder at the same time! And withal, after such audacious acts, they, lost to all shame, attempt to call themselves a "Catholic Church". (Ref. VIII, chapter 7).

If we disregard the venomous polemics of that rigorist predecessor of the conscientious Pope Paul VI we find here a most illuminating example of the ethical conflicts in which Christian women found themselves 1,700 years ago in the problems of childbirth and birth control. The offspring of their ecclesiastically valid marriage would never be able to inherit their own and their family's fortune. No public career would be open to such a child. And yet they loved their Christian husbands and desired a child, as every healthy woman does, a child who from the very beginning of his existence in his mother's womb would be God's beloved child. What terrible conflict! Can we imagine that indeed some of these women succumbed to the temptation of an abortion? Who is here prepared to throw the first stone? Hippolyt, of course, knows what the solution to the problem is. This rigorist and all his successors, all the Hippolyts up to our time, have a very simple advice: Stay unmarried, or do not consummate the marriage. It is very simple, too simple!

The Task of The Church

What has the Church to learn from these centuries when it was thrown into a sex-obsessed world, full of adultery and murder of the unborn? The Church at that time did not try to make the world a better place to live in. How should she have been able to do it? This is never the task of the Church. We live in a world cursed by the sins of many generations. To this world we have to proclaim God's Word in Law and Gospel. We have to show how a Christian individual and the Christian congregation has to live and can live so as to be a living witness to the eternal truth of God. As citizens we have to share in the responsibility of making the laws for the State in which we live.

What Must We Do?

First of all, we have to witness to the eternal truth, which has not been invented by the Church, that abortion means to kill a human person. There are cases when a human being has to die in the interest of preserving other human lives. So there may be cases where the termination of a pregnancy is the means to save another life. These are, however, exceptional cases, carefully to be decided by a jury or impartial doctors. The 90,000 cases of abortion which are supposed to occur in Australia in a year are, as the corresponding cases in other countries, apart from the exceptional cases mentioned, mass-murder with all the consequences for the nation concerned. This we shall have to tell the world on the authority of the living God.

To prevent this crime and to discourage the terrible practice, a thorough instruction on all matters of sex is required. Such instruction is valueless if it is not based on clear concepts of what is right and what is wrong in these matters. One need not be a Christian to know that any extra-marital sexual intercourse is fornication. One need not be a Christian to know that the foetus is more than a part of the body of the mother to be removed at will.

It will be up to the Church to instruct first of all its own members, married and engaged couples, young people and the Christian congregation as a whole. The doctors, lawyers and law-makers who belong to the Church, but also others, may benefit from it, as they should share in an enlightened Christian instruction on these problems. What we have to give up is the utopian idea that our society will suddenly accept the ethical standards of the Church if it will not accept even standards and rules that are written in all men's hearts. We do not live any longer in a Christian society, if ever such a society has existed. We are in the same position in which the ancient Church found itself.

Study Questions

1. Abortion in the sense of artificial or induced termination of pregnancy is never ____.
2. Is rape a valid reason for abortion? ____
3. Who was Acesius? ____
4. According to the New Testament every extra-marital sexual intercourse excludes from ____.
5. Abortion in the sense of willful termination of pregnancy is ____.
6. What does Jeremiah 1 teach about the embryo in the mother's womb? ____
7. The oath of Hippocrates goes back to ____.
8. One of the great contributions of Christianity to human civilization was ____.
9. Any extra-marital intercourse is ____.
10. Is the fetus just a part of the body to be removed at will? ____

§

SOLA SCRIPTURA

(Letter from 1971)

June 23, 2004

Dear Pastor and Grace Otten,

After seeing Dr. Hermann Sasse's picture in the June 7th *CN* and the reprinting of the article about your Testimonial Banquet in Chicago where my father Al Wagner spoke, I thought to send you Dr. Sasse's letter we have preserved from 1971. It must have been intended for the "*Sola Scriptura*" publication of FAL at that time and perhaps you already have it in your files. At any rate I was touched by Dr. Sasse's great earnestness and concern for Lutheranism as he discusses the theological problems and situation of the Church which are still pertinent today.

We wish to tell you also that our family has been blessed by your faithful witness....

Kay Ulrich

Editor's note: The cover and masthead of Sola Scriptura follows the article. Al E. Wagner was an executive editor of Sola Scriptura and Hermann Sasse was an Editorial Representative. Sola Scriptura was published by Lutheran News, New Haven, Missouri.

x x x

North Adelaide
6-2-70

Dear Brother Wagner:

Here is my reply. You are free to make any use of it. Perhaps there is a possibility of having it duplicated. The enclosed is my own responsibility, food for thought.

God bless you all,

Yours in Christ,

H. Sasse

x x x

Hermann Sasse
16 Wellington Square,
North Adelaide, South Australia 5006

25th January, 1971
Editors, "*Sola Scriptura*"
P.P. Box 1377
Studio City
California 91604
U.S.A.

Dear Brother Wagner:

Your letter of the third Sunday in Advent reached me with considerable delay which I cannot explain — even not from the many postal stamps. This explains my belated reply. Besides I wanted to talk over the matter with Bro. Bruce Adams. We both are heartily endorsing the aims of *Sola Scriptura* as a theological paper. But we cannot, of course, subscribe to statements and proposals that refer to the immediate steps which have to be taken in your Church. I for one do not even know the decisions of Denver with the exception of the declaration of fellowship with the ALC which was of great importance to us Australians, because one of our Churches was in fellowship with Missouri and the other with the ALC. At present we must live in a state of neutrality. We are deeply concerned about the future of American Lutheranism, though at present the situation in all conservative Churches is in a state of flux.

I myself am not able at present to take part in your discussions, though we are facing the same problems. I am now emeritus, nearly 76 of age, and working under extremely difficult conditions. I am trying hard to finish my last book which requires a lot of research. I am no longer able to answer all letters I receive from America. So allow me to put before you some thoughts which may be of help to you and others. I assume that you have no objections if I send this letter also to Bro. Werning and to President Preus.

Doctrinal Substance Vanishing

If we want to understand our tasks, we must realize that the situation of the Lutheran Church today must be seen against the background of a development that is going on in all Churches of Christendom. The doctrinal substance of the faith is vanishing everywhere. It may have been a great surprise to many of us that even Rome is experiencing this loss. It may help us to understand the doctrinal decay in Lutheranism if we observe the process going on everywhere. Almost fifty years ago I was a witness of the disintegration of the Presbyterian Church in America. Only remnants of the Church of the Geneva Reformation have been left today. In 1968 the Lambeth Conference met for the last time. The Anglican Communion is vanishing. It is the conviction of Archbishop Ramsay that Anglicanism may remain in England. But the member Churches of the Anglican Communion are being encouraged to join the local unions. The disintegration of these Churches began with the loss of their doctrine. The decay of Roman Catholicism is obvious. The old discipline is breaking down in a shocking way. But behind the crisis of discipline stands the breakdown of the doctrine. "Time Magazine" published recently a picture showing a Lutheran pastor and two Catholic priests con-celebrating mass.

"Yielding to temptation" read the caption. They yielded to the temptation to break the law of their Churches and their ordination vows because they had lost the doctrine of their Churches. "Doctrine divides, service unites" was to be read on a backdrop in large letters. It is an old slogan from the beginning of the century when in America the social gospel began to replace the gospel of the New Testament. The Second Vatican

109

Council has indeed produced some achievements which never should be lost again, e.g., a new mutual relationship between the Churches of Christendom or certain reforms within the Catholic Church. But much of what has been greeted as a renewal of the Church has actually been a revolution which is bound to destroy the Church unless it is checked in time. The deepest nature of this revolution is the abolition of the concepts of orthodoxy and heresy. Probably John XXIII himself has opened the gate to a flood of heresies when in his opening speech he defined the task of the council to make use of the medicine of mercy rather than that of severity, to demonstrate the truth of the Church's teaching rather than by condemnations, as though truth can be confessed without rejecting the opposing error. In any case his successor, the conscientious Paul VI, has to carry a burden as perhaps no pope before him seeing tremendous amount of heresies which is sweeping through his Church. Even the simplest truths of the creeds seem to be vanishing among theologians and even bishops. He knows what his duty is as pope. He ought to excommunicate the heretics. But there are too many of them. The majority of the Catholic bishops in Holland, and a good number in America too, ought to be deposed. But he seems to be powerless. Small wonder that he speaks of his own future in terms of the cross in a way as perhaps no pontiff before him.

The Crisis of the Lutheran Church

It is only against this world-wide background of the crisis of the Christian faith that one can come to a fair and just understanding of the crisis of our own Lutheran Church. Unbelief is certainly the grave sin of the individual. At the same time it can be and in many cases is the result of movements which are, humanly speaking, beyond the control of the individual. If you send a young man to a liberal or modernist seminary, how can you expect him to come back with an orthodox theology? Of course, we have to send our young men abroad. But we must look after them. They must know what they will encounter. There must be guidance by an experienced Lutheran scholar and pastor. If we send them to non-Lutheran faculties like Heidelberg, Tübingen, Basel, Münster and they come back with an un-Lutheran theology, you cannot axe them as some people seem to think. This is no solution to the problem. What would be required is at least a post-doctoral year under real guidance. I think one of the reasons for the failures in our faculties is the superstitious belief of the Americans in German doctor's degrees. Th.D. of Heidelberg or Tübingen is not a very high degree, formerly called the Lic. theol. Such a degree proves nothing but that there is a man who once in his life has written a thesis which was just sufficient for a pass. The whole system of theological training must be overhauled. I often ask myself why all sorts of sciences are flourishing in America, except theology. This is true of the theology of all Churches. If you want to study good Catholic theology or philosophy, you must at least cross the border to Canada. What strange institutions are the "Theological" faculties in the great universities like Harvard, Yale, Princeton, Union Seminary (Columbia), Chicago.

They have all the facilities for research and teaching. They have even some outstanding scholars, mainly in the historical subjects. But they have no theology and cannot have it, for there is no theology without a Church. A theologian must know the Word of God (not only the Bible as religious literature). Here lies the main reason for the absence of real theology in these institutions. You have in America great scientists in chemistry, physics, mathematics etc. If the faculties of science were as bad as the theological faculties in your universities, no American would ever have reached the moon. America has excellent archaeologists, historians, philologists. You have produced some of the best editions of Patristic texts. But where are the theologians? Theology, being a function of the Church, had to be taught and cultivated in denominational seminaries. These seminaries have done and are partly doing a tremendous work. Where would the Lutheran Church be without them? By all means Lutheran seminaries must be maintained. In an era when the universities, the state universities in Europe as well as the free institutions in America, are disintegrating into clusters of departments when whole sciences are migrating from the universities where they can no longer be adequately dealt with, when student rioting and other revolutionary movements are indicative of a profound crisis of our scientific culture we must build up what we have. Perhaps the future belongs again to the small seminary not to institutions such as Concordia, St. Louis.

What the American seminaries have done for the Lutheran Church is the faithful tradition of the classical Lutheran theology. The danger of these institutions was that their theology consisted mainly in the faithful passing of the theology of the past. The great crisis was bound to come when Lutheran theology had to leave the ghetto in which it had lived for too long a time and had to take issue with the great problems of our age. Whatever the merits of dogmatics by Pieper, Jacobs and their contemporaries may have been, these men did not know and could not take in account the issues of today. One of the reasons for the crisis of doctrine in all Churches in the breakdown of Aristotelian philosophy. Aristotle has played a role even in American philosophy at the time of Pieper. Pieper himself seemed not to be aware of this. But modern mathematics and physics have definitely destroyed Aristotelianism as it has also destroyed and definitely refuted the philosophy of Kant. Historical research has definitely entered also the Lutheran seminaries. I know several seminaries of the LCA. I have lectured in all seminaries of the ALC and Missouri. I have visited Mankato and Mequon and have good friends in these faculties. If I admire one seminary it is Mequon with its excellent tradition in the Biblical languages. But apart from the institutions of these rightwing Lutherans they all have gone through the same development. When the generation of Knubel, Jacobs, Reu died out, the great change came everywhere. The students were supposed to read the orthodox books, but Tillich and Bonhoeffer* were the men who fascinated them. They read them as the students at the seminary of the Brüdergemeine read secretly, as Schleiermacher tells us, the rationalists of their time.

111

Walther and Old Missouri

We shall never understand the true causes of the decay of conservative Lutheranism if we find fault only with other people. Without trying to minimize the influence which secular powers and false teachers have exercised on whole generations of our pastors, we must ask why they found so little resistance. Something must have been wrong with our own theology. It is really touching to see how faithful pastors and congregations are fighting for the preservation of the faith of the fathers in the Lutheran Churches in Europe and America. If in some cases the zeal of the fighters is greater than their wisdom, if uncharitable words are spoken and untenable statements are made, we should not forget that this has happened in the Church at all times since the days of the apostles. On the whole I can only with admiration look at those people who, often in great loneliness, some even with great sacrifices, are giving their witness to the faith of the fathers and are trying to maintain on their part the orthodox Lutheran Church. But why is it that these groups cannot agree in so many cases? If we all believe in the Bible as God's Word, full of grace and truth, why is it that these groups are so often divided in doctrinal questions?

Among the issues that divided conservative Lutherans in the 19th century there was at least one question in which the Gospel itself was at stake, the doctrine of election and predestination. It was to the credit of Walther and old Missouri how they dared to maintain Luther's "De servo arbitrio" over against that synergism which secretly had crept into our Church as a result of the old "Intuitu Fidei" and later of the Pietistic movement. It is doubtful whether this issue is still understood. It is doubtful whether this issue is still understood by modern Missourians. We all have been deeply influenced by that Pelagianism which, e.g. in certain un-Lutheran forms of Stewardship and Evangelism, is pervading all Churches.

When Missouri parted from Iowa and Ohio on this issue, the separation was justified because the articulus stantis et cadentis ecclesiae was at stake, the Gospel itself. This was not the case in the problems of the relationship between Church, local congregation and the origin of the ministry. This whole controversy was obsolete already in 1883 when the newly discovered "Doctrine of the Apostles" was published.

Since that time we know that in the early Church there existed side by side different forms of Church and ministry. The New Testament does not know of an "ordo quo Dominus ecclesiam suam gubernari voluit" (Calvin). Even the Roman Church has meanwhile learnt something of this truth. But we Lutherans seem to have overslept a century. We know that in the early Church some local Churches elected and ordained their own leaders, while others received their ministers from an apostle. The New Testament does not differentiate between the local Church and the Church in a certain district (Acts 9:31), or the Church universal. The Twelve were the ecclesia repraesentativa and the first office-bearers. One of the drawbacks of Missouri's "Ubertragungslehre" is that it makes it very hard to refute the ordination of women. Since also the women share

112

the universal priesthood why should they not share its public exercise? The passages 1 Cor. 14 and 1 Tim. 2:12ff. should, of course, be sufficient. In the latter passage, however, it is not quite clear whether or not the apostle gives a divine injunction or an order on the basis of his apostolic authority, 1 Cor. 14:37. Paul refers expressly not only to the custom of all Churches, but to a commandment of the Lord. This is confirmed by Jesus Himself.

His disciples were well organized. There were the Twelve with an inner circle of the Three. We hear on one occasion of a wider circle of the Seventy. Another group were "the women" who accompanied Him and served Him and probably the apostles too. They play a great role in the history of the passion and of Easter. Why did Jesus not admit at least one of them to the Last Supper? Is it because the solemn command to celebrate the sacrament and the transmission of the office of the Keys John 20 were at the same time acts of ordination? However that may be, it is clear that Jesus Himself acted in this way. If He did, we have to accept it, even if we do not understand it. He must have His reasons. Paul (1 Tim. 2:13 f.) suggests that they are rooted in the mystery of the creation of man and woman. Later generations will see the tragic consequences of a revolutionary movement for the "liberation" women which no longer respects certain divine orders. To "improve" the institution of Christ so as to make it more acceptable to modern man in a secularized world is a direct attack on Christ's authority.

If you take up in "*Sola Scriptura*" this burning issue, make this clear to the Lutherans in America. The LCA and the ALC in your country have now, persuaded by a clever propaganda from Germany and Sweden, introduced this blasphemous revolution in the Church. They have started a development which cannot be revoked. I cannot see how by way of a dialogue this movement can be stopped. It is too late. *Jacta est alea.* The dices are cast. If Missouri wants seriously to be a sound Lutheran Church it must declare that it cannot have fellowship with these Churches as long as this scandal continues. Such declaration must be made in a Christian way, without the slightest trace of pharisaeism, in the spirit of humility and repentance. For our testimony to the truth of Scripture was obviously not strong enough. Any protest must be accompanied by practical suggestions how to limit the damage done by these rash and inconsiderate decisions made by incompetent pastors, professors and Church presidents who uncritically followed the bad example of European Churches. Since all Churches in the LWF accept the female pastors and since a frank discussion of this vital question was impossible within the LWF (they left the decision to each member Church), membership in the LWF has become impossible for a Church which is not only nominally Lutheran.

Romans 16:17

The question of the ordination of women is one of the cases where the serious admonition of Rom. 16:17 applies. Since you mention this much debated passage as one of the subjects which "*Sola Scriptura*" is going

113

to discuss, I want to say a word on the exegesis of this passage. Why is it that confessional Lutherans who want to speak where Scripture speaks, and to be silent where Scripture is silent, have been divided on the understanding of this simple text? Is perhaps something wrong with our exegetical methods? You propose to publish an article "Grammatical Study of Rom, 16:17".** This is certainly necessary and good. I have read such a study. Exact grammatical study is certainly necessary in the case of any study of Scripture. But we should be aware of the fact that grammar and dictionary, even if the best available are used, are not always sufficient to elucidate a certain passage. In the case of Rom.16, 17 f. the question is what the "doctrine (didache) which you have learned" means. Who are the errorists hinted at? What did they teach or not teach? To find that out, one must read the "verses" 17f. (The introduction of "verses", not yet known to Luther, was not an unqualified blessing) in their context, in the context of the chapter and in the context of the whole Corpus Paulinism.

Rom. 16 is one of the most interesting and touching documents of the New Testament Church. Traces of the earliest Eucharistic liturgy are recognizable. Wherever the admonition is given: "Greet you one another with the holy kiss" (Rom. 16:16; 1 Cor. 16:20; 2 Cor. 13:12; 1 Thess. 5:26 comp. 1 Peter 5:15) we should remember that the holy kiss, the kiss of peace (the "Pax") belongs to the celebration of the Lord's Supper, even today still in all Catholic masses, Eastern and Western. It is the expression of full peace and community within the Church as the body of Christ. Since it is a greeting it is connected with ("aspasmos" of those who are absent, but in full fellowship with the celebrating local Church. "All the Churches of Christ" are united with us when we celebrate the sacrament (comp. Rom. 16:16 with 1 Cor. 16:19f.). These greetings are more than mere human greetings which they, of course, are too, especially when definite personal greetings by the writer or his secretary are added.

This unity in the Church is a gift of the Holy Spirit (Eph. 4) and consequently also the unity in the one faith. In the Eastern liturgies still today the Creed is introduced with the words: "Let us love (kiss) one another that we may confess unanimously" (spoken by the deacon). "The Father, the Son and the Holy Spirit, the one and indivisible Trinity" (sung by the choir). Then the doors are closed and the Nicene Creed is spoken in unison by the celebrant and the people. The "Pax" is followed by the "Anathema" (l. Cor. 16:22). Only those are admitted to the Lord's Table who are united in the true faith. The anathema is directed 1 Cor. 16: 22... against those who split the Church by lack of love for the Lord, against the schismatics, this having been the great sin at Corinth: "If anyone does not love the Lord, let him be anathema". Rom. 16:16 it is directed against heretics "who create dissensions and scandals in opposition to the doctrine which you have been taught." In view of the very grave danger which these heretics mean to the Church, Paul warns against them with very strong words: "avoid them". They have obviously not yet appeared in Rome at the time when the apostle writes this letter. But they are coming and will try to be admitted to the Church.

114

One must compare the whole setup of Rom, 16 with that of l Cor.16 in order to understand the liturgical background of Rom. 16. In 1 Cor. 16 we find still another liturgical word, the prayer, in the form of an acclamation, "Maranatha", our Lord come. This must go back to the oldest Aramaic speaking Church. It is the prayer that He may come soon in His glorious parousia, in the Second Advent. At the same time it is a petition for His coming in the sacrament.

For each Lord's Day is an anticipation of the great "Lord's Day", the day when the Messiah will come, mentioned already in the Old Testament (Amos 5:18). The first "Lord's day" of the Church was Easter Sunday when Christ came back from the dead and appeared to His disciples (John 20). Since that day the Church regularly celebrates the sacrament. On the Lord's Day, probably at the same time when the Churches of Asia assembled around the Lord's Table, John had his great vision at Patmos. There he saw the heavenly worship going on in heaven. He heard the great hymn that is sung by heavenly beings in the presence of the Lord, the Sanctus in the New Testament form Rev. 4:8. The Sanctus belongs from the very beginning to the Liturgy of the Lord's Supper, either in the form of St. John or according to Isaiah 6. (The Church had later two more forms, the Trishagion of the old Greek liturgies and the *Te Deum*).

It is, by the way, the strongest proof that the doctrine of the Real Presence belongs to the Church from the beginning. It is also remarkable that the Revelation of St. John has the same background as the passages quoted from St. Paul. Also the conclusion of Revelation (ch. 22) contains the warning against falsification of the Word of God, the "marana-tha", now in Greek translation and a formula which we find in various forms in the Pauline epistles. "The grace of the Lord Jesus be with all the saints." (Rev. 22:21). The usual form with Paul is: "The grace of our Lord Jesus Christ be with you" (Rom. 16:20 comp. l Cor. 16:23). In its fullest Trinitarian form it appears 2 Cor. 13:13. The dialog which precedes the Preface and Sanctus, which is opened in the Western Church with "The Lord be with you", begins in all Eastern liturgies with the charis-formula in its full Trinitarian Pauline form 2 Cor. 13:13.

The Right Praise of God

This is the background of Rom. 16:17f. The early Church was a teaching Church, confessing the truth and rejecting error. She was at the same time a praying Church.

Doctrine and prayer, dogma and liturgy belong inseparably together.

When a letter like Romans or 1 Cor. was read to the assembled Church, it was read as the proclamation of the Apostolic Word and immediately followed by-the celebration of the sacrament. This connection of word and sacrament, dogma and liturgy has to be kept in mind, if we want to understand what the New Testament teaches on pure and false doctrine.

This the Eastern Church has never forgotten. It calls itself "orthodox" not only in the sense of "keeping the right doctrine", but also as "keeping the right praise of God". All great churchmen of all ages have known of this connection between doctrine and praise.

The Lutheran Church in the period of Orthodoxy in the 16th and 17th century was the Church in which the great Lutheran liturgy was flourishing, when the great hymns of our Church were created . The apostle John is called "Joannes ho theologos" (see the old manuscripts of Revelation) not because he was a great teacher of theology, but because he was "the liturgist"... "With never ceasing theologies" sing the angels in heaven the Sanctus, as the old prefaces have it. All truly great theologians have also been great liturgists. What would Thomas Aquinas be without his hymns, what Luther without his hymns and his entire liturgical work. What Johann Gerhard without the Meditationes Sacrae and the hymns and prayers by the Fathers and even the Medieval schoolmen which he quotes in his Loci? One of the reasons why our conservative Churches have not been able to revive orthodox theology in our time more powerfully is certainly the failure to realize the liturgical and sacramental character of the Christian doctrine. The dogma is the doctrinal content of the liturgy, the prayer of the Church. The liturgy is the dogma in form of prayer. Long before there was an explicit doctrine of the Trinity, this basic doctrine of the Church was expressed in the formula of Baptism, in the Sanctus, in such words as 2 Cor. 13:13. A Christian congregation is not a school in which doctrines are taught and learnt, as Melanchthon the great schoolmaster thought. It is the Church of Christ in which the great mysteries of the Christian faith, as revealed in Holy Scripture, are believed, confessed in creeds and prayers, preserved and passed on in the true worship in which the Church in heaven and on earth are one (Rev. 4).

The Church of Rome

What, then, was the doctrine which the Christians in Rome had learnt and which they are admonished to faithfully preserve when soon false teachers would turn up? And what would be the doctrine of these heretics?

To answer these questions we must have a look at the Church of Rome at the time when Paul wrote his letter in the early years of Nero's rule, probably around 58 A.D. The long list of greetings indicate that the Church of Rome at that time was large, composed from people of different walks of life, many slaves among them who by way of the flourishing slave trade had come to Rome. They came from various provinces of the East, many come from Asia, others from Syria and Egypt. There are a few Latin names. But the language of the Church in Rome was and remained for at least two centuries Greek. Who had taught them? There were some who had learnt their faith in the East from Paul, but probably only a few, which may be the reason why he, announcing his intention to go via Rome to the Western provinces, gives in this letter such a comprehensive presentation of "his gospel" (16:25 comp. 2:16). Some of them may probably have gone through a very short catechumenate.

What did they learn in their Church services which had to be held in private houses or secret places in the early morning or late at night? A full meeting of the entire Church of Rome was probably impossible. There was not such a thing as a Catechismus Romanus, no written Gospel except the earliest beginnings of what later became a written Gospel (Luke 1, 1f.) With the astonishing memory of ancient and Eastern people they kept in mind stories from the life of Jesus, especially the story of his passion, his logia and parables. There was not yet a Creed except such short formulas as 1 Cor. 15:3ff.; Phil. 2:5-11. Their Bible was the Greek version of the Old Testament or parts of it... as it was used in the dozens of synagogues of the city. Many of these Christians came from the "God fearing" people, the outer circle of the synagogues, men and women of pagan origin who, attracted by the power of the Word in the Old Testament, attended regularly the Jewish service. In these synagogues the discussion began whether or not Jesus, who recently had been crucified at Jerusalem, was the Messiah of Israel. The theological discussion of this question was continued in street riots which led to the interference of the police, to anti-Jewish demonstrations and sometimes to the expulsion of the Jews. These riots lasted till the third century, as the history of Kallistos and his counter-bishop Hippolytos shows. As long as the Christians were regarded as a Jewish sect, they enjoyed the religious privileges granted to the Jews. When the Jews informed the authorities that the followers of Christ were not Jews at all and hinted at the crimes committed in their service (ritual murder for what else can it mean for a Roman policeman that the flesh of the son of man is eaten and his blood is drunk) and incest (the holy kiss), the persecutions began. A few years later Peter and Paul died as martyrs in Rome. Then followed the great Neronian persecution in which a "vast multitude" (Tacitus), probably the majority of the believers in Rome perished. Among the names mentioned in Rom. 16 there may have been some of these future martyrs.

All this must be kept in mind if we want to answer the question what "the doctrine which you have been taught" was. It was the doctrine of the Gospel in its simplest form as it was contained in the apostolic kerygma and in the liturgy of the Church, "that Christ died for our sins according to the Scriptures, that he was buried, that he was raised on the third day according to the Scriptures..." (1 Cor. 15:3ff.). The "doctrine" which the Church of Rome had learnt was contained not only in the catechetical instruction, not only in the sermon — both may have been in many cases very weak—, but it was contained and expressed in the liturgy. Such formulas as 1 Cor. 15:3ff. or the *"carmen Christi"* (Bengel) Phil. 2 or the Christian version of the Old Testament Creed, the *"Schama Jisrael"* of Deut. 6:4 given by Paul 1 Cor. 8:6 and similar passages, used in the liturgy, contain indeed the whole Christian faith. They resound in the great Creeds of the later Church. The doctrine of the *Homousia* of Father and Son, the vere Deus, vere homo of the Christological dogma is already contained in the simple New Testament Creed: *Kyrios Jesus Christos*, Jesus Christ is Lord. As soon as the Aramaic *"Maran"*, our Lord, is rendered in Greek, the holy name of God in the Greek Bible, *Kyrios* (the rendering of *"Jahue"*) is applied to Jesus.

Luther found the articulus stantis et cadentis ecclesia: in the words of the Nicene Creed, "Who for us men and for our salvation came down from heaven" and *"crucified pro nobis."* These early Christians had not yet a system of dogmatics, but they possessed the entire dogma of the Church of all times.

To "sing praise to Christ as God" is according to the report of the governor of Bithynia the essential content of the Christian worship. It is completely wrong to say: The early Church had not yet a dogmatic creed, they were satisfied with the simple statement that Christ is Lord. So let us be satisfied with that. The entire dogma of the Church was already present. If they called Jesus "Lord" they confessed his full divinity. For *"Kyrios"* is in the Bible the name of God in His revelation. To deny or even to question the full divinity and the full humanity of Christ, or the blessed Trinity would come under the Anathema of Rom. 16:17f. In other words, the "doctrine" is here the doctrine as the apostles proclaimed it. By contrast, the doctrine rejected is any doctrine which destroys the Gospel as proclaimed by the apostles. For Paul the Church destroying heretics were first of all the Judaizers who demanded circumcision and the keeping of the Old Testament Law. They followed him on all his mission fields in Galatia, Asia, Macedonia and would soon make their appearance in Rome. It is worth noticing that there is a close relationship between Rom. 16 and the corresponding passages in Philippians, the latter having been written a few years later in Rome. Even the terminology is very much the same, including the "belly" of the heretics (see Phil. 3;2ff.; 6ff). With great passion Paul rejects these enemies of Christ. With the same passion he speaks in the Pastoral epistles against the gnostics who deny the real incarnation. He sees behind them Satan (comp. Rom. 16:20 with 1 Tim.3;15). In this he agrees fully with John's fight against the gnostic deniers of the Incarnation as inspired by Antichrist (John 4: 1ff).

To sum up, every doctrine which destroys directly or indirectly the Gospel comes under the Anathema of Rom. 16. This does not mean that every theological error, exegetical or otherwise, is Church destroying. It has never been easy for the Church to find the borderline between that which can be tolerated and that which cannot. Not every exegetical statement of the *Book of Concord* is binding on us. Luther's exegesis of John 6 as not referring to the sacrament is not tenable. The same is true of his understanding of *"parelabon apo tou kyriou"* (1 Cor. 11:2) as referring to a direct revelation. The apostle uses here the terminology of Jewish theology. What he means is that the tradition he has received and passed on goes back to the hour in which the Lord instituted the sacrament. It has been frequently observed how patiently Paul can deal with errorists, not only as a good pastor helping them to give up their errors, as he did in his arguments with the deniers of the resurrection at Corinth, but acting as a real churchman who knows that an absolute uniformity of opinions on every question is neither possible nor desirable in the Church of Christ. His urgent appeal to the Corinthians, (1:10) "that all of you agree and that there be no dissension among you, but that you be united in the same mind and the same judgement" is directed against the schisms in which that Church indulged. He was fully aware that there were differ-

118

ent theological emphases between him, Peter and Apollos.

Over against the tendency at Corinth to exaggerate these differences and to regard them as basis for a Pauline, a Petrine, and an Apollonian group and one which simply wanted to be "Church of Christ", Paul makes it clear that the different apostles preached one and the same Gospel and shared the same work given them by God. This broadmindedness distinguishes the Church from the sects. The Jehovah's Witnesses, the Christadelphians, and the Christian Scientists have all the same doctrinal opinion. They require acceptance of a certain exegesis on any point. A "watch tower" censorial board sees to it that no deviation from the official doctrine occurs. This is not the unity of the Church as taught by Article 7 of the CA on the basis of Eph. 4: "It is sufficient for the true unity of the Christian"— which means Catholic — "Church that the Gospel is taught unanimously in its purity and the sacraments are administered according to the divine Word". Also this has been understood differently.

According to the Lutheran understanding, the administration of the sacraments is inseparably bound up with the doctrine contained in the sacramental words. The Gospel is not taught in its purity if it is not understood in its relation to the Law. It has repeatedly happened in the Church that only in the course of whole generations and centuries the proper understanding of an aspect of the Gospel has been reached. Athanasius remains to us the great fighter for the orthodox faith though he, like most of the Oriental fathers, remained in his doctrine of sin a Pelagian. The great sequence "Lauda, Sion, salvatorem", written by Thomas Aquinas for the liturgy of the feast of Corpus Christi was still sung in Latin in the 17 century in the Lutheran Churches with a slight alteration of one verse where the transubstantiation is mentioned. Still today this hymn, like other hymns of the Ancient and the Medieval Church, resound in our services.

The question whether a certain theological opinion destroys or tends to destroy the Gospel, as it was proclaimed by Jesus and the apostles and the sacraments, cannot, as initiated by Christ, always easily be answered. There is on the one hand the great danger that the broadmindedness of the Church becomes unionism and loss of the truth.

On the other hand looms always the great danger that the Church becomes a narrow minded sect which makes a theological opinion not directly taught in Holy Scripture an articulus stantis et cadentis ecclesiae. Many Lutherans in the 16th century deplored the broadmindedness with which Luther tolerated certain deviations of Melanchthon. But without this patience there would never have been possible a Formula Concordiae. We all are confronted today with the problem where Church fellowship is possible and where not. This is the issue which at present divides conservative Lutherans. The principle is clear since the beginning of the Church. There ought not to be "communicatio in sacris cum haereticis at schismaticis". According to the usage of the Roman Law the "sacra" are the religious rites characterized of a religious society, (see the Act of the Martyrs of Scili). To the Church the "sacra" were mainly the celebration of the Mass, in a special way the participation of the body and blood of

119

Christ which presupposes, as we have seen, the full unity of faith and brotherly love. For us Lutherans it means the administration of the means of grace, the proclamation of the Gospel and the administration of Christ's sacraments. But what about prayer outside the solemn service of the Church? Since the "Apostolic Canons" also private common prayer with heretics and schismatics was forbidden again and again. However the constant repetition of this rule seems to indicate that it was not always kept. In the last great persecutions it sometimes happened that Christians of various denominations were waiting in prison for their execution. Could they who in a few days or even hours would stand before Christ and live in the fellowship of the Church Triumphant pray together or not? Some did it, others refused it.

Even the great Church fathers were not united in this question. While the Donatists did not recognize the Catholics as Christians, men like Optatus and Augustine regarded their Donatist adversaries as brethren, as "fratres sejuncti", separated brethren (this is the origin of the modern term of "separated brethren" which Cardinal Bea has taken from Augustine). As a matter of fact, no one has ever been able to define with absolute certainty the borderline between that which is tolerable and that which is not. This is true also of exegetical problems such as presented by the first chapters of Genesis. What is a "day" of creation? To some it is an "ordinary day" of 24 hours. But no one can say what evening, morning and day mean before there could be sunrise and sunset. The same applies to other passages. There are questions to which we do not have and cannot have a definite answer. The Church has never dogmatized on them, and should not try to dogmatize on them either. It is easy to say: A story is either true or not true. Gen. 1-3 is either history or legend and myth. It is history, but history seen and told in forms different from our traditional forms of literature. But we do not want to repeat what has been said in another conflict on the strange form of the Biblical books. The clarity of Scripture is not the clarity of scientific and historical textbooks. This is what Luther told Erasmus in "De servo arbitrio".

Conclusion

It is time to conclude this letter which already has become too long. Its purpose was to encourage you, Brother Wagner, and your friends and co-workers to continue the work you have taken up. This is one of the times in the History of the Church when Christians in all denominations are in danger of despairing of the future of the Church. This is true also of Lutherans who see the terrible decay of the Church of the Augsburg Confession. A process of de-confessionalization of the Churches which once were the stronghold of our confession is going on everywhere in Europe. The "Evangelical Church in Germany" which comprises Lutheran, Reformed, and United Churches is going to be organized into a unified Church which nominally is supposed to be a Church of the Augsburg Confession. But it will be a Variata, worse than all previous attempts to alter and "improve" the CA. It may be compared with S.S. Schmucker's "Definite Platform" in America, but still more "ecumenical". First the profes-

120

sors of theology gave up the old confession, then followed the pastors whom they had educated. Now everyone makes his jokes about confession and confessionalism. Even bishops and Church presidents speak openly of a "pluralistic" Church in which all sorts of doctrines must be tolerated as they are tolerated in the modern "pluralistic state".

The ordination vow has become a mere formality. Many demand that it should be abolished. In wide parts of Germany Infant Baptism and Adult Baptism are accepted as alternatives, which means an abolition of the Catechism. Intercommunion is practiced everywhere, sanctioned by new formulas on the sacrament which — give up the old doctrines of the Lutheran and the Reformed Churches. This is the situation in Europe, but the Americans follow that example. Who in America has loudly protested against the report "Marburg Revisited" and its conclusions? The Lutheran Church-Missouri Synod, which likes doctrinal discussions, has taken part in the negotiations and seems to have given a more or less quiet agreement at its convention in New York. Will your Church have the courage to reject the whole enterprise at the next convention? If not, Missouri will be swallowed by the great union of American Protestants which is coming. What is still more alarming to many of us, is the silence of Wisconsin on this point. We must be very grateful that the Lutheran Congress at Chicago, 1970, has taken up the matter. Where the sacrament of the Altar dies, the Church must die.

The Apology ad CA 7/8 has this to say about the "comforting article" in the Creed on the Church: "We see the infinite dangers that threaten the Church with ruin. There is an infinite number of ungodly within the Church who oppress it. The Church will abide nevertheless; it exists despite the great multitude of the wicked, and Christ supplies it with the gifts he has promised — the forgiveness of sins, answer to prayer, and the gift of the Holy Spirit. The Creed offers us these consolations that we may not despair..." This "ne desperemus" of our confession should resound in our hearts, in our manses, in our congregations and synods. It should sound in our sermons, in our Bible classes, in our hymns, in our entire worship.

If anything is encouraging, it is the fact that everywhere, in Scandinavia, Germany and America a confessing Church is awakening, still weak and often perplexed by the multitude of problems it is facing. This is the Holy Spirit's work, as all true confession is a gift of the Spirit. Let us strengthen this movement wherever we can. Let us do our work with patience, in a spirit of repentance and humility. Let us avoid the great mistake made so often in our circles that we split up on minor issues, hurling anathemas against a brother whom we see caught up in what seems to be, and perhaps is, an error. Much hard theological work has to be done, mainly in the study of the Bible and the confessions. We have to study Luther and not only to search for fitting quotations. We all are deeply indebted to you and your brethren for "*Sola Scriptura*". It is a good beginning, as also the Congress of Chicago was a promising sign of a new theological awakening of confessional Lutheranism. Out of these beginnings a new movement may arise, which across our synodical borders will gather the confessors of the Lutheran faith. Long range plans may be necessary. Perhaps the year 1977 with the fourth centenary of the Formula of Concord may see an assembly or at least gatherings in various countries of those who still believe, teach and confess the old faith of our Church.

It will be different from the celebration by the Synodical Conference of 1877. Much hard theological work will be necessary. This work cannot consist in a repetition of the theology of the old Synodical Conference. New questions have come up which demand new answers. Courageously we must examine our theological methods, and the philosophical presuppositions of our theology. One of the reasons for the crisis in the Roman Church is the breakdown of the Aristotelian philosophy which was the basis of Thomism. Can we retain this philosophy without re-examining it? Such questions have to be faced. Have we not been in the danger of perpetrating certain traditions of our theological schools which we unconsciously equated with the doctrine of Holy Scripture? Christ, says Tertullian, has called himself "veritas", not "consuetudo". The Church has the promise that the Paraclete, the Spirit of truth will guide her into all the truth. This promise will be fulfilled if we let all our theological traditions, even the most cherished ones, be tested again and again by the source and rule of all Christian doctrine: Scripture alone.

With all good wishes for your work and fraternal greetings,

Yours in Christ,

(Hermann Sasse)

Study Questions

1. Hermann Sasse and Bruce Adams endorsed the aims of ____.
2. What is vanishing everywhere? ____
3. The Anglican Communion is ____.
4. The decay of Roman Catholicism is ____.
5. "Doctrine ____ but service ____" is an ____.
6. What seems to be vanishing among theologians and even bishops? ____
7. The majority of Catholic bishops in Holland and America should be ____.
8. Is the Th.D. of Heidelberg of Tübingen a high degree? ____
9. What must be overhauled? ____
10. A theologian must know ____.
11. "Where are the ____?"
12. Perhaps the future again belongs to ____ rather than institutions such as ____.
13. Where did Hermann Sasse lecture in America? ____
14. "The students were supposed to read the orthodox books but ____ and ____ were the men who fascinated them."
15. Walther and old Missouri dared to maintain Luther's ____.
16. Missouri's parting from Iowa and Ohio on the doctrine of predestination was justified because ____.
17. In the early Church there existed side by side different forms of ____.
18. What Paul writes in 1 Cor. 14:37 about women refers not only to the

122

custom of all Churches but to ___.
19. What is a direct attack on Christ's authority? ___
20. Missouri cannot have fellowship with the ALC or LCA as long as the scandal of ___ continues.
21. All Churches of the LWF accept ___.
22. The first "Lord's day" of the Church was ___.
23. All truly great theologians have also been great ___.
24. The liturgy is the dogma in form of ___.
25. Luther found in the Nicene Creed ___.
26. Every doctrine which destroys directly or indirectly of despairing the ___.
27. This is a time when Christians in denominations are in danger of despairing the ___.
28. Where the Sacrament of the Altar dies, the ___ dies.
29. What will abide despite the multitude of the wicked? ___
30. ___ is the source and rule for all Christian doctrine.

Editor's note:

* Dietrich Bonhoeffer has been praised by Concordia Theological Seminary, Ft. Wayne as a theologian faithful to the Word of God. Concordia Seminary, St. Louis said Bonhoeffer was the greatest Lutheran theologian since Martin Luther. Lutheran Church-Missouri Synod, President Matthew Harrison, in his *Little Book of Joy,* presents Bonhoeffer as a faithful Lutheran. The LCMS's *Lutheran Witness* said Bonhoeffer was a confessional Lutheran. *Bonhoeffer and King*, published by *Christian News*, documents the fact that Bonhoeffer supported evolution and denied such doctrines as the virgin birth and resurrection of Jesus Christ.

** "A Grammatical Study of Romans 16:17 by Dr. Robert Hoerber was mailed to all the clergymen of the Synodical Conference in 1947. "Twenty-five Years In Retrospect", *Christian News*, December 9, 1974. *Christian News Encyclopedia*, p. 1215.

§

AN INTERNATIONAL VOICE OF AUTHENTIC LUTHERANISM

SOLA SCRIPTURA

Vol. 1, No. 6 May-June 1971

SOLA SCRIPTURA

AN INTERNATIONAL VOICE
OF AUTHENTIC LUTHERANISM

II Tim. 1:13

Box 1377 – Studio City, Calif. 91604

JULY-AUGUST 1970 — VOLUME 1 NO. 1

EDITORIAL OFFICE

Sola Scriptura
Box 1377
Studio City, Calif. 91604

Published bi-monthly by Lutheran News, Inc., a non-profit organization at Trinity Lutheran Church, Box #168, New Haven, Mo. 63068.

Send all sub. and address changes to Sola Scriptura, Box 168, New Haven, Mo. 63068. Subscription rate of $3.00 includes 6 issues of SOLA SCRIPTURA and 46 issues of CHRISTIAN NEWS.

Second Class Permit pending at the post office at New Haven, Mo. 63068 and at additional mailing offices.

Editors and Contributors to SOLA SCRIPTURA are not responsible for CHRISTIAN NEWS.

IN THIS ISSUE...

SOLA SCRIPTURA

A BI-MONTHLY JOURNAL OF AUTHENTIC LUTHERANISM

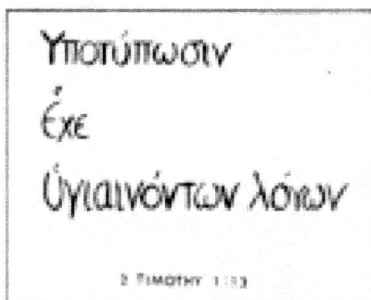

Ὑποτύπωσιν

ἔχε

ὑγιαινόντων λόγων

2 TIMOTHY 1:13

126

JAO PREUS

To set the record straight for the benefit of my learned friends, the students of Concordia, St. Louis, and others: JAO is the name of the most famous emperor of ancient China in the third millenium B.C. The Chinese have always gratefully remembered him. He saved his people from a devastating flood (Schu-king I, 3, 11 see edition by James Legge in the Chinese Classics, 1865, the English translation also in "Sacred Books of the EAST" vol. III, 1879).

Sincerely yours,
Hermann Sasse
16 Wellington Square
North Adelaide,
South Australia
(Christian News, June 21, 1971)

§

"THE BIBLE AND LUTHER"

By Sasse
Christian News, September 6, 1971

Festschrift in Honor of David Hedegard

On November 29, 1971, David Hedegard, doctor of theology, will complete his eightieth year. Some of his friends have contributed essays for a *Festschrift* in his honor. For a whole generation David Hedegard has fought for faith in God's word in his teaching, proclamation, and translation work and in writings of both a scientific and a popular nature. He has won an international reputation through his works and his lectures. It seemed self-evident to us that a *Festschrift* dedicated to him should deal with the Bible. Thus we determined to publish a Bible handbook in Swedish, to include contributions from leading theologians from far beyond Sweden's borders. The *Festschrift* will include the following articles:

The Inspiration of the Bible
Prof. Siegbert W. Becker

The Authority of the Bible
Cathedral Provost Gustaf Adolf Danell

The Bible and the Congregation

Prof. Hugo Odeberg

The Bible and the Question of the Canon
Prof. Allan A. MacRae

The Bible and the Synagogue Worship Service
Tryggve Kronholm, teol. Kand., fil. Mag.

The Bible and Archaeology
Prof. Aapeli Saarisalo

The Bible and Science
Prof. Seth Erlandsson

The Bible and Human Language
Prof. Harold O.J. Brown

The Bible and Luther
Prof. Hermann Sasse

The Bible and the Lutheran Confessions
Prof. Robert Preus

The Bible and Its Defense
Prof. John W. Montgomery

The Bible and Tradition in Ecumenical Debate
Prof. Carl Fr. Wisloff

The Bible and Its Use
Rev. Herman Otten

Life and Bibliography
Rev. Lars Engouist

The *Festschrift* will include a *Tabula Gratulatoria* listing the names of those who wish to join in giving David Hedegard a well-earned tribute and in assuring the publication of the book. All those interested are invited to send, as promptly as possible but no later than September 10, 1971, the sum of thirty-five Swedish crowns (SKr 35.00) for which they will receive the book postpaid upon publication. The contributions should be sent to Prof. Seth Erlandsson, Regins vag 5, S-754 40 Uppsala, Sweden, Postal Checking Account 74 76 40-1 (Stockholm).

The book will have in a fine cloth binding a number of about 300 pp. A small edition will be sold in bookstores for about SKr 53.00.

Uppsala, August 1971

Gustaf Adolf Danell - Hugo Odeberg - Carl Fr. Wisloff - Sir Erlandsson - Lars Engquist

128

Ed. (SKr 35.00) is about $8.00. *Lutheran News* and now *Christian News* has published a number of articles by Dr. David Hedegard. Dr. Hedegard was our reporter at the last assembly of the World Council of Churches in Uppsala, Sweden. He was one of the first prominent Lutheran theologians to consent to write for us when we began publishing in 1962. We were privileged to have him as our guest in New Haven in 1963. Dr. Hedegard was formerly an instructor of New Testament Isagogics at Lund University. He is the president of the Bible League of Sweden and editor of "For Biblisk Tro" (For Biblical Faith). He is the author of a new Swedish Bible translation and has written textbooks in religion for Swedish public schools. Dr. Hedegard is the co-editor of Biblisk Uppslagsbok ("Biblical *Encyclopedia*"), author of numerous pamphlets and books and translator into Swedish of Wilhelm and Hans Moeller's "Einleitung in das Alte Testament" and "Biblische Theologie des Alten Testaments in heilsgeschichtlicher Entwicklung."

Study Questions
1. Who was Dr. David Hedegard? ____
2. What was the title of Sasse's contribution to the Hedegard *Festschrift*?

____

§

A PUBLIC THANKS TO RICHARD JUNGKUNTZ

Christian News, January 24, 1972

Herman Otten
Christian News, New Haven, Missouri

Second class mail from U.S.A. to Australia was very slow these last months, due probably to several strikes. So I received several copies of "*Christian News*" simultaneously. I read them, as always, with great interest, but also with deep distress. I fail to see how the rift that goes through your Church can ever be healed. I saw the tragedy of Missouri since 1948. I know only of one parallel to the development of your Church. This is the tragedy of Rome. But let us not despair, I personally endorse wholeheartedly the endeavors of your presidency to bring about a reconciliation.

When perusing the latest copies I found my name mentioned in connection with the attempt by Dr. Richard Jungkuntz to publish a series of articles of mine. The writer explained this as attempt to use me for Church political purposes. I want to assure you that nothing can be farther from the truth. The idea was not only an idea of my friend Dr.

Jungkuntz. Others supported him and helped him with translations and with making ready the manuscript. Their motive was true friendship and the conviction that articles that had appeared in other languages and in the periodicals of other Churches should be made available also to Lutherans in America, and especially to readers among your pastors. If European Modernism is now making its inroad into American Lutheranism with the active support of the leaders of Lutheran Churches in America, why should the voice of conservative Lutheranism be silenced?

I do not know what has happened to Dr. Jungkuntz. I was not happy when he took over the office of the secretary of that Commission on Theology because I was convinced that he would not be able to carry out the Herculean task to create or restore a true theological consensus among people divided by what seem to be irreconcilable contrasts in the midst of your Church. I have not heard from him since some years. I cannot judge the rights or wrongs of his activities nor the wisdom or otherwise of the decision which removed him from that secretariat. Your presidents must have had their reasons, which I do not know. I know from my own bitter experience what can happen if theology and Church politics are bound to clash. I use this opportunity to thank publicly Dr. Jungkuntz and all those in your Church who in these critical years, when the Church of the Augsburg Confession is dying in many parts of the world, have been listening to the voices of their brethren in the confessing Lutheran Churches overseas.

If on the threshold of a new year we look into the future and ask the Lord for a renewal of our Churches let us remember that as the Gospel began with the call to repentance, so every new epoch of the Church has begun as a great repentance. There is no hope for a renewal of our Churches until we all have learned again to speak in view of the desolate state of Christendom: Mea culpa, mea culpa, mea maxima culpa.

Yours in Christ,
Hermann Sasse
North Adelaide
South Australia

Study Questions
1. Hermann Sasse was not happy when _____ became secretary of the LCMS's Commission on Theology.
2. Every new epoch of the Church has begun as _____.

§

ST. LOUIS SEMINARY JOURNAL ATTACKS INERRANCY OF BIBLE

Christian News, December 13, 1972

THE CONCORDIA THEOLOGICAL MONTHLY, which is "A Theological Journal of the Lutheran Church Missouri Synod Edited by The Faculty of Concordia Seminary Saint Louis, Missouri," continues its attack upon the doctrine of scriptural inerrancy.

Rev. Traugott H. Rehwaldt, long a defender of the liberal professors at the St. Louis seminary, takes issue with the orthodox doctrine of the inerrancy of the Bible in an article titled "The Other Understanding of the Inspiration Texts." Rehwaldt's article appeared in the June *CTM*.

The LCMS clergyman writes: "Whoever makes either the Law or the entire content of Scripture the object of faith introduces the monster of uncertainty into the life of the Christian and robs the guilty conscience of any possible comfort. It is surely unfortunate that in his comments on John 10:35 Pieper really goes beyond this principle and introduces a concept of absolute inerrancy, which, as we have tried to indicate, goes beyond what Scripture says of itself. The doctrine of the absolute inerrancy of Scripture has a way of bringing with it legalism, for example, the demand that one believe in a 24-hour creation day."

Rehwaldt maintains that the scriptures are theologically inerrant but not in other areas such as history. He favorably quotes such liberals as Kent Knutson, Fredrik Schiotz and Helmut Thielicke. He fails to note that Knutson and Thielicke have not only questioned the inerrancy of the Bible but have cast doubt upon such doctrines of the Christian faith as Christ's vicarious satisfaction, the virgin birth of Christ, and Christ's deity. Rehwaldt favorably quotes Thielicke's words to "Bible-believing Christians" as they are published in *Between Heaven and Earth – Conversations With American Christians*. In this book Thieliecke denies the scriptural doctrine of the virgin birth of Christ. Thieliecke suggest that possibly the primitive Church fabricated the doctrine of Christ's virgin birth, (74). While the *CTM* article praises leading liberal theologians who deny historic Christianity, it criticizes such orthodox theologians as Francis Pieper, J.T. Mueller, and E.W. Koehler. The *CTM* reviews at considerable length the oft-quoted November 14, 1950 letter of Dr. Hermann Sasse.

Dr. Sasse informed Concordia Seminary a number of years ago that he has withdrawn his November 14, 1950 letter and asked the seminary to discontinue distributing it. The seminary still offered Sasse's letter for sale even after Sasse's request that it no longer be sold at the seminary. Now the *CTM* again uses the withdrawn letter. When former ALC president Fredrik Schiotz attempted to use some of Dr. Sasse's writings to support his denial of inerrancy, we wrote to Dr. Sasse. Dr. Sasse replied: "If I may say a word in reply to your request I should like to point out that I am not quite happy about the way Dr. Schiotz has selected passages from my articles. Taken out of their context they might suggest that I reject the inerrancy of the Scriptures. The contrary is true" (*Lutheran News*, January, 1967).

Anyone seeking documentary evidence showing that a good percentage of the members of the faculty of Concordia Seminary no longer accepts the inerrancy of the Bible just has to read the *CTM*. Unfortunately, very few pastors and laymen ever receive the *CTM*. Most members of the LCMS don't know what the *CTM* is publishing.

The *CTM* is neither a scholarly nor a scriptural journal. It has become rather useless. Reports indicate that even very few officials of the LCMS bother to read it. We wish more would.

Ralph W. Klein, one of the liberals teaching at the St. Louis seminary, again reveals his destructive higher-critical views in the current *CTM*. He says in a review of *An Introduction to Source Analyses of the Pentateuch*: "A person will get a clearer understanding of the evidence for the composite authorship of the Pentateuch by working through this program... One thing, however, is certain: a person who works through this program will have great difficulty in maintaining the unitary authorship of the Pentateuch!"

Study Questions
1. The June 1972 *Concordia Theological Monthly* of the St. Louis seminary attacked ____.
2. Helmut Thielicke denied the ____ of Christ.
3. What writing of Sasse did the *CTM* use again? ____
4. Did many members of the LCMS know what the *CTM* was publishing? ____
5. What did Concordia Seminary Professor Ralph Klein write about the authority of the Pentateuch? ____

§

FOCUS ON THE LUTHERANS
Christian News, December 18, 1972

The June, 1972 *Concordia Theological Monthly* published an article by Traugott H. Rehwaldt attacking the inerrancy of the Bible. The *CTM* is edited by the faculty of Concordia Seminary, St. Louis and is "A Theological Journal of the Lutheran Church-Missouri Synod."

The July 3 *Christian News* quoted from the *CTM* article to show that Rehwaldt rejects the inerrancy of Holy Scripture. The *CTM* author maintains that the Scriptures are theologically inerrant but not historically inerrant. He favorably quotes such liberals as Kent Knutson, Fredrick

Schiotz and Helmut Thielicke. The *CTM* reviewed at considerable length the oft-quoted November 14, 1950 letter of Dr. Hermann Sasse.

The July 3 *Christian News* noted: "Dr. Sasse informed Concordia Seminary a number of years ago that he has withdrawn his November 14, 1950 letter and asked the seminary to discontinue distributing it. The seminary still offered Sasse's letter for sale even after Sasse's request that it no longer be sold at the seminary. Now the *CTM* again uses the withdrawn letter. When former ALC president Fredrik Schiotz attempted to use some of Dr. Sasse's writings to support his denial of inerrancy, we wrote to Dr. Sasse. Dr. Sasse replied: 'If I may say a word in reply to your request I should like to point out that I am not quite happy about the way Dr. Schiotz has selected passages from my articles. Taken out of their context they might suggest that I reject the inerrancy of the Scriptures. The contrary is true' (*Lutheran News*, January, 1967)."

We are photographing below an important letter by Dr. Sasse which was published in a conservative Swedish journal which reprinted Rehwaldt's *CTM* attack upon scriptural inerrancy. We have not yet seen Dr. Sasse's letter in the *CTM*. The ethical standards of Concordia Seminary don't appear to be very high. Liberal theology and the new morality walk hand in hand. Dr. Sasse has repeatedly asked the seminary not to use his 1950 letter because he has corrected some statements in it. The St. Louis seminary simply ignores these requests. Will the LCMS Council of Presidents unanimously repudiate the *CTM* because of its low ethical standards and because it repeatedly attacks God's truth?

Brev till SPT
The Inspiration of the Bible

A friend of mine in Sweden sent me by letter a copy of your article *Om Skriflems Inspiration* in SPT nr 40/72 (my own copy has not yet arrived in Australia). Since I am not a reader of *Concordia Theological Monthly*, I had to go to the library to have a look into their issue of June. I think I owe it to you in view of a possible ensuing discussion to make a clarifying statement. I do not know the venerable author of *The Other Understanding of The Inspiration Text* and do not blame him for having written bona fide on my doctrine. But if he regarded me as so important he should have consulted not only an article written almost a quarter of century ago but at least some of my later publications (he mentions briefly an article of 1960 in which I have corrected some thoughts, but without noticing this.) The whole argument is based on a letter which appeared in 1950, just before our great discussions of the doctrine De sacra Scriptura in the Lutheran Churches of Australia began. During these discussions and in thorough investigations connected with them I withdrew certain statements made in that letter. I stopped, or rather tried to stop, the reprinting of the old document. But meanwhile the students of Concordia, St. Louis, USA, had come across it and found it to be a most lucrative business to reprint and even to sell it to anybody. When I protested with the then president of St. Louis against this literary piracy, he answered to the effect that boys are boys and you cannot do anything. When the scandal went on I appealed to the professor who was at that time acting president. He stopped the matter, but the damage was done. I do not know from which dark source Pastor Rehwaldt had his copy of the old article. I am not angry with him. He meant it obviously well. But literary manners have never been very high in American Lutheranism.

I am sending a copy of this letter to Rev. Rehwaldt and to the editors of *CTM*. I thank you very much that SPT seems to be interested in the great issue which has become vital for our Church.

Hermann Sasse

Photographed from Svensk Pastoraltidskrift 46/1972.

• • •

Comment by *Christian News* editor (*Christian News*, December 18, 1972):

The vast majority of laymen are still unaware of what is going on theologically within their Churches. We have had considerable difficulty in getting laymen to learn that there is such a publication as *Christian News*. Unfortunately, even many conservative pastors hesitate telling their members about *CN*. These pastors tell us that they read *CN* and basically agree with it but they feel that they can't ask their members to subscribe to a publication which has been repudiated by President Jacob Preus and the entire LCMS Council of Presidents. *CN* has repeatedly asked all those who signed the repudiation either to show us where we were not telling the truth or to withdraw their signatures from the repudiation. So far not one of the signers has shown us where we were guilty of untruths. None has withdrawn his signature. *(Ed. Several later withdrew their signatures.)*

Dr. Roland Wiederaenders did tell us that we had greatly wronged Dr. Oliver Harms and Dr. Walter Wolbrecht. We offered to publish any statement he might send us on this matter but he has not yet sent us a statement. Dr. Wiederaenders said that we were at least in part responsible for the defeat of Dr. Harms because of information we had published.

CN has tried to advertise in some Church papers. The *Spectrum* of Concordia Seminary, St. Louis, refused to publish the advertisement printed on this page. Several years ago *The Lutheran Laymen* refused a simple advertisement from *CN* but at the same time published an advertisement praising a book which attacked the Christian faith and taught that Jesus Christ was not God. Since the November 5, 1972, *Lutheran Witness* published a full page advertisement for Dr. Martin Marty's expensive little newsletter, we again attempted to advertise in *The Lutheran Witness*. We wrote to the editor of *The Lutheran Witness* on November 28: "We wrote to your advertising sales director on November 7 for your advertising rates. We would like to place an advertisement in *The Lutheran Witness* for *Christian News* as soon as possible. We have not yet heard from your advertising department. Could you kindly see to it that we are sent a list of your rates.

"Several years ago you refused to advertise *Christian News*. If this is still your policy, why did you publish a full page advertisement for Dr.

134

Martin Marty's *Context?*"

We have not yet heard from *The Lutheran Witness*. Twenty-two issues of Marty's six-page newsletter cost $16.50.

Marty is a theological liberal who despises the scriptural theology of the Lutheran Church-Misscuri Synod. He rejects what God's Word teaches about adultery. He says that "I could conceive, from the pastoral point of view, the legitimacy of something like adultery in extreme situations." (See "Formal Charge vs. Martin E. Marty" *Christian News*, November 13,1972).

Concordia Publishing House, which publishes *The Lutheran Witness*, tells us that it cannot send us review copies of their publications because President Preus and the LCMS Council of Presidents have repudiated *Christian News*. CPH sends review copies to all sorts of publications which attack the scriptural theology of the LCMS. Now it even publishes a full page advertisement for an editor who has viciously attacked the LCMS's theology in *The Christian Century*.

Study Questions
1. Liberal theology and the ____ walk hand in hand.
2. Did the LCMS's Council of Presidents repudiate the *CTM*? ____
3. How did the president of the St. Louis seminary respond to Sasse's complaint of literary piracy? ____
4. Many conservative pastors in the LCMS did not tell their members about ____ .
5. Who refused to publish advertisements from *Christian News*? ____
6. The LCMS's *Lutheran Witness* published a full page advertisement from ____ .

§

REPLY TO "LUTHERANS DOWN UNDER"
The Lutheran, September 23, 1974

It was an unexpected pleasure to meet Dr. John Garrett in the hospitable columns of the *Lutheran World*. Years ago, when he was just about to leave Australia for his new appointment at Geneva, we met in one of the centers of our Church in South Australia in the company of one of the outstanding laymen in what at that time still was our sister Church. As an "Unrepentant Congregationalist", as he called himself, he discussed with me, the equally "unrepentant" Lutheran, in the most friendly way the question which he now takes up again - the relationship of the Lutherans in Australia with the Australian Council of Churches and the Ecumenical Movement as a whole. I gladly make use of the permission of the Editor to say a few words in reply, especially since the question is repeatedly addressed to us.

No Uncharitable Isolationism
It would be quite wrong to interpret our attitude as an uncharitable isolationism. We do not want to live in a confessional ghetto. There may sometimes be differing opinions among us on how we can best make manifest the solidarity which Christians must and can show at a time when anti-Christian powers threaten the very existence of the Christian faith in the world. So I should like to ask Dr. Garrett not to single me out, even in the most friendly way and with the best of intentions from my colleagues in our Faculty, to which I still belong as an emeritus, and from my brethren in the ministry.

All our pastors, as far as I know, belong to the local fraternals in which ministers of all denominations meet. Our Faculty has always made its contributions to a famous "Theological Circle" which was for many years under the leadership of the great Congregationalist, Dr. Kiek. We have accepted invitations to lectures and discussions throughout Australia and New Zealand. We had our share in the building up of the Church in New Guinea. Our Church is proud, to speak of another field of ecumenical activity, of the great work which is being done by our brother, Dr. Muetzelfeldt, in the service to refugees and to starving people in the Near East.

We are aware of our limitations and shortcomings, which are partly due to the fact that we are a comparatively small and poor Church. This is no excuse for the sins of omission and commission that have weakened our life and our witness. Visitors from the European establishments and from rich Churches in America have often wondered how it was possible that this minority Church was able to cater for a continent of the size of the USA, to maintain so many congregations with Churches and schools, to create administrative facilities, and to care for mission fields in Australia and abroad. If one considers all this, it is obvious that our theologians could not sit all the time in comfortable studies and libraries. Ecclesiology which was their favorite subject was for them more than theoretical speculation on the ideal Church and its constitution.

Our First Task—Lutheran Union
What we have been able to contribute to ecumenical problems had a very practical background. Our first task was to unite the Lutherans of Australia and New Zealand who had come from various countries—not only Prussia—and from different theological schools of thought. For generations they were striving for unity. They had to prove that the great doctrine of the Seventh Article of the Augsburg Confession, which underlies all ecclesiologies of Christendom since the 16th century was more than a nice theory. When around 1926 the then United Evangelical Lutheran Church of Australia was invited to join the German Evangelical Church Federation, which would have meant the end to poverty and

need, only one congregation accepted the offer. The others declared that their Lutheran Confession was not for sale. This decision was the basis of our union that brought together all Australian Lutherans. It was my good fortune that I was called into this Church and was able to help finalize the endeavors of several generations. The papers which I wrote in this connection together with my lectures are behind the publications which Dr. Garrett mentions in such a kind way. They did not come only from a "pen-house". Written on the basis of the experiences of the "Confessing Church" in Germany, and from years of work in the World Conference on Faith and Order, they were given again in lectures which I could present in the framework of the universities from Perth to Brisbane, from Canberra to Dunedin, which to my knowledge is the southernmost university of the world, and in theological seminaries of various denominations, in ministers' conferences and, with special joy and satisfaction, in groups of Christian students. So the "mouth-house" was wide open.

A Decisive Battle To Be Fought

As an Australian—as far as a "migrant" after 25 years can be regarded as an Australian—I have often meditated on the situation of Christianity in our country. Some years ago the Social Justice Statement of the Catholic bishops compared modern Australia with Ireland at the dawn of the Middle Ages. As Ireland became the starting point for the Christianization or re-Christianization of Northern, Central and Western Europe in the Dark Ages, so Australia may become the starting point for the encounter of the Church with the great rising religions of Asia, with Islam in Indonesia and Pakistan, the new Hinduism of India, Buddhism in the Far East and the great counter-religion of Chinese Communism. One of the most decisive battles of the spiritual history of mankind will be fought at our doorstep. The bishops asked whether Australia's Christianity is strong enough for that battle. Today, after the mission conference at Bangkok, which was held under the auspices of the World Council of Churches, they may ask whether the Christian faith, or what is left of it in Europe and America, is stronger than ours. They might even extend their soul-searching query to their own Church and ask whether Rome is really so much stronger than Geneva. For us Australians, whatever our Church affiliation may be, the question should burn in our consciences: Are we prepared?

Church "Should Make Their Contribution"

We all have to admit: we are not. This, Dr. Garrett would say, speaking of his rich experience at the WCC Headquarters at Geneva and from his experience as professor of theology, is the reason why I make my suggestions. What Australia needs is closer co-operation in a more comprehensive Australian Council and in the WCC. All Churches should make their contribution. By a thorough discussion of their respective traditions in a profound dialogue they would discover the basic unity which binds them together in the Church as the body of Christ, in spite of certain varieties

137

which at first sight might seem to be irreconcilable. Patient and charitable discussion of our doctrines would show them to be either shades of one and the same truth, or misunderstandings thereof. This will lead to the mutual recognition of the Churches and to the visible manifestation of its lost unity.

The Ecumenical Movements Of Our Age
This theory goes back to the Pietistic movements in the Protestant Churches, especially to the great mission work and the youth movements of the 19th century. It has produced the ecumenical movements of our age and is now getting more and more hold also on the Roman Catholic Church. It is based not on experience but on an axiom which is so evident to those who hold it that no experience of its failure has been able to refute it. It has become an article of faith. Has not our Lord Himself promised that there will be one fold and one shepherd? Has He not prayed in the most solemn prayer before His passion that they all may be one? This is true, but the question ought to be raised whether we understand these and similar words correctly. In our day the Eastern Orthodox Church has reminded Rome that the New Testament doctrine of the one flock in which Church and mankind will have become one under one shepherd will find its fulfilment after the Parousia in the world to come. Should not we evangelical Christians examine the Gospel a little in the light of our experience?

Disappointments And Frustrations
May I appeal to Dr. Garrett's own disappointments. For many years he has been active in the union movement in Australia. With great hopes and great seriousness the prayerful work went on to unite the Churches in this country. A united Church after the pattern of the union in South India was envisaged, a Church united in a common confession, a Church which would comprise those who had accepted the "historic episcopate" and the Protestants of Free Church tradition. But the Anglicans would not accept the watered-down concept of an episcopal office of South India and other unions, while the Presbyterians refused an episcopal office, despite all endeavors of the Presbyterian Bishop Newbigin in Madras. What remained was the scheme of a union of the Presbyterians, the Congregationalists and the Methodists in a "Uniting Church" which later might be joined by others. A common confession was framed, discussed, redrafted and again thoroughly discussed by all involved, a tremendous theological work which went on for about a generation.

The Uniting Church—A Partial Success
But this holy and peaceful Thirty Years War ended in what the world would call defeat. Since no Church likes to confess defeat, as this could be understood as a defeat of Christ, it might be called a partial success. The last version of the new confession was accepted as the basis of further negotiations. The real confession could be made only by the new Church itself. Now the mills of the law courts are grinding to settle the problems

138

posed by the external assets of the Churches involved. The decisive synods have been held. The result will be the same as it was forty years ago when the Methodists and Congregationalists with the majority of the Presbyterian Church formed the United Church of Canada, while a great number of Presbyterians remained outside and continued the old Presbyterian Church of Canada. So also in Australia, not all Presbyterians will join the Uniting Church. They will form a Continuing Presbyterian Church—if it will be one Church, because there are different motives behind the resistance, doctrinal and legal ones. It may well be that the Continuing Church may be, as in Canada, the spiritually stronger Church because the heritage of the old Free Kirk of Scotland and the Reformation of old Geneva will be kept. These continuing Churches which survive the modern unions deserve more attention than they usually get. I have met the continuing Anglicans in South India and I am convinced that the great Azariah Vedenayakam, the Bishop of Dornakal, who since 1910 was the soul of the union movement in South India, but who is hardly remembered by the present CSI, would either belong to the continuing Anglicans or stand behind them. He and Archbishop Temple have been spared the torture of the acceptance or non-acceptance of the final constitution of the CSI in 1947. This union was the pet child of William Temple, the great testing case of the Faith and Order program. When he died during the war, after he had to say No to the final solution of the problem of the episcopate in India, he was according to his biographers in a similar mood as Bishop Charles Brent, the father of Faith and Order, was at his death shortly after the conference at Lausanne.

In his closing words at Lausanne he hinted at the magnitude of the tasks still before the conference. He did not despair. This great Christian knew what it means: *"In te speravi, Domine, non confundar in aeternum"* (I have hoped in Thee, O Lord; I shall not be eternally confounded).

He who has seen the face of this great churchman which bore already the marks of his approaching death, the eyes wide open as if he was looking into the distant *future of* which he spoke in his closing address, and has heard the words which he afterwards spoke to his closest co-workers, understands what the French call "la tristesse ecumenique" (the sad ecumenicity) and without which there is perhaps no true ecumenicity.

Loss Of Doctrinal Substance

What is the reason for the deep ecumenical disappointments experienced by the—most serious—churchmen and theologians in all Churches? It is the loss of doctrinal substance. Innumerable new confessions have been written and have been solemnly accepted by the respective Churches, hailed as the beginning of a new era of Christian faith and confession. But most of them have very soon lost the power to attract and to bind together the Christians in a true unity. They were felt to be insufficient and had to be replaced by better ones. It seems that this time of astonishing productivity in the field of doctrine is drawing to an end. The famous Declaration of Barmen, imitated by younger Churches throughout the world, seems to have been almost forgotten in Germany. It has been incorporated in the "Book of Confessions" issued by the

United Presbyterian Church in America, which contains all classical creeds and confessions of the Reformed Churches. But who reads such books today? What is a confession which is no longer confessed? This is a question which also we Lutherans should ask ourselves very seriously. If at first sight it seems to denote great progress if a Church has got rid of the old creeds and confessions, and claims to rely solely on the Bible as the Word of God, it soon becomes evident that with the authority of the confessions the authority of Holy Scripture also lapses. Already now it must be asked whether or not perhaps the Catholic Churches, Eastern and Western, are the better heirs of the authority which the Reformation ascribed to the Bible.

Lines Of Demarcation Fading

With the authority of the confessions, the borderlines between the Christian denominations are lapsing. This seems to be at first sight a great advantage. The way is open for that unification of Christendom which today is regarded as the fulfilment of the great petition of our Lord, *ut omnes unum sint* (that they all may be one). But the fact remains that wherever the walls between the Christian Churches lapse, the border also lapses which separates Christianity from the other religions. An Anglican archbishop who has the broadest knowledge of the mission fields of Asia was asked when he visited the Church of South India: "Why is it that you Anglicans no longer send your young men to study at our seminary at Bangalore?" He replied: "We can no longer send our converts to a seminary where the new missionary method of dialogue with the pagans is taught. We have examples of young men who were converts to the Christian faith. After two years at your seminary they are either agnostics or they have lapsed back to Hinduism."

This is the most serious problem for all missions in East Asia, including the mission work of the Roman Church.

There are similar cases of syncretism (unionism) in Japan. The worst example is perhaps the solemn address with which a princess of the Royal House of Thailand, who happens to be President of the World Alliance of Buddhists, was to open the World Missionary Conference held under the auspices of the WCC at Bangkok in 1973. She did not speak herself, but the message was read. It is not contained in the official report, but was published in the daily paper of that conference *(Yesterday,* January 1, 1973). It is the worst example of syncretism and sounds as if it had been written at Geneva. There at the end all possible "trinities" are invoked to bless the conference.

Such syncretism will certainly not happen in Fiji where all the great religions of Asia meet in the streets and on the market places in their colorful costumes, most of them simple tradesmen and merchants. Nor would it happen when we Australians meet in our universities Islamic scholars and Buddhist priests. But this syncretism is a sign of warning to all of us who still know that there is salvation only in Christ, the Savior of the world.

Ministers Of The Word

Let me, in conclusion, briefly state what our seminaries, our lecturers and students should do. We have no objection to our students meeting students of other Churches. But we want them to be students of theology, in preparation for a lifelong service as ministers of the Word. Dialogues may come their way and should not be avoided. But we must not forget that for all great theologians, even for Thomas Aquinas, the study of the *sacra Pagina* (sacred page) was the main task of the theologian. Such study requires time. Our seminary in Adelaide is one of the few institutions which still teaches and requires the three Biblical languages, Hebrew, Greek and Latin (for after all the Latin Bible has been the Bible of our fathers for a thousand years and still resounds in our Confessions and Liturgies).

The Problem Of Linguistic Studies

What can be done to save something of the basic values of the ancient languages? This has become a problem even for Rome. I have often discussed this problem with professors of classics and tried to encourage the Churches to keep the closest relationship with the respective Departments of our universities. While the universities in Eastern Europe have experienced a great revival of classical studies, many of our Departments of Classics are empty. I found one Department in New Zealand which had become a center of Biblical Studies. In another university in a city which is famous for the strict atheism of political circles, I had a most valuable discussion with the professor of classics on the problem of how methods of linguistic studies could help. When he showed me over the library I noticed a gap in a series of books. Nilsson's *History of Greek Religion* had been removed by unknown atheists who from time to time were purging the library of all literature which seemed to smell of religion. Now an indispensable tool of studies in ancient literature and philosophy had fallen a prey to their efforts. This was before the time of the great unrest in the Western universities.

Thorough Biblical Theology

From the library I went down to the basement where the Christian students had their den, well protected by the authorities. This "catacomb" had once been the laboratory of the great Rutherford, a cradle of nuclear physics. Here we held our lectures and discussions. My experience has shown me that what really attracts students and satisfies their needs is a thorough Biblical theology. For many this was quite new, and the most attentive hearers were students from various countries of Asia. It was surprising to me to see their interest in the Gospels, especially the Gospel of St. John, which seems to speak in a special way to the soul of Asia.

The Future Of Christianity "Down Under"

In this direction I see the modest contribution which our Church and our theology can make to the common tasks that lie before the Churches of Australia, New Zealand and the vast Pacific world. We do not want our people to become Europeans or Americans, grateful as we are for everything we can learn from all Churches abroad. Nor do we want to make the Melanesians and Indonesians Westerners. We know that we are a small Western minority on the fringe of the hundreds of millions of Asia.

If I ask myself how I would envisage the future of Christianity in this part of the world with its vast distances and limited means, with its various racial, social and political structures, I see Christian Churches before me with various traditions, doctrinal and liturgical, cultural and constitutional, more or less independent, but united in a federation, as probably the entire ecumenical movement will have to give up the chiliastic dreams of a general organic union and will have to return to the great program of a federation of Christian Churches as it was proposed in 1920 by the Ecumenical Patriarchate of Constantinople.

Exchange Of Theological Thought

In such a federation, certain common activities would be possible, especially in the way of mutual help in times and situations of need. There would be a possible living exchange of ideas, practical forms of Church life and, most important, an exchange of theological thought in thorough dialogue. This federation would be united in the bond of mutual respect and Christian clarity. It might grow in a way we cannot foresee into a fuller understanding of the Word of God that binds us all. In this sense a co-operation of our seminaries might be feasible, a mutual fraternal sharing of the special gifts entrusted to each of them. In this sense Adelaide greets its sister in Fiji.

Dr. H. Sasse.

Study Questions

1. What is the reason for the deep ecumenical disappointments experienced by the – most serious – churchmen and theologians? ____
2. The Declaration of Barmen seems to have been almost ____.
3. Wherever the walls between the Christian Churches lapse, the border also lapses which separates Christianity from ____.
4. There is salvation only in ____.
5. The main task of the theologian is the study of ____.
6. Why should Hebrew, Greek and Latin be required for seminarians? ____

§

THE WELS —
HOLY COMMUNION —
TOM HARDT

Christian News, October 28, 1974

Prof. Hermann Sasse
16 Wellington Square
North Adelaide. South Australia 5006
October 7. 1974

The Rev. Herman Otten
Editor, *"Christian News"*
New Haven. Missouri. U.S.A.

Dear Brother Otten:
You may have wondered that you did not hear from me for so long a time. The reason is my state of health which made it almost impossible for me to attend to my correspondence. That little time I could spare was entirely taken up by my duties here — even an emeritus has to be a busy man — and by urgent theological work. But I must thank you for the Christian patience with which you took my silence.

When you started your paper you could not anticipate what a tremendous work you were undertaking. Future generations only will be able to gauge the share you have had in the attempts to revive Lutheranism from its sleep. You will also find the recognition on the part of future Church historians who will have to write this sad chapter in the history of our Church.

You had the freedom to speak out what the official Church paper —this refers to all papers in all Churches of our time – had not the freedom to say even if their editors wanted to tell the truth, the whole truth and nothing but the truth. Also you had not the *charisma numquam deficients, veritatis* on which the theologian gloriae of official Church papers rests. But you have never been ashamed to correct and retract what turned out to be untenable and even wrong. We all owe you a great lot of gratitude, hoping that the volume of collections which you have published will be followed by continuations.

The matter which causes me to steal the time for this letter is our common concern for Lutheranism in Sweden. In spite of all Swedish theologians of glory there is a general conviction that not all is well with this old nominally Lutheran Church—though the word Lutheran does not belong to its official designations and that on the contrary, the Swedish Church is an outstanding example of what a Church can become in this age of secularism and vanishing Christian substance. The late Father Gabriel Hebert of the Anglican Society of Sacred Mission was one of the English friends of Sweden. He had learned Swedish so well that he could

143

act not only as interpreter, but also as translator, e.g. of Brihoth's book on the Eucharist. He has repeatedly told me how deeply disappointed he was with this Church which once had been to him the ideal of a Lutheran Church. In Sweden itself the dissatisfaction with the state of the Church was growing among pastors and laymen, bishops and students. Many laymen found their real spiritual home in the pietistic groups which play such a great role in the Scandinavian countries where Pietism seems to have played a role as a second Reformation. Suggestions have been made to bring about a separation of Church and State—in Sweden the clergymen are at the same time public servants of the country or at least to soften the yoke of the political powers which became more and more leftist and enjoyed obviously the status of the Church as a tool of the government. The Church was so accustomed to its slavery that as soon as the Swedish Parliament, the Rijksdag made a law which would open the ministry to women, the Kyrkomota at once followed suit and changed the ordination liturgy accordingly. The official legend is that they were compelled by the state. But the secular authority declared that they did not compel the Church but even if this had been the case, no Church government has the right to sacrifice a divine law to the wish of a government.

It was the case which caused the greatest unrest in the Church. Pastors gave up their ministry and became teachers of religion in the state schools which in Sweden teach officially "religion" in a neutral, non-committal way. Others thought of leaving the state Church and forming or joining a free Church. Why have so few thus far done that, our American brethren might ask. For them it presents no insuperable difficulty to change one's Church affiliation. It means to switch from one parish to another parish, from one synod to another synod. Also this can involve not only inner struggles, but also sacrifices. But it cannot be compared with leaving a state Church. "A person who leaves the state Church is practically ostracized by his fellow Swedes" we read in the *Wisconsin Lutheran Quarterly* 1974, p. 58. This applies more or less to all European established Churches.

Our American brethren would do well to remember more than they usually do the tremendous sacrifice made by their own fathers when they migrated for their faith's sake. In our century the sacrifices are still greater because our life has become more complicated. That "ostracism" is perhaps today easier to bear in our pluralistic societies. But to leave the established Church for the Free Church can mean for a theologian the death sentence for his wife. It may mean that he can no longer afford a decent education for his children. It is not the refusal to make sacrifices on the part of the pastor only. It means that he demands tremendous sacrifices from those for whom he is obliged to care.

I am grateful that "*Christian News*" has always recognized that. You have done what, as far as I know, no other Lutheran Church paper has done by giving your readers an insight into the situation of the faithful confessors in the Church of Sweden. You have especially helped Pastor Tom Hardt and his small flock. I want to thank you publicly for that and can only encourage you to continue this fraternal support. I know a little of his work, having worshipped in his congregation and having followed his theological work. I often wondered how he could combine a very conscientious ministry in a congregation and an extended pastoral care for lonely Lutherans throughout his country with his theological research which has earned him two academic degrees, the licentiate and the doctorate at Uppsala. His doctoral thesis is an astonishing book, based on careful historical research which has disclosed hitherto almost unknown sources.

Everyone who wants to pass a judgment on Dr. Hardt should first have studied this book, written in Swedish but with digests of the individual chapters in German. Professor Gyllenkrok, his adviser and examiner, was full of praise for this outstanding achievement. We all who know it regret that at a time when so much theological rubbish finds publishers this work could not be printed. The Lutheran Church has never been grateful to its faithful scholars. Apart from this theological work Dr. Hardt had spent a lot of time of the great problem of education the Christian children of Sweden who are compelled by the law of the state to attend a religious instruction in the state schools which is bound to destroy whatever the child may have learnt at home and from faithful pastors of the Christian faith. Together with Dr. Gunnar Karnell, Professor of law, and a faithful member of St. Martin's congregation, he has successfully fought the appeal to the highest authorities and institutions in the field of international law. It was this small free Church which has compelled the Swedish state to alter its legislation concerning the freedom of Christian parents to secure a Christian education to their children.

It was a great surprise to me to read in the *Christian News* a letter from Professor Becker, Mequon, in which he attacks Dr. Hardt. Since some time another small free Church has arisen in Sweden under the patronage of the Evangelical Lutheran Church Wisconsin. The "Quarterly" of Wisconsin reports on this in November 1, 1974, p. 60ff. I do not know whether really everything has been done to prevent this split which can only be detrimental to the cause of the Free Church in Sweden. I know a little of WELS and belong to those who have tried to heal the split in the Synodical Conference which was a tragedy for confessional Lutherans in the world. I admire the missionary zeal of this Church which is obviously convinced that it is their great task to save orthodox Lutheranism in the world. I had good friends among the older pastors of Wisconsin, men of deep Lutheran piety, genuine Lutherans also in that they saw the dangers which were threatening also their Church. There are many Lutherans in Wisconsin who are aware of those dangers.

When this Church recently celebrated the 125th anniversary the call to self-examination and repentance was not missing. One of their dangers is the great hurry with which they try to build up orthodox Lutheran Churches also in competition to Lutherans who are in their opinion not Orthodox.

If we pass such judgement on another Church we should always first examine our own orthodoxy. We should ask whether the men we send out to establish a truly Lutheran Church or congregation have the abilities to do that. How many or how few of the graduates of Mequon have the necessary training?

In my encounter with Lutherans of various denominations in America I found a remarkable difference between the older generation which had been educated in the old Lutheran faith and the younger generation who had no longer a real understanding of the old confession of our Church. One of them complained that he had tried in vain to find in the *Book of Concord* that doctrine of Holy Scripture which is regarded by American Fundamentalists and their disciples as the mark of true orthodoxy. I could answer only: You have looked into the wrong confession. What you are looking for is to be found in the Westminster Confession.

Also for the Lutheran confession as the Bible is the inerrant word of God, but you have to understand them first to find the doctrine of our Church. 26 years ago I visited for the first time their seminary, at that time still in "Thiensville". When I was shown over the library we came across the Weimar Edition of Luther's Works. Who reads these books, I asked. The reply was: We do not want to train professors, but pastors. I could only answer what I said a few days later at a seminary of the ULC: You will not get Lutheran pastors unless you have first Lutheran professors.

The result of such training is now before us. It is the new "This we believe", a handy substitute for the book of Concord for the layman and his pastor who has been trained in a few years in all subjects of theology. This new confession or substitute for a confession is now treated as the basis of the mission work throughout the world. We cannot review it here, nor would it be worthwhile. It should be forgotten as soon as possible, for it is no confession at all — who would be prepared to die for it. It is a summary of what is taught nowadays as Lutheran theology in your Church. It contains, of course, also good and correct statements. But there are gaps. How was it possible to leave out the article on confession and absolution? One must know the Lutheran congregations in America to know what little has been left of the office of the keys which in the Augsburg Confession is still treated as sacrament. And what about the Lord's Supper? Does this confession still contain what Luther teaches in the *Large Catechism* on this sacrament and its importance for the life of the Christian? Or is it only the doctrine of the Real Presence which has been preserved as a mark of orthodoxy? In any case one cannot build a Christian congregation on this basis. There are, of course, pastors who hold still the old faith as a living possession and preach it faithfully. But also they are confronted with the fact that the members of their congregations and especially their converts from other denominations have first to learn the Lutheran faith.

It seems to me that the disagreement between Dr. Hardt and Prof. Becker lies just in this field of the sacraments and the liturgy, for, as far as I know, there is no other disagreement between them apart from certain complaints on the mission methods of the Wisconsin Synod, and especially the way how Prof. Becker gathered the members of his new Church and the issue of the *Biblicum* on which we cannot speak here. It

146

would be up to Dean Dannell to give an opinion on that. Brother Hardt is a priest in the way of the Swedish Church with a profound sense for the liturgy of the Church and its sacramental life. WELS stands on the opposite pole of Lutheranism. One has to look into the chapel of St. Martin at Stockholm and into the interior of most of the Wisconsin Churches to see the difference. Why do our American brethren no longer have a crucifix on their altar, but instead that terrible naked cross of American Protestantism which means nothing at all, but is a substitute for what even Karl Barth unashamedly called "das Gotzenbild"? The Lutheran Churches in America look like Methodist temples until they become super-catholic. The Northwestern Lutheran presented recently a picture of a young pastor on one of their American mission fields, baptizing a baby on the kitchen sink.

The kitchen seemed otherwise well equipped. There should have been a more dignified vessel as substitute for the baptismal font. But no one seemed to be shocked by this display of neglect of the sacrament. Such things are, of course, adiaphora but they are indicative of a lack of understanding of the sacrament. It may be that but Dr. Hardt goes sometimes in one expression or another too far in the opposite direction at least for the tender ears of pietists and unconsciously Calvinized American Lutherans. I for one would not speak of "this bread which has created this world," but rather of the body of Him who created the world. But I cannot find that any of the other sentences goes beyond that which can be laid in the Lutheran Church. What he says about the polemical tongue which belongs to the marks of the Church should evoke a loud Hallelujah on the part of Professor Becker. What he says about the Lamb of God which lies on the altar is good Lutheran. Elevation with ringing of the bells was regarded by Luther as an adiaphoron as every student knows. If Prof. Becker wants to criticize Romanism, he has ample opportunities in America where this plague is spreading from the center of the forty self-canonized martyrs in St. Louis and Valparaiso through the Lutheran world. He has not to travel to Sweden to meet this danger which is threatening our Church. In fact his criticism is applicable to Martin Luther himself who in this respect differs from Melanchthon with his humanistic fear of artolatreia. Nowhere, as far as I can see, does Hardt go beyond the rule which Johann Gerhard has established so well in the 21st of his Loci. He was not Romanizing when he concludes this great chapter with the prayers and hymns of the Middle Ages. If he quotes at the end the great hymn "Adoro te devote, latens Deitas" by Thomas (my students were supposed to know it by heart as one of the greatest documents of genuine Christian Faith), he did no more than our brethren in Wisconsin when they sing in English some of these Eucharistic hymns among others our hymn "Schmucke dich o liebe Seele" in which the sequence of Corpus Christi still resounds.

Let us all be a little more tolerant and not dogmatize on questions which are neither directly nor indirectly decided in Holy Scripture. Otherwise we would have to excommunicate Martin Luther. It was on his way to Eisleben shortly before his death that he celebrated the sacrament

— probably for the last time — at Halle, waiting for the opportunity to cross the Saale which was flooded by ice as he described it so nicely to his wife. It happened to him that during the celebration in the icy cold Church some of the consecrated wine was spilt. The congregation has never forgotten the scene when the old man knelt down and licked the wine from the floor! Let us not be more Lutheran than Luther was and not wiser than God's Word is. What it teaches us is dogma of the Church, but it does not answer our every question.

Before burning Tom Hardt as heretic and destroying this beginning of a small Lutheran Free Church let us at least study his books. I must leave it to your wisdom, Brother Otten, to deal with this question in such a way that the cause of the free Lutheran Church not suffer irreparable damage.

Yours sincerely in Christ,
Hermann Sasse

Hardt's "Romanism"

I would like you to inform your readers that I have checked the quotations of the Reverend Professor Dr. Siegbert W. Becker in *Christian News* September 23rd, where he wishes to prove my "Romanism". I am quite sure that your readers have already received sufficient materials for the refutation of that accusation, but I still wish to inform them that Professor Becker has committed a mistake when quoting "Take now this bread, which has created the world". It does not refer to the baked communion bread (!) but to the Bread of Life, present as God's gift both in Gospel and Sacrament. The sermon is on John 6, divided into three parts: "I. The true heavenly bread is demanded only by the spiritually hungry. II. The true heavenly bread is the Son of God, the Savior of the world. III. The true heavenly bread gives us all that is good."

The quoted words are found in the second part, explaining the words "I am the Bread of Life". It is said that it is the contents of the Gospel and that it has a concrete form in the sacrament, "when the Word has assured us that the body of blood of Christ are the antidote of my sin". Thus it can be said "whenever the table of the Lord is laid": "Take now this bread which has created the world, which wipes out all unrighteousness..." As this saying seems to be the only one that could be misunderstood. I wish your readers to know the context of it. By the way there is no Roman Catholic theologian who ever taught that the communion bread created the world. The false doctrine of trans-substantiation removes the bread entirely from the sacrament according to Roman doctrine.

Tom G. A. Hardt
Pastor, teol. dr.
Scheelegatan 17, 3 tr.
S-112 28 Stockholm
Sweden

Professor Becker's "Lamentable Letter"

Prof. Siegbert Becker's lamentable letter attacking St. Martin's Lutheran Church in Stockholm and its pastor, the Rev. Tom G. A. Hardt (September 23, *CN*), necessitates a reply, however much one is disinclined to break into print. The use of a pejorative phrase such as. "Romanizing view of the Lord's Supper," cannot but grieve the judicious, since it tends to close minds without giving thoughtful consideration to the facts.

By now the readers of *CN* have been informed that this independent congregation and its pastor accept without reservation the inspired Scriptures and the *Book of Concord* as a true exposition of the doctrines of Scripture (See *CN*, October 14, p. 14. for specific details). One could add to the information given there that St. Martin's congregation and its pastor reject the so-called High Church notion, found in some parts of Lutheranism in Europe (including Sweden), that the Office of the Public Ministry is dependent in some vague way on the Apostolic Succession. St. Martin's demonstrated their confession by practicing what we might call "lay-ordination" or "congregational ordination" when Pastor Hardt was called and ordained a dozen years ago without the benefit of any kind of clergy.

In their congregational usages, St. Martin's tries to approximate the actual liturgical rites which Martin Luther used. Surely, this doesn't bring one a day's march closer to Rome especially when we know that the congregation really confesses with Luther and our Confessions that it is "not necessary that human traditions. That is, rites or ceremonies instituted by men should be everywhere alike."

Prof. Becker's letter is also puzzling because it seems to be out of tune with the new Lutheran Confessional Church in Sweden with which Prof. Becker is closely associated (See *CN*, October 14. p. 16). Dr. Hardt dedicated his major work on the Lord's Supper to Dr. Hermann Sasse and Dr. Sasse commends the book as presenting the orthodox Lutheran position on the doctrine of the Lord's Supper. The *Biblicum* of which Dr. Seth Erlandsson is the Executive Secretary and who is also one of the founders of the new Lutheran Confessional Church in Sweden, likes very much Dr. Sasse's book, *This Is My Body*. In fact, the *Biblicum* thinks so much of this work and sees such a need that this point of view be now publicized for the sake of true Lutheranism, that it apparently commissioned Pastor Per Jonsson (one of the co-founders of the new Confessional Lutheran Church in Sweden, with which Prof. Becker is closely associated) to translate into Swedish Chapter VII of Sasse's book. *The Sacrament of the Altar and the Lutheran Church Today*. If the readers of *Christian News* have friends who read Swedish, we would urge them to procure this neatly printed Swedish translation from *Biblicum*, which will undoubtedly lead them to a renewed study of the doctrine of the Lord's Supper. All confessional Lutherans not only need this doctrine for their personal comfort and assurance, but also because today this Lutheran doctrine is under severe attack even among some Lutherans.

149

This can be seen from the Presbyterian-Lutheran rapproachement in this country revealed in the Marburg Revisited essays, and in Europe by the Luenberg Theses, newly agreed to by many Lutherans and the Reformed. Indeed, we must all of us examine ourselves to see whether or not we have inadvertently stumbled a couple of furlongs toward Geneva.

Sincerely,

(Prof.) B. W. Teigen

Mankato, Minnesota

Study Questions

1. Sasse wrote that when Otten started *Christian News*, he could not anticipate ____.
2. Otten had the freedom to ____, according to Sasse.
3. The volume of collections *Christian News* had published should be ____.
4. The Swedish Church is an outstanding example of ____.
5. To leave the established Church for the Free Church can mean for the theologian ____.
6. What had *Christian News* done, according to Sasse, that no other Church paper had done? ____
7. What had Tom Hardt done in Sweden? ____.
8. Sasse tried to heal the split in the ____.
9. Sasse said that you will not get Lutheran pastors until you first have ____.
10. Should a Lutheran Church have a crucifix? ____
11. Let us not dogmatize on questions which ____.

§

CONGRATULATIONS ON 80ᵀᴴ BIRTHDAY

Congratulations to Dr. Hermann Sasse, 6 Wellington Square, North Adelaide, South Australia. Dr. Sasse is one of the leading orthodox Lutheran theologians of this century. He celebrates his 80th birthday on July 17.

Christian News, July 7, 1975

§

PRAYING FOR JUSTICE FOR TRINITY LUTHERAN CHURCH, NEW HAVEN AND OTTEN

63 Clifton Street
Prospect, S.A.
Australia
22-7-67

Dear Friend,

Thank you for your kind wishes. This was only congratulations I have so far received from America.

I hope and pray that justice may be done for your congregation not only but also for you personally – in the interest of Missouri. Your apology was completely sufficient. You could not do more at the time.

With kind regards,
Yours in Christ,
H. Sasse

§

THE GREAT ECUMENICAL CREED
Dr. H. Sasse.
Christian News, December 29, 1975

On June 19, 1975, a remarkable service was held in the *Marktkirche,* the oldest and largest of the Churches of Hanover. Clergymen of various Churches, Eastern Orthodox (Greeks, Russians, Ukrainians, Serbians). Roman Catholics and Old Catholics, Lutherans and Anglicans, Presbyterians, Methodists, and representatives of minor Protestant groups entered the crowded Church in solemn procession. The Roman Catholic Bishop of Regensburg, Dr. Rudolf Graber, well known as one of the most conservative leaders of the Catholic Church in Germany, preached the occasional sermon from the pulpit from which otherwise the message of the Lutheran Reformation is proclaimed.

Commemorating the Nicene Creed

It was a memorial service to commemorate the 1,650[th] anniversary of the day when the First Ecumenical Synod accepted the **Nicene Creed**, the most important creed of Christendom which is common to all Christian Churches with the exception of some modern communities which have abolished all creeds. Our **Apostles' Creed**, the old baptismal creed of the Western Church, as also the Athanasian Creed, are not known to

151

the Churches of the East. As we confess the **Nicene Creed** at every celebration of the Sacrament of the Altar, so it has been chanted in every Mass of the Churches of the Catholic traditions throughout the world for many centuries.

The Ancient Synods of the Church

A synod - we should keep this in mind - is not a parliament but a solemn assembly of the Church dominated by the worship which is an essential part of such an assembly. In the ancient Church it was an assembly of bishops who represented their local Churches whose chief pastors they were. Ministers of lower rank, as for example deacons and laymen, could be invited as guests but without voting rights. Such "pastors' conferences" as we would call the ancient synods, were from the time of the second century regularly held on a provincial level to discuss and decide ecclesiastical and theological matters, often very important ones as, for example, the question as to which writings had to be regarded as the canonical books of the New Testament.

An Ecumenical Synod

The synod of 325, however was to be an ecumenical synod. The word *oikoumene* (Luke 2.1) denoted at that time the world as far as it belonged to the vast Roman Empire. To organize and to finance such an assembly was beyond the capacity of the Church, especially in an era of persecution. Who else could summon and arrange such a meeting? This was done by Constantine, one of the greatest rulers of all time. After years of civil war he had become the sole ruler of the empire and was faced with the task of reorganizing it. Constantine was not a Christian, but a friend of the Church. He had been enrolled as a catechumen, but was baptized only on his deathbed in 337. Otherwise a ruthless ruler, he had made the great decision to terminate the persecutions of the Christians which had been going on for centuries on a more or less local and temporal scale and had found its climax after the year 300 in the thoroughly organized attempt to eradicate the Church once and for all.

Turning-Point in History

It was a turning-point of world history when Constantine decided to recognize Christianity and to use its religious and moral strength in building the new state. At the time of his conquest of the western provinces he had begun to favour the Church. To his great disappointment he discovered that the Church was divided. Two Churches were competing in the African provinces divided over issues of Church discipline which had arisen in the persecution. His attempt to heal the split failed. In the following generations neither the wisdom and power of the rulers nor the endeavours of great theologians such as Augustine were able to restore the lost unity. It was a divided Church which later was extinguished in the onslaught of Islam: Constantine had a similar experience in the East after his final victory. There, also, Christendom was divided. Even in the city of Byzantium which was to be rebuilt as the

"New Rome" and was then called Constantinople there were two Churches divided on matters of Church discipline. This split was never healed.

Doctrine at the Seat of Controversy

But a far more serious problem turned up soon, a schism in which the most important doctrine, the very heart of the Church was at stake. It began with a controversy at Alexandria, the second largest city of the empire. Alexander, bishop or "pope" as he was called, and as his successor is still called today, had, with the approval of the synod of Alexandria, excommunicated Arius, one of his presbyters, the parish priest of one of the big city Churches. He was a popular preacher, a gifted poet and a learned man, though not a great theologian. In Antioch, at one of the few great theological schools, he had been trained in what was regarded as the most modern theology. Its aim was to make Christianity acceptable to the pagan academics of that time. One must keep in mind that the Christian faith was no longer the faith of the lower classes. In the third century it had penetrated into highly educated circles and had won some outstanding academics who now tried to convert the adherents of the philosophy of that age.

A Strange Christology

Applying this philosophy to the Christian faith, Arius and some of his fellow students, even among the bishops of the East, had developed a strange Christology. They taught that Christ, the Word of John 1:1 was "divine", and should be called Son of God, but only in a figurative sense. He was the first and highest creature through whom God had created the world. This spiritual creature had assumed in Jesus a human body, but not a human soul. Alexander realized that this was the end of the Christian faith. Christianity would lapse into paganism if such doctrine was tolerated, for no creature can be our Saviour. Christ would become a mythological being, neither God nor man, and the entire liturgy of the Church in which He is worshipped would be one great lie. Expelled from Alexandria, Arius went to the East, seeking and finding allies among the bishops who had been trained at Antioch. His doctrine was even approved by a synod at Antioch. So the controversy began to develop into a real schism which threatened to divide the Church even more seriously than the controversies on matters of Church discipline. This was clearly seen not only by Alexander. Even the emperor began to realize that the existence of the Christian Church and with it the well-being of the empire was at stake.

Constantine Calls a Great Synod

Constantine decided to do all in his power to settle the dispute at a "Great Synod". He summoned the bishops of all provinces of the empire and even from some mission fields beyond the borders to a synod to be held at Nicaea, a city in northern Asia Minor, south of his residence at Nicomedia. He owned a palace there which could accommodate a large

153

assembly. More than 300 attended! He treated them as his beloved and honoured guests. Many still bore the marks of persecution. He himself played the role of a humble catechumen and interfered only occasionally by giving advice. Minor matters of practical importance such as the date of the Easter festival and questions of Church constitution were settled without difficulty.

The Great Doctrinal Issue

The main concern was the great doctrinal issue. It soon became evident that what was required was a unanimously accepted creedal statement on the person of Christ. Such a statement was accepted with only a few opposing votes on June 19, 325. It is the first form of the **Nicene Creed**. Arius had many sympathizers among the bishops, but it soon became clear that what the vast majority wanted and the Church needed was an unambiguous confession of the divinity of the Saviour. The Church, of course, had creeds especially for us at Baptism. They differed locally, though the great truths of the faith were confessed in each of them. Traces of such early creeds are still extant in our liturgy, for example in the Great Gloria which we sing in the Sunday service or in the *Te Deum* which originally was used at the Eucharist, while our *Apostles' Creed*, the baptismal creed of the Western Church, was unknown in the East. One such creed was reaffirmed and augmented mainly by the addition of a word which Constantine himself favoured and which then became the watchword of Christian orthodoxy, the famous *homoousion*.

Watchword of Christian Orthodoxy

"We believe in one God, the Father Almighty, Maker of all things .... And in one Lord Jesus Christ (compare I Corinthians 8:4), the Son of God, begotten of the Father, only-begotten, that is, of the substance (essence) of the Father, God of God, Light of Light (Hebrews 1:3), very God of very God, begotten, not made, of one substance (*homoousion)* with the Father, through whom all things were made; who for us men and for our salvation came down and was made flesh, and became man . . . . And in the Holy Spirit."

It is clear what the new term, *homoousion,* means. It expresses the full divinity of Christ who is eternal God as is the Father. Alexander could be satisfied, especially since, at the end of the creed the views held by Arius and his friends were solemnly anathematized.

Controversy Continues

At first it seemed that the split in the Church had been avoided. The condemnation of Arius was expressly upheld and the few bishops who still supported him were compelled to give up their sees. However, it soon became evident that the decision could not be regarded as final. Many of the bishops had not been able to understand the subtle distinctions and the scholarly words used. They were simple country parsons who could preach to their flocks, administer the Sacraments in the small congregation or diocese, and celebrate the liturgy. Deeper theological studies lay

154

outside their ministry, so they left it to their "more learned" brethren to make the decisions — which is always a dangerous thing.

St. Paul had to fight the pride of people who rightly or wrongly regarded themselves as great theologians. "**Knowledge puffs up**", he said, and pointed out that God has revealed His mysteries not to the great scholars of the world, but to the **"foolish"**. All really great theologians have known that. Luther said that one must first become a good fool in Christ before one can philosophize without danger. Thus the controversies went on after Nicaea. The proud friends of Arius had accepted the *homoousion* because His Majesty wanted that. But they were already well versed in the art of interpreting any word in their sense.

Subsequent Generations Face the Issue

A real theological problem arose among the bishops who did not deny the full divinity of Christ, but found a certain danger in the doctrine of Alexander and his theological adviser, the learned deacon Athanasius, who had accompanied his bishop to Nicaea and in 328 became his successor. Could not *homoousion* be understood in such a way that the distinction between the person of the Father and the person of the Son would vanish? This would contradict the passages of the Gospels in which Father and Son are clearly distinguished. How can Gethsemane and the cry on the cross be taken seriously if Father and Son are of one substance? This was to become the issue of the theology of the subsequent generations.

Political Interests and the Church

Meanwhile, the fact that it had been the wish of the emperor which had introduced the *homoousion,* began to create the troubles under which the Church had to suffer for several generations. The political interests of the empire demanded the unity of the Church. If this unity could not be reached by Nicaea and its creed, other methods might be more successful. When Constantine realized that the adherents of Arius had been stronger than he had believed, he sought a reconciliation with them. He went so far that he even demanded and achieved reinstatement of Arius in his office. This was refused by Athanasius who was now the Patriarch of Alexandria. He now became the leader of orthodoxy, who would not yield to the wishes of Constantine and the rulers who followed him. All attempts to settle the matter by political means or by Church/political compromises failed. It is no exaggeration to state that the unshakable firmness of this man saved the Church in the terrific fights of the 4th century. When he fell into disgrace at the imperial court he went into exile and was replaced by a loyal patriotic creature of the emperors. He spent years in exile, either in the deserts around Egypt in Rome or in Germany (Trier). He left his flock to the care of the great shepherd in heaven and trusted in Him who would lead the Church into all truth.

The Struggle of the Church

It would be beyond the scope of this article to describe the details of the struggles in which the Church sometimes seemed to perish. It was only when Julian, who had lapsed into paganism and wanted the Church to perish by its own inner struggles had become the ruler of the empire that the Church regained its freedom. A free synod not influenced by political powers at Alexandria in 362 was the turning-point. Again the greatness of Athanasius became evident. This staunch defender of the *homoousion* this unshakable character was able to come to an agreement with those who in serious and thorough theological work had found another solution to the great problem of Nicaea.

A New School of Thought

A new school of thought had developed in Cappadocia in eastern Asia Minor represented by great churchmen and theologians such as Basil the Great and Gregory of Nyssa. They had come to the conclusion that one had to teach the full divinity of Christ in the sense that the Son is **equal** with the Father. When the question arose whether the *homoousion* of 325 could be also understood in this way, Athanasius was ready to give in. The debate was not, as one sometimes reads and as the pagan critics put it, about the addition of an "i" (*homoousion* or *homoiousion*) but about the recognition of a twofold understanding of the divinity of the Son. One can say with Athanasius **of one substance with the Father or of equal substance with the Father** (*Homoios* in these debates never means *similar* but always *equal*). In this sense the decision of Nicaea was reaffirmed. The Arians, of course, remained excluded. But the full divinity of Christ was recognized. *Homoousion* could now be understood as expressing not the oneness, but the equality of Father and Son.

Two Forms of the Creed

At Alexandria the question had arisen whether the *homoousion* had to be extended also to the Holy Spirit. This was recognized. Thus the way was paved for another Great Synod at Constantinople in 381, which accepted the **Nicene Creed** in a new form. It is the text which we confess in all Christian liturgies. The first creed which gave expression to the Christian doctrine of the blessed Trinity. Scholars used to call this second form the "Constantinopolitanum." But the Church has always called it the **Nicene Creed** which thus exists in two forms, that of 325 and that of 381, both being regarded as of equal meaning and importance.

Fifty Years after Stockholm

Why do Christians in Germany, France, and other countries commemorate Nicaea and its creed in 1975? A 1,650[th] anniversary is not usually the occasion for a jubilee. But it is exactly fifty years ago that one of the great ecumenical world conferences was held at Stockholm — the **Nicaea of Ethics** as the then Archbishop Soderblom of Upsala, called it. His idea was that the unity of Christendom can never be reached by discussion of dogma. "Doctrine divides, service unites" was one of the slogans of that time. Let us abstain from doctrinal discussions and controversies and rather unite in common service. What we all can do is to follow Christ in common service to mankind in carrying out the great commandment of love which our Saviour has left to all His disciples. "Follow Me!" in unselfish care for the poor people in fighting hatred and the spirit of war, in improving the moral climate of the world. Nothing must be said against this program of **Life and Work**.

Nicaea of Ethics - Nicaea of Doctrine

However, in the five decades which have elapsed, it has become clear that the **Nicaea of Ethics** is not possible without the **Nicaea of Doctrine**. Certainly, we all must follow Christ. But why just Him? Innumerable millions in Asia hear the voice of other great leaders and follow Buddha as their teacher of the holy eightfold path of salvation from the sufferings of this world. Follow me! was his admonition. Is there salvation? Yes, but you must do it yourself. You must follow me and keep my commandments. "Strive unremittingly" were the last words he addressed to his weeping disciples.

"My Lord and My God!"

"Let not your heart be troubled", said Jesus when He took leave of his disciples. **"Believe in God, believe also in Me .... I am the way, and the truth, and the life."** He had not only admonished them to follow Him, but had also asked them: **"Who do you say that I am?"** He demanded the confession of faith: **"Whosoever therefore shall confess Me before men, him will I confess also before My Father which is in heaven"** (A.V.). The answer of His disciples, their confession and the confession of all His disciples was: **"You are the Christ, the Son of the living God"**. Even the doubting Thomas had to confess: **"My Lord and My God!"** This is the confession of Nicaea.

The Crisis of the Ecumenical Movement

That Christians of many denominations today repeat the old confession can readily be understood. Our age is an age of uncertainty and doubt. The doctrinal substance of the Christian faith is rapidly vanishing in all Churches. This is the underlying reason for what is called "the crisis of the Ecumenical Movement". Every revival of the faith began with the rediscovery and reaffirmation of the old creed. Not only our Augsburg Confession, but also the confession of the Reformed Churches begin with the reaffirmation of the great decision of Nicaea. As all the Churches of the 16th century, even Rome, had to reject the "new Arians", so today we have to fight the most dangerous form of Arianism which has ever appeared in Christendom. No great heresy ever dies completely. It comes back again and again, dressed in the latest philosophical fashion of the time. So we also have to fight the great enemy of the Christian faith. Are we prepared for that?

"God in Three Persons, Blessed Trinity"

"In the name of the Father and of the Son and of the Holy Spirit." Thus our Christian life began at our Baptism when for the first

157

time we confessed the faith through the mouth of our parents and god-parents.

"In the name of the Father and of the Son and of the Holy Spirit." Thus every Sunday service begins as it calls us back to our Baptism.

"In the name of the Father and of the Son and of the Holy Spirit." Thus will our funeral service begin as we leave this world to see, by the grace of God, the glory of Him who is God in three Persons, blessed Trinity.

(Originally photographically reproduced from *The Lutheran*, November 3, 1975)

Study Questions
1. What took place on June 19, 1975 in the Marketkirche? ____
2. What is the most important creed of Christendom? ____
3. Who arranged the Ecumenical Synod of 325? ____
4. What was a turning point of world history? ____
5. The city of Byzantium which was rebuilt was then called ____.
6. Who excommunicated Arius? ____
7. Arius taught that ____.
8. The doctrine of Arius was approved by ____.
9. What does homoousion mean? ____
10. What is always a dangerous thing? ____
11. God has revealed his mysteries to ____.
12. Who was Athanasius? ____
13. What saved the Church in the 4th century? ____
14. Athanasius spent years in ____.
15. The Nicaea of Ethics is not possible without the Nicaea of ____.
16. Buddha taught that ____.
17. Thomas confessed ____.
18. Our age is an age of ____.
19. What is the great enemy of the Christian faith?____
20. Our Christian life began at ____.
21. Our funeral service as we leave this world begins ____.

§

HERMANN SASSE: SACRA SCRIPTURA
Evangelium, April 1984

Hermann Sasse, the Lutheran theologian and Church historian who died in 1976 at Adelaide, South Australia, was unable to publish these

"Studies on the Doctrine of Holy Scripture," on which he had worked for a number of years. A volume he had planned on the authority of the Bible in the Church, particularly in the Lutheran Church, remained incomplete. Pastor Friedrich Wilhelm Hopf, D.D., published some of Sasse's studies and suggestions on Holy Scripture from materials Sasse left behind. Individual articles by Sasse on the doctrine of Scripture, already known from years past, have now formed Part II of the book, "Sacra Scriptura". The publisher's preface of May 18, 1981, in which Sasse himself is given a broad chance to speak, clarifies both the goal and the tendency of the entire work: A doctrine of Scripture should be formulated which, as much as possible, steers clear of the old dogma of inspiration and which can create a new consensus on the nature and authority of Holy Scripture among Churches of the Augsburg Confession.

In discussing Sasse's work, which contains numerous valuable insights into the whole area of historical development, we hope to concentrate on his primary theme, the doctrine of Holy Scripture, and to evaluate it on the basis of Luthernism's Biblical principle, according to which the Bible is God's own "unerring Word". If the Bible and its message are recognized as the sole source of Christian faith and as the highest norm for Church teaching, then this would presuppose that the Bible was given word for word by God's Spirit to the holy writers (Moses and the prophets, the evangelists and apostles). Without acceptance of the full inspiration of the Bible by the Holy Spirit (plenary or verbal inspiration), the Bible then fails to serve as the infallible norm of Christian doctrine and is itself in need of some other higher, final norm. Sasse sees the dogma of verbal inspiration as mere "pious opinion" or a "shrewd theory", certainly not as a binding plank of faith and confession. He claims it to be of Jewish rabbinical or even heathen origin and therefore inferior and damaging (see p. 215). Such a historical tracing of the doctrine of verbal inspiration from Judaism and the heathen world is unacceptable, since it simply smooths over the most divergent views of inspiration. Sasse especially fails to see that the verbal inspiration of Holy Scripture by the Holy Spirit rests on the Bible's own testimony concerning itself and therefore needed no assistance from a heathen religious environment. For this and yet another reason the teaching of verbal inspiration is for each orthodox Christian and confessional Lutheran an absolutely binding matter of Biblical and confessional teaching. After all, Jesus Christ Himself and His apostles never saw their Bible (the Old Testament) as anything but the inspired, inerrant Word of God to people- how could a Christian possibly take any other position on the Bible?

Sasse, however, emphasizes again and again that the doctrine of plenary inspiration is un-Biblical, un-Christian and un-Lutheran. One can only wonder why Sasse would not, in holding this view, be consistent enough to push for the exclusion of all who accept verbal inspiration from the Lutheran Church. He further claims that a christological heresy corresponds to the doctrine of verbal inspiration, namely, that of monophysitism: Here the "divinity" of the Scriptures is overemphasized, while its "humanity", of which the fallibility of the human writers in the act of writing is part and parcel, is largely denied. Therefore, Sasse accepts only the religious and theological statements of the Bible as inspired, while the scientific, historical and geographical statements in it could easily include errors and misjudgments (pp. 232-3). For Sasse, the Bible becomes a book in which truth and error saturate one another.

Two things are particularly disturbing in Sasse's work on the doctrine of Holy Scripture. First is the distorted picture which he paints of verbal inspiration, which one would scarcely expect from a Church historian of his calibre. The second is the more or less openly admitted lack of faith in numerous statements of the Bible. This has the result of negating the Biblical Lutheran Scripture principle.

(Translation: R. Bugbee)

§

THEOLOGICAL OBSERVER
A TALE OF TWO BOOKS

Concordia Theological Quarterly, July-October 1986

A recent publication of Concordia Publishing House is Hermann Sasse's *We Confess Jesus Christ* (St. Louis, 1984). A very different volume is by John H. S. Kent, *The End of the Line?* a product of Fortress Press (Philadelphia, 1982). Few may realize it now, but in fact these two books are nearly perfect paradigms of what the publishers' respective Churches really stand for. The sharply contrasting books, both as it happens by historical theologians, represent, of course, not the average or typical theologies of their Churches, but the latters' basic directions and ultimate destinations, given their present courses. "Missouri's" average theology is hardly as good as Sasse's, nor can that of the New Lutheran Church possibly be as bad as Kent's. Rather, the two books represent the two polarities or centers of gravity round which North American Lutheranism is resettling at present. If the Missouri Synod is serious about reclaiming its confessional heritage, it will continue to pursue the path so conscientiously charted by Sasse. And if the merging synods insist on letting historical criticism dominate their seminaries, Kent's "end of the line" will be the logically foreseeable outcome.

The five Sasse pieces are translations by Professor Dr. Norman Nagel of Concordia Seminary, St. Louis — of material selected from the collection of essays by Sasse which had appeared in two German volumes under the title *In Statu Confessionis* (1966 and 1976). The English paperback is the first of three in the *We Confess* series, of which the second, dealing with the sacraments, has already appeared. A third volume, on

Church and ministry, should be out by the time this article appears in print.

The center-piece of this first Sasse volume, and possibly of all three, is the essay on Luther's theology of the cross. Here Sasse, beginning with a panoramic survey of the cross in Church history, plumbs the depths of what it means to be Lutheran. "The cross demands faith *contrary to what our eyes see"* (p. 50). This is not a summons to intellectual irresponsibility. Faith must not escape from objective reality into subjectivity. On the contrary, faith defies and unmasks our own illusions. Heaven cannot be stormed by feats of philosophy or religion. It is freely given to a faith which, taking God at His Word, believes His power where it sees weakness, knows His love when it experiences anguish, and finds glory in the cross under the mask of shame. God hides Himself not in high abstractions, but in lowly, visible things like baptismal water, absolving words uttered by sinful lips, and consecrated bread and wine-and this all the better to reveal Himself there. This is not a theory or a game: "A yes to the cross of Christ is also a yes to my cross" (p. 52). This article is preceded by a study on "Jesus Christ is Lord" and is followed by an essay commemorating the fifteenth centenary of the Council of Chalcedon and by two essays on the Church as a confessing entity and as itself also an article of faith to be confessed. A brief biography of Hermann Sasse concludes the volume.

As it happens, Kent's book also consists of five main parts. The first two chapters trace the retreat of Christian dogma before rationalism and historicism of the eighteenth and nineteenth centuries respectively. Chapter Three discusses the fate of the doctrine of the Church from John Wesley's time to the present. The next chapter treats of the "social theology" of that same period, and the last chapter deals with the twentieth century. Where Sasse was able to confess, because he was conscious of standing on the firm rock of God's Word, Kent, a professor of theology in the University of Bristol, can only debunk, retreat, question, criticize, and deny. For him there is no truth, no dogma, no Word of God at all in the old, traditional sense " . . . the study of modern historical theology which I have attempted here suggests that if Christianity is nearing the end of its main, public line, this is because it has exhausted ways of keeping its images alive" (p. ix). Although Kent punctuates his title, *End of the Line,* with a question mark, an exclamation point would have been more fitting. To show that things are not as hopeless as they seem on his account to be, Kent offers this piece of bravado (p. x):

> For the critical theologian, for the Christian humanist, the assertion of belief, of belief in God, in human creativity, in the Gospels as one sign of that human capacity to make peace instead of a desert, is now more than ever a matter of faith: faith in the underlying rationality of the universe ... faith in the quality of life commended in what seems to have been the teaching of Jesus ... faith in reason, however unfashionable reason may have become in the sick romanticism of today.

To paraphrase Antony Flex, how does a Christianity so defined differ from no Christianity at all? It is not surprising to find Kent criticizing J.A.T. ("Honest To God") Robinson's "crude reinterpretations" for still having kept too much of the old mythology. Of Robinson's redefinition of Christ's divinity in evolutionary terms, without any personal pre-existence ("God raised Jesus up through the normal process of heredity and environment and made him his decisive word to men"), Kent says: "neither biology nor the doctrine of the divinity of Christ had suffered much so far" (p. III)!

Kent is quite right, no doubt, in seeing the collapse of the Church's accustomed social support, in an increasingly secularized Europe, as the fundamental reason for the urgent preoccupation with the question of what it is that legitimates the Church's existence and authority. Rome's answer was to anchor the whole system in papal infallibility at Vatican 1: The Anglican Oxford Movement turned to the historic episcopate for support. In this context Kent's judgment makes very good sense: "the modern ecumenical movement partly originated in the anxiety of Church leaders to replace the vanished social order in which the Churches had played an accepted part with a united ecclesiastical institution capable of holding its own as an independent structure with the increasingly independent and secular state" (p. 63).

Is it really true, however, that those who, in the various Churches, stood for a "fixed dogmatic orthodoxy of the past" saw their main problem as one of "how to restore the Church's past ascendancy in western society" (p. 1)? Kent's rather too easy identification of the cause of "orthodoxy" with that of the ecumenical movement is an optical illusion due to Kent's extremely liberal perspective. After all, when observed from great astronomical distances, two stars which are actually very far apart, may seem to be quite close. There is also a Reformed Anglo-Saxon bias which makes it seem self-evident that the Church is essentially a "visible" institution.

Here Sasse and Kent take antipodal positions. Walking by faith, not by sight, Sasse points to the pure Gospel and sacraments, that is, to the pure marks of the Church, as the sole guarantors of the Church's presence. Kent, together with the ecumenical movement he criticizes for being insufficiently liberal, treats the Church as a part of this world, with reformist social and political duties. The Church is thus an article of sight. Perhaps Kent's skepticism needs also to be seen, however, as an understandable reaction to an impossible "ecclesiology of glory." Focusing narrowly on Anglican and Roman pronouncements, Kent takes "orthodox theologians" to be advocating a belief in "the indefectibility of the [visible] Church, which Christ will never desert and which the Holy Spirit will lead into all truth" (p. 80). Sasse's sober and sobering theology of the cross can help to purge our proclamation of "human illusions" such as all delusions of grandeur about external historical institutions and, thus, to inoculate our theology against the grim fate of being swept away in the "general disillusionment" (Sasse, pp. 36, 37) of our time.

Since my esteemed colleague, Dr. Eugene Klug, has raised the issue of Dr. Sasse's orthodoxy in respect of biblical inerrancy *(Concordia Journal,* July 1985), a comment or two may be apropos. I fully share Dr. Klug's dismay at some of the statements in Sasse's posthumous *Sacra Scriptura* (Erlangen, 1981). It is a great pity that an unfinished manuscript by Sasse was printed after his death, together with some previously published material. The book ignores the development over the years of Sasse's position on inerrancy and thus leaves an unfair overall impression. For instance, when President F. Schiotz of the American Lutheran Church had cited Sasse against inerrancy, Sasse complained that "selected passages" from his articles "taken out of their context... might suggest that [he rejected] the inerrancy of the Scriptures. The contrary is true." Sasse tried repeatedly to stop the reprinting and sale by the St. Louis seminary bookstore of an English translation of his "Letter to Lutheran Pastors on Holy Scripture" of 1950. In deep humility Sasse wrote to *Lutheran News* (7 August 1967), enclosing a copy of a letter to the bookstore manager, in which Sasse said that "the essay, written during our Australian discussions of the doctrine of Holy Scripture, contained formulations which [he] could not maintain," and that he had "corrected what had to be corrected." In his essay of 1950 Sasse had, in effect, limited biblical infallibility to "articles of faith." In the July 1960 number of *The Reformed Theological Review,* however, Sasse clearly confessed: "one thing Christian theology can never admit, namely, the presence of 'errors' in the sense of false statements in Holy Scripture."

Soon after he became president of the Missouri Synod, Dr. J.A.O. Preus wrote to Sasse for advice on the inerrancy question. Sasse replied under date of 24 February 1970, urging the Missouri Synod to do serious theological work on this topic, since hardly any help was to be found elsewhere. Barth, wrote Sasse, had tried, but ended in *Schwaermertum,* and Elert's doctrine of Holy Scripture, despite some "excellent paragraphs", was "terribly weak." Sasse compared inerrancy to the ancient Church's *homoousios* and urged: "The term *inerrantia* cannot and should not be given up-the meaning is quite clear, the absence of real error in the Bible."

Nevertheless, it is true that a certain ambiguity haunted Sasse's writings on this subject. If a grateful pupil be permitted to conjecture about a venerable and learned master's oversight, I would say that Sasse never succeeded in applying his deeply incarnational, Chalcedonian theology of the cross to Holy Scripture with the same consistency with which he had applied it to the sacraments and to the Church . The theology of the cross demands that the mysteries of God acting under earthly "masks" —including, therefore, Holy Scripture — be taken not at their apparent face value, in terms of human phenomena, but at their real face value, as given by God in His Word. Theology, also bibliology, must be done "from above," that is, in reliance on God's authority alone, without substantive admixtures "from below," that is, from the wisdom and philosophy of this world.

The sole point of these digressions is to commend the present *We Con-*

fess series. It would be tragic if we refused to learn from Sasse on Church, sacrament, ministry, and confession, simply because there were inadequacies in his writings on Scripture. Where, after all, is the theologian who has no "blind spots"? Dr. Norman Nagel has rendered the Church an enormous service with his masterful English renditions of Sasse's essays, which rank already as classic contributions to the genuinely Confessional Lutheran theology of the twentieth century.

With John Kent's *The End of the Line?* one shudders on the brink of the bottomless abyss. The critical religious ideology-one can no longer call it theology-presented there with all due academic elegance, betokens a background of super-human powers, hissing, as it were, through Pontius Pilate: "What is truth?" Sasse, whose illusions perished at the front in World War I, exorcises the hissing, in *We Confess Jesus Christ.*

K. Marquart

Study Questions
1. If the Missouri Synod is serious about reclaiming its confessional heritage, according to Kurt Marquart, it will continue to pursue the path ____.
2. For John H. D. Kent there is no ____.
3. Sasse points to the ____ as the pure marks of the Church.
4. Marquart shared Klug's dismay at some statements in Sasse's posthumous ____.
5. The book ignores the development over the years of Sasse's position on ____.
6. Sasse wrote that "one thing Christian theology can never admit, namely, the presence of ___ is the sense of false statements in Holy Scripture."
7. A certain ___ haunted Sasse's writings on the inerrancy of the Bible.
8. Where is the theologian who has no ____.
9. With John Kent's the End of the Line? one shudders at ____.

§

HERMANN SASSE AND THE LCMS
INERRANCY OF HOLY SCRIPTURE

Christian News, September 29, 1986

We wish we could say that all the liberals within the Lutheran Church-Missouri Synod, who rejected the inerrancy of the Bible, left the LCMS in 1974 with the formation of Seminex and then the Association

164

of Evangelical Lutheran Churches. Several hundred pastors and professors did leave, but many still remain. A recent *Christian News* survey showed that there are still plenty of liberals on the LCMS clergy roster who deny the inerrancy of the Bible and accept some of the destructive theories of historical criticism. These liberals were strongly opposed to Dr. Robert Sauer and wanted a president who would allow them to remain on the LCMS clergy roster.

Some Lutheran liberals have long used writings of Dr. Hermann Sasse to defend their denial of the inerrancy of the Bible. While *CN* often promoted the work of Dr. Sasse, we regretted that some of his writings on the inerrancy of the Bible were not consistent and even attacked scriptural inerrancy.

Dr. Sasse told us at the LCMS's convention in San Francisco in 1959 how thrilled he was that the LCMS reaffirmed the binding nature of the *Brief Statement,* which clearly confesses the inerrancy of the Bible in all matters. He said that Church history was made when a large Lutheran body took such a confessional stand with the adoption of the famous San Francisco Resolution No. 9 which was so bitterly opposed by the LCMS liberals and then later declared unconstitutional. Some liberals even blamed a group of young students and pastors from Concordia Seminary, St. Louis, for creating an atmosphere which opened the door for such a resolution. The students told various LCMS leaders that the doctrine of the inerrancy of the Bible was being denied by liberal professors at the St. Louis seminary. Sasse made it clear to us that he definitely opposed the position of these St. Louis liberals. Unfortunately, some of Dr. Sasse's writings did give aid and comfort to the liberals who now again still like to use his writing to defend their denial of the inerrancy of the Bible.

Dr. Eugene Klug of Concordia Seminary, Fort Wayne, discusses Sasse's position on inerrancy in "Holy Scripture: The Inerrancy Question and Hermann Sasse" in the July, 1985 *Concordia Journal* of Concordia Seminary, St. Louis.

Klug, who rightly recognizes that Sasse was a great defender of the Christian faith, writes:

"To understand the Bible correctly, Sasse holds that the early chapters of Genesis must be understood not only as prehistory, but as 'history of a different sort than we find in the books of Kings and Chronicles.' Sasse contends, therefore, that Luther construes these opening chapters of Genesis as factual historical reporting by Moses. According to Sasse, Luther fails to see that he is more dependent upon an ancient pre-historical tradition than upon God's Word as such (pp. 91-111). Sasse comes very close to supporting the views — if in fact he does not do so- of the school of thought which finds these accounts, including also that of Jonah and other stories like it, to be mythological reporting for the sake of the Heilsgeschichte, the saving message, or salvation history of God toward sinful mankind.

"Actually this is not a new position which Sasse adopted only in his later years. Some of the chapters in this volume were presented earlier, for example, 'Luther and the Word of God.' In Sasse's considered opinion the defense of Scripture's inerrancy was not only futile but also an evident surrender to Fundamentalism. He minced no words in faulting the LCMS for defending Scripture's inerrancy, openly criticizing theologians like Franz Pieper, Theodore Engelder, Paul E. Kretzmann, and William Arndt, for leading Missouri down the primrose path to an impossible, absurd, and naive position on Scripture. Instead of trying to reconcile Scripture's so-called 'problems,' or discrepancies, one should simply live with them as phenomenological happenings. Sasse felt that he had the mind of Luther here. The facts are, however, that Luther can only be claimed for the Pieper-Engelder-Arndt side of the matter."

Klug concludes: "Sasse's motives were, no doubt, good. He did not intend to hurt the Church of his day. In fact he sincerely believed, as his writing attests, that the way to peace and unity within the Christian Church on earth lay with a correct interpretation and understanding of God's Word, Holy Scripture. He thought that he was rendering a service by showing the Church how and to what extent it ought to accommodate itself to some of the conclusions of the historical-critical methodology. No doubt other sincere Christian-theologians have approached the matter in the same way, without devious intent to overturn the Scriptures or trouble the Church. Right motives do not right the wrong, however. The question of Scripture's inerrancy cannot blithely and lightly be swept under the theological rug. Scripture's authority is grounded on its divine inspiration. Inerrancy is integral to the mortar of inspiration. A man's avowal of support of Scripture's inspiration and authority becomes empty denial when he disavows inerrancy."

Study Questions

1. A survey showed that even though several hundred liberal clergymen in the LCMS left in 1974 to form Seminex, several hundred who denied ____ remained in the LCMS.
2. At the LCMS's convention in 1959 Sasse said he was ____ that the convention reaffirmed the binding nature of the ____.
3. Klug observed that Luther can only be claimed for the side of ____ on the inerrancy of the Bible.
4. "Inerrancy is integral to the mortar of ____."

§

LOSING A FATHERLY FRIEND

N. Oddo, 5-45200 Stramstad
August 16th, 1976
Dear Herman,
Our Dear friend, Hermann Sasse, died on the 9th of August. He was found dead in his home, apparently having suffered a heart-attack in the early hours of the morning. We have lost a fatherly friend, both of us. How we shall miss him.
Yours in Christ,
Tom Hardt

Editor's Note:
At the LCMS's convention in San Francisco, California in 1959, Sasse told *CN* about some "lonely Lutherans" faithful to God's Word. One of them was Tom Hardt. When Grace Otten, along with Kurt Marquart, were reporters at the Fourth Assembly of the Lutheran World Federation in Helsinki, Finland, she had dinner in the Hardt home in Stockholm, Sweden on her way to the LWF Assembly.

Hardt and Sasse exchanged many letters. Hardt is the author of "In the Forecourts of Theology: The Epistemology of Hermann Sasse and the Relationship between Philosophy and Theology and between Natural Theology and Revelation in His Works" presented at the Sasse Symposium held from October 30 to November 1, 1995 at the centenary commemoration of Sasse's birth. The essay was published in 1998 by Concordia Academic Press, 3558 S. Jefferson Ave., St. Louis, Missouri 73118-3968, in a 271 page book titled "Hermann Sasse: A Man For Our Times?" edited by John R. Stephenson and Thomas M. Winger. Other contributors are Ronald R. Feuerhahn, Lowell C. Green, John W. Kleinig, Edwin Lehman, Kurt Marquart, Gottfried Martins, Norman Nagel, John Stephenson, John R. Wilch, and Thomas Winger.

Feuerhahn concluded his essay by quoting Richard Jungkuntz, who had served as the Executive Secretary of the LCMS's CTCR when it began in 1962: "But there are Lutherans in America, as there are in Europe and Australia, who today thank God that from Hermann Sasse they have learned in a better way than they knew before – 'was heist Lutherishch' what it means to be Lutheran" (p. 29). Stephenson says in the "Editorial Foreword: "We would also voice appreciation for financial assistance from the Luther Academy, whose then president, Dr. Robert Preus, participated with gusto throughout the Symposium, which ended just three days before his sudden death." *Marquart's Works* published by *Christian News* includes some essays Marquart wrote about Preus.

The back cover of "Hermann Sasse: A Man for Our Times?" quotes William H. Lazareth, Bishop Emeritus, Metropolitan New York Synod, Evangelical Lutheran Church in America: "Here is a fascinating review of 20th century international Lutheranism as dramatically personified in the Germanic jeremiads of one of its most controversial and influential participants, Hermann Sasse." Robert Mayan, President of the Lutheran Church-Canada, is quoted: "Hermann Sasse, through his writings, continues to influence Confessional Lutheranism around the world." Roger D. Pittelko, President Emeritus, The English District, The Lutheran Church - Missouri Synod, LCMS Vice-President, 1998-2001, a classmate of the *CN* editor, is quoted: "It is evident that Hermann Sasse is indeed a theologian and a man for our time. The theological issue that he dealt with...Pastors, theological students, and informed laity would do well to 'take and read' this volume."

Here are some of the articles Tom Hardt sent *Christian News* for publication which are in the *Christian News Encyclopedia*: "Baptism and the Holy Trinity", translated by Peter Krey, p. 145; "Om Altarets Sakramen," a summary of Hardt's doctoral thesis "Venerablis et Adorabilis Eurcharitia" reviewed by Peter Krey, 488; "Lutherans Differ on Moment of Real Presence In Sacrament" on pp. 489-490 has a response to Hardt from Kenneth Miller, who became moderator of the Lutheran Church of the Reformation; "The Lutheran Church and Birth Control – The Family in Natural and Revealed Law," 930, 931; "Dean Danell Attacks New Swedish N.T. Translation," 1671; "No Archaeological Evidence for Female Clergy in the Ancient Church," 1726-1728; "The Church of Sweden," *Lutheran News*, November 16, 1964, pp. 7-9, *A Christian Handbook on Vital Issues*," p. 669-674.

§

WE SHALL MISS HIM
Christian News, August 30, 1976

Dr. Hermann Sasse, one of the world's leading Lutheran theologians, was called to his eternal home this month. Dr. Tom Hardt of Stockholm, Sweden, sent us this notice in a letter dated August 16: "Our dear friend Hermann Sasse died on the 9th of August. He was found dead in his home, apparently having suffered a heart attack in the early hours of the morning. We have lost a fatherly friend, both of us. How we shall miss him."

We first met Dr. Sasse at the Lutheran Church-Missouri Synod's 1959 convention in San Francisco. Several of us who had just recently graduated from Concordia Seminary, St. Louis or who were still students there, met with some of the officials and leaders of the LCMS and shared our concerns about some theological trends at the St. Louis seminary. Dr. Sasse was the guest essayist at the convention and was sympathetic to our concerns. Professors Kurt Marquart and David Scaer were among those of our friends who had lunch with Dr. Sasse. Augsburg Publishing House had just released Dr. Sasse's book, This Is My Body. He signed our copy "Verbum Domini manet in aeternam! San Francisco, June 23, 1959."

Dr. Sasse later gave us valuable advice in our case with Concordia Seminary. Professor Marquart conferred with Dr. Sasse during the 12 years he was a pastor in Australia before he was called to Concordia, Springfield. *Christian News*, through the years, has published some of the writings of Dr. Sasse. A few appear in our *Christian Handbook*. (The Sacrament of the Altar, pp. 99-101; Christian View of Abortion, pp. 225-227.)

Some Lutheran liberals frequently quote Dr. Sasse on the inerrancy of the Bible. They use letters he had written many years ago. Although he withdrew certain statements he had written on inerrancy and asked that these statements no longer be published, liberals continued to publish them and use Dr. Sasse to support their attack on the inerrancy of the Bible. (*A Christian Handbook*, p. 559.) When Dr. Fredrik Schiotz, the former president of the American Lutheran Church, used some writings of Dr. Sasse to defend his denial of the inerrancy of the Bible, Dr. Sasse wrote us on December 19, 1966: "I should like to point out that I am not quite happy about the way Dr. Schiotz has selected passages from my articles. Taken out of context they might suggest that I reject the inerrancy of the Scriptures. The contrary is true."

Dr. John W. Behnken, former president of the Lutheran Church-Missouri Synod, wrote shortly prior to his death in 1968:

My personal friend, Dr. Hermann Sasse, who sacrificed much, even his professorship at Erlangen and could today draw a fine pension, left the Bavarian Landeskirche when it linked up with EKiD and joined the Breslau Synod, which is in fellowship with us since 1947, sent me a letter recently from Germany where he has been visiting from Australia. He stated: "The general theological situation in Germany is hopeless. The gulf between the congregations and bishops on the one hand and the radical theology on the other is widening. Attempts made by Lilje and others to minimize the differences were unsuccessful. But the Lutherans in America seem to side with the radicals rather than with the Confessing Church."

"In a week's time we shall stand again at the manger of our Lord. I would rather be an ox or an ass in Bethlehem than one of those demythologizers, who rob the Christian people of the wonderful message of Christmas." What a marvelous statement!

This is the good Dr. Sasse, who did so much to persuade the two Lutheran bodies in Australia, the ELCA, and the UELCA, to enter fellowship, yet, form one Lutheran Body on sound doctrinal agreement. This is the good Dr. Sasse, who warned his "Landesbischof" Hans Neiser not to become a member of EKiD. This is the good Dr. Sasse who cannot favor membership in the Lutheran World Federation.

Nor do I favor membership. I am opposed to it not only because of

169

Dr. Sasse's influence, but also because I attended two of the LWF Assemblies. The first in Hanover. The chief topic was THE LIVING WORD IN A RESPONSIBLE CHURCH. I spoke in the Sectional Meeting on Theology and pleaded that they should center their attention not merely on the person of Christ, but also on the written Word. They should adopt a resolution about God's Word. I got a rousing applause. Dr. Hoopmann of Australia spoke along the same line. So did an ALC professor from St. Paul, Minnesota. But nothing happened. The second was at Minneapolis with the topic: "Christ Frees and Unites." Again some of us pleaded for some definite resolution. Nothing happened. The Standing Committee for the next few years came up with nothing acceptable. The third was at Helsinki. I did not attend. The topic was JUSTIFICATION. It hurt me that even on this cardinal doctrine of Scripture and the Lutheran Church nothing was adopted which could be told to the world to be the teaching of the Lutheran Church. Too bad! I know what was claimed about saying things in relevant language. That's not an excuse. We want something Scriptural, something truly Lutheran. May God graciously keep our beloved Synod on sound and solid Scriptural grounds! May He preserve the purity of doctrine for us which He has so mercifully bestowed on us!

Dr. Sasse was an authority on the ecumenical movement in which he was extremely active in its formative years. In 1933 he was called to the chair of Church history and symbolics at Erlangen University in Germany. In 1960 he wrote in a published letter (Una Sancta, St. Luke the Evangelist, 1960, 19): "In Germany the Lutheran Church, as it was understood by our fathers, also by your fathers, has ceased to exist apart from the Free Churches. Everyone is free to teach and do what he pleases. There is no longer a doctrinal discipline in an evangelical sense. You can be a Unitarian, or you can be a man of Roman convictions. The Church in Europe has reached the state of the Anglican Church where practically all persuasions are tolerated provided they do not interfere with the ecclesiastical organization."

This issue includes some of the writings of Dr. Sasse which previously appeared in *Christian News.*

Along with Pastor Tom Hardt of Sweden and loyal Christians all over the world, we shall miss him and his valuable suggestions but one day through faith in the same Christ in which he placed all his hope for eternal life we shall be with him in heaven.

Study Questions
1. When did Marquart and Otten first meet Sasse? ____
2. What did Sasse write about Schiotz's use of his writings? ____
3. Sasse wrote to Behnken that the general theological situation in Germany is ____.
4. According to Sasse, the Lutherans in America generally appear to side with ____.
5. Sasse wrote that he would rather be an ____ at the manger in Bethle-

hem than a ____.

6. Both Sasse and Behnken opposed membership in ____.
7. Sasse wrote that in Germany the Lutheran Church has ceased to exist apart from ____.

§

A PASTOR DIES

Sermon preached by Dr S.P. Hebart at the Funeral of
Dr. H.O.E. Sasse on August 12, 1976
The Lutheran, Australia, September 20, 1976

"We are more than conquerors through him who loved us." For I am sure that neither death, nor life, nor angels, nor principalities, nor things present, nor things to come, nor powers, nor height, nor depth, nor anything else in all creation, will be able to separate us from the love of God in Christ Jesus our Lord. Romans 8:37-39

'We are more than conquerors.' Is that true? How can we say that in this sad moment when we are here to take leave from Hermann Sasse; when you, his family, who were so close, so dear to his heart, are saddened by the death of your father and grandfather? How can we, his colleagues, his brethren in the ministry, the whole Church, say that, when we think of all that he gave us as scholar, thinker, theologian, pastor and teacher, when now we must realize that he has been taken from us, inescapably? There is so little we can say to one another, even though it helps to know that others are here, because they, too, were close to him, and it means something to them to have come here. We have sorrow, true enough, but is that the expression of a conqueror?

Besides the sorrow, there is a deep sense of **gratefulness** for all he did for you, his family, and beyond that for countless others, encouraging them, admonishing them through an endless flow of letters that went to all parts of the earth, stimulating, educating, counselling, and warning them and enlightening many through his books and articles, pointing them to the unshakeable truths of God's Word, wrestling with them when, as it seemed, they were in danger of sacrificing truth and weakening in the confession of their faith, speaking kind words, speaking hard - even harsh - words, because it was truth that mattered, whether that was in his German homeland, or in this country of Australia, his adopted land; whether it was in Munich or Berlin, in Geneva or Rome, in Minneapolis or Uppsala, in Adelaide or St. Louis; whether it was as a fearless confessor in the Church in the midst of persecution, peril and sword under Nazi suppression, or as meditation, pleading brother whose theological insights did so much to bring about the cherished union of our two

171

former Lutheran Churches in Australia.

Yes, we are grateful for all that. God knows it, too, and even when we have forgotten, God will still remember. But does that make us conquerors? Hermann Sasse is no longer with us, so near still in a way, but really so irrevocably distant. There is something hateful about death, something with which we cannot come to terms, something we would rather not talk about, but push back into the far recesses of the mind. We would rather let the dying die their lonely death alone, as he died it alone. But he wanted to be alone; no one could persuade him to go elsewhere and leave his beloved books behind. He knew he might one day die alone.

And yet he was undaunted. Was it merely his amazing willpower that commanded his ailing body to perform tasks against which it consistently rebelled? We know it too well, no will-power, no gratefulness of ours, could produce in Hermann Sasse, or in us, that overwhelming, amazing sense of hope, joy and conquering self-assurance which pervades the whole New Testament, especially these verses from St Paul's letter to the Romans, a highlight in the New Testament, a mighty, confident message of victory, in the face of overwhelming odds.

What gave St Paul such joy, even in the face of death, when he exults: 'I am sure that neither death nor life ... will be able to separate us from the love of God in Christ Jesus our Lord.'? Don't mistake this for some kind of self-hypnosis, or a whistling in the dark which pretends the awful reality is not there. I know we tend to do that, and the nagging question keeps coming back at us: is it true that there is a shore beyond that mighty ocean which we call eternity, is there something there, are we going to meet again, are we more than conquerors?

Surely we need an answer to all this. For whatever St. Paul says here, what we will see today is: earth to earth, ashes to ashes, dust to dust. We visit the graves of our loved ones; we want to be close to them; we are sure they are there, and of course they are not there — earth to earth!

And that is not all. Besides death, other formidable powers and uncanny forces are arrayed against us, says St. Paul. Accusers stand up and bring charges against us in final judgment; God's law condemns us: our conscience joins in. And there is distress, persecution, nakedness, peril, the sword, when God seems far distant and we are sure we are victims of a blind fate. Still more, beyond these blows of fate are gruesome, dark, evil, cosmic forces, mysterious, destructive powers, that disrupt God's good creation, that make their presence felt in the great historical events among the nations, in the Church, in our individual lives. We shudder as we think of them. Hermann Sasse was very much aware of the presence of these demonic forces in history, and of their threat to the Church of Jesus Christ. With the fervour of an Old Testament prophet he predicted developments in history and issued his clarion call to the faithful to assemble for battle, to stand, to fight and not to be daunted by these powers of the old aeon.

Why could he do that? Because he knew that, indeed, we are more than conquerors, that neither death nor life, neither God's law nor our conscience, neither accusers nor tribulations, neither persecution nor famine nor peril, nor nakedness, nor distress, neither things present nor things to come, neither angels nor principalities nor powers, can be the ultimate. God's steadfast love in Christ who died, yes who was raised from the dead, is greater than death, greater than fate, greater than the total army of evil and chaos.

Here is the basis for our certainty that we are conquerors, that Hermann Sasse was a conqueror: the unshakeable, eternal love of God, the ultimate of all ultimates, the strongest force there is, the expression of an unchanging will, far more permanent than those laws of nature which the scientists discover and use, and which will pass away.

This love means us, seeks us, wants us, keeps us. Long before we were born, God called us by name, in the same way as we give our children a name. We could give them a number, but the name expresses the fact that each of us is unique and irreplaceable; each of us is a person in his own right, with his own dignity. If we were mere numbers, we would be anonymous, an 'it' to be programmed in a computer. To have a name is to show that we are people, members of a people. And if God calls us by name, he indicates that he is not a God of anonymous masses, but the Father of each one of us. For him, too, each of us is unique, irreplaceable; he loves each one of us as if there was no one else to be loved.

To that God and his love, demonstrated to us on the cross of Christ, *in* the love of Christ, each one of us, also Hermann Sasse, was linked inseparably in baptism, when our given name was coupled indelibly with that of the holy Trinity. We can deny that link; we can regret it; but we cannot unmake it. To be linked with God is to be linked with him who is immortal. The love of Christ has placed us into a relationship with God from which we cannot flee. That is the ground of all Christian hope, the basis of the new, the Messianic age.

What guarantee have we for that? Most of all, St. Paul reminds us of the historical fact of the resurrection of our Lord, that one spot in history where a hole was blown into the iron wall of death. Ever since, we speak of death swallowed in victory, and of the certainty that we, too, will be raised from death.

The other guarantee is the great company of the 'we' who are more than conquerors, of the 'us' whom nothing can separate from the love of God in Christ, the one, holy, catholic, and apostolic Church, present and hidden in the several denominations that divide us, the body of Christ, the communion of forgiven sinners and saints. This Church catholic was a matter of passionate concern for Hermann Sasse; that is why he was so hostile to Church unions which sought concord at the expense of truth. That is why he was so exclusively Lutheran, and yet paradoxically so close to his fellow-believers in other Churches. That is why there was such a broad sweep in his vision of the Church. Many are grateful to him for teaching them loyalty to their denomination, coupled with that true ecumenical openness which is ready to teach out for the hand of the brother across the dividing wall.

The third guarantee for St Paul is given in those decisive words 'in

173

Christ our Lord' (v. 39). In a very special way we experience the significance of those words in that pure gospel, the Lord's Supper, where, in union with our Lord, ages and eons are spanned, and where we are raised beyond time and space and the terrifying realities of this world to be one with all the saints in heaven, beyond life and death. Nothing can separate us from the eternal oneness given to us in the Lord's Supper. Hermann Sasse knew that, and his constant watchfulness over the truth of what it means: 'This is my body' was in keeping with his heroic faith.

It is this faith that made of him a conqueror, that makes all of us conquerors. It is with this heroic faith that we will leave this Church and the graveyard, knowing that the last is not earth to earth, but the love of God in Christ Jesus our Lord from which nothing can separate us in all eternity.

Hermann Sasse knew that he would live on, enshrouded, as Luther once said, in the mind and memory and Word of God, in the presence of God, even though he slept the sleep of those who have died and who look for that great awakening, the resurrection of the dead and the life of the world to come. Let Hermann Sasse himself speak to us once more and tell us of this heroic faith. In a sermon he once wrote he said of the Church Militant, of the pilgrim people of God surrounded by the dust and din of battle:

'From afar we hear the hymn of victory. Now, however, we still belong to the age of burdensome struggle, when we can be grateful if we can hold our ground. Our eyes see nothing of that victory now ... but the Church knows that victory belongs to him, our Lord, when he comes again. That is the faith and hope of the Church, as the battling army of God in this world: victory will be ours when the battle is done.'

Study Questions
1. Why was Hermann Sasse a conqueror? ____
2. Paul reminds us of the historical fact of ____.
3. While Sasse was so exclusively Lutheran he was close to ____ in other denominations.
4. The Christian leaves the cemetery knowing that the last is not ____.
5. "As the battling army of God in this world: victory will be ours when the battle ____."

§

A TRIBUTE TO DR. SASSE

Dr. L.B. Grope
The Lutheran (Australia), September 6, 1976

'Whosoever therefore shall confess me before men, him will I confess also before my Father — which is in heaven.' Matthew 10:32.

In recognition of Dr. Sasse's 70th birthday a book was published in 1966 consisting of important letters written by Dr. Sasse to pastors in many parts of the world on a variety of theological topics. The book is entitled: *In Statu Confessionis.*

In his introduction, the compiler gives the reason for the rather unusual title. He contends that almost every utterance made by Dr Sasse, whether from the pulpit, in the lecture hall, or in his letters and books, was *In Statu Confessionis* that is, in a situation when he was witnessing to and contending for the truth, when he was making a good confession.

Our departed friend and brother was a confessor of Christ. No matter what the occasion or circumstance, no matter how lowly or how exalted his audience, Dr. Sasse confessed the Lord whom he so dearly loved and so faithfully served. A great multitude of people in many lands and of a variety of religious persuasions will readily testify to this fact: Hermann Sasse confessed the Christ of the Holy Scriptures as few learned men have done in our generation.

What is more, the departed made his confession fearlessly and courageously, irrespective of the consequences. In the process he won many admirers, and also inevitably made some enemies. But it was the price he was prepared to pay. He dearly loved his Lord and Saviour, the Holy Scriptures, the Holy Sacraments, the Liturgy of the Church, the Lutheran Confessions. These were his life, and he was prepared to make great sacrifices for their sake.

For him, confessing Christ was not merely a matter of saying the right words at a Sunday morning service. He has written:

> According to the New Testament, to be a confessor means more than to express a religious or theological conviction ... A real confession of faith is always made before God and all the world, and therefore it bears an eschatalogical character. When a confession is demanded of us — and it is demanded by Christ himself of all who meet him, believers as well as unbelievers — nothing less is at stake than life and death for time and eternity.

Now he who took the Christian privilege and duty of confessing Christ so seriously is in the nearer presence of him who has promised to acknowledge his faithful ones before the Father in heaven.

We rejoice that our dear departed is now among those of whom it is written:

'He who conquers shall be clad in white garments, and I will not blot his name out of the book of life; I will confess his name before my Father and before his angels.'

Despite the irreparable loss that we have suffered, Dr. Sasse, though dead, will continue to speak to us through his writings in the years that lie ahead. He will continue to encourage us to be confessors, whether we be pastors or parishioners, professors or presidents. He will continue to call on us to be faithful:
faithful to the Lord;
faithful to his Word;
faithful to the Holy Sacraments;
faithful to the Church which Christ loved and for which
he gave himself.

To confess Christ means to speak to others of the love of God revealed in Jesus Christ; but it means much more: It means
to live a life that is in consonance with our words;
to fight the good fight, even unto death;
to hold fast to God's Word and the Sacraments, no
matter how high the price we have to pay.

Let this be our response to the Lord who so graciously gave Dr. Sasse as his precious gift to the Lutheran Church of Australia.

Study Questions
1. Sasse confessed the ____ of Holy Scripture.
2. Sasse dearly loved ____.
3. Sasse will continue to speak to us through ____.

§

GOD TOOK HIM
Pastor H.F.W. Proeve.
The Lutheran, September 6, 1976

'Those who are wise shall shine like the brightness of the firmament; and those who turn many to righteousness, like the stars for ever and ever.' Daniel 12:3

Hermann Otto Erich Sasse was born on July 17, 1895, at Sonnewalde, in Lower Lusatia, Germany, as the son of Hermann Wilhelm Heinrich Sasse and his wife Maria Magdalene, née Berger. He was baptized in the Church of his birthplace on August 2, 1895, by Superintendent Hengstenberg, and on March 22, 1910, he was confirmed in Berlin-Friedenau by Pastor Görnandt.

Meanwhile his education had begun in the public school at Laage, in Mecklenburg, and continued on the secondary level at Lubeck-Krotoschin, Breslau, and Berlin. His years of studies at the University of Berlin in the faculties of theology and philosophy culminated in his passing the first theological examination in 1916, and— following war service 1916-1918 — his second theological examination *pro ministerio* (for the Ministry) in 1920. Continuing his academic studies during his ministry, he obtained the degrees of Licentiate (now called Doctor) of Theology in Berlin, 1923, and Master of Sacred Theology following studies at Hartford Theological Seminary, Connecticut, USA, 1925-1926. In addition, the University of Erlangen conferred on him a Doctorate of Theology *(honoris causa)* in 1933, and more recently, in 1967, Concordia Theological Seminary, Springfield, Illinois, conferred on him a Doctorate of Divinity.

Following his ordination to the Holy Ministry on June 13, 1920, in the *St. Matthai* Church, Berlin, by General Superintendent Kessler, Dr. Sasse first served for about 14 years in the parish ministry. Initially an assistant pastor in *Advent* Church, Berlin, and at Templin (1920-1921), he took over his first pastorate in Oranienburg, north of Berlin, where he had a parish of 10,000 souls in two Churches (1921-1928), and then served as the pastor of *St. Marien* Church, Berlin, and the *Sozialpfarrer* (welfare pastor) of Berlin (1928-1933). Even after his parish ministry ceased, the theologian remained in heart a pastor who cared for souls. During the Second World War, 1939-1945, he was a part-time hospital chaplain, and here in South Australia it was a constant burden on his heart that his compatriots who were post-war immigrants should receive adequate spiritual care in their mother-tongue, in which he himself gave the local pastors of his Australian spiritual home, *Immanuel,* North Adelaide, as much assistance as possible.

During his studies at Hartford, and strongly influenced by his reading, particularly in Wilhelm Löehe's *Three Books on the Church,* a theological development began which was to have a profound influence on Dr Sasse's own life and career, and through him in wider circles. He had been born and had been serving within the circles of the Evangelical Church of the Union (the Prussian State Church), but his continued studies made him a convinced confessional Lutheran.

In May 1933 he took up duties as Professor of Church History, History of Dogma, and Symbolics in the University of Erlangen, Bavaria, serving there for about 25 years, until he emigrated. These were the years in which he was personally and deeply involved in the confessional aspects of Church activity in Germany. He was one of the leading men in the establishment of the Confessional Church in Berlin in 1934, and provided the preparatory work on which its Bethel Confession was based. When the debate and negotiations of succeeding years culminated in the formation of the Evangelical Church in Germany in 1948, Dr. Sasse became a member of the Lutheran Free Church, and in the following year accepted a call as lecturer at *Immanuel* Theological Seminary of The United Evangelical Lutheran Church in Australia. He took this step under the conviction, in his own words, that 'where the Altar of our Lutheran Church is, there is our home'.

With his wife and family he arrived in Melbourne on September 11, 1949, on the *Surriento,* and was installed in his lectureship in the field of Church History on October 12. When the seminaries of the two former Lutheran Churches were amalgamated to form Luther Seminary of the Lutheran Church of Australia at the beginning of 1968, he continued to serve for another two years until the end of 1969, thus completing 20 years of service in the Australian institutions. Until his death he was an honorary and honored member of the Faculty.

Dr. Sasse's retirement was not a signal for him to enter into inactivity. Although increasing age brought with it a handicap of physical infirmity, it did not dim his mental and spiritual keenness, and his written contributions in particular continued to make him a teacher in the Church. The books, pamphlets, articles, reviews, and editorial work that came from his pen in the past 56 years, as listed in a recent bibliography, total almost 450 entries. They include such valued books as *Vom Sakrament des Altars* (Concerning the Sacrament of the Altar) which he edited and to which he contributed; *Here I Stand; This Is My Body;* and articles in the monumental *Theological Dictionary of the New Testament* (editor, Kittel) and in a number of theological encyclopedias. He shared his theological insights and his assessment of ecclesiastical developments through contributions to a wide range of periodicals and other publications, both Lutheran and non-Lutheran, in Europe and England, North America and Australia, and for varying periods of time during the years 1929 to 1938 he edited three or four periodicals. A selection of his articles was published in Germany, under the title *In Statu Confessionis,* as a 70th birthday tribute, and reissued last year with additions as a two-volume 80th birthday tribute.

The breadth and depth of his knowledge and learning was known and appreciated in wide circles throughout the Christian Church. In 1927 he attended the World Conference on Faith and Order at Lausanne, Switzerland, and edited the German report of this Conference; he was a member of the Faith and Order Continuation and Executive Committee until 1936, and a member of the British-German Theologians Conference till the same year. He was active in the Lutheran World Convention, but was prevented by police action from attending its Assembly in Paris, 1935. He served as a guest lecturer at the Wartburg (Dubuque) and Concordia (St Louis) Seminaries, and twice at Concordia (Springfield) Seminary. He lectured to many Church groups and at many tertiary institutions in the cities of Australia, and in New Zealand centres. Through his voluminous correspondence he maintained close contact with eminent churchmen of many branches of the Christian Church in the world.

We remember with gratitude to God that in our Australian Church we were privileged to benefit from his presence in our midst. The universal respect in which he was held by all Lutherans in this land, his knowledge of the Scriptures and of the dogmas of the Church, enabled him as a member of the Inter-synodical Committee of the UELCA to make a very substantial contribution to the discussions which by God's grace led to the establishment of one Lutheran Church of Australia in 1966. Since then he served as a consultant of its Commission on Theology and Inter-Church Relations.

It was in the difficult inflationary years, while he was the pastor at Oranienburg, that Dr. Sasse married Charlotte Margarete Naumann, the date being September 11, 1924. The marriage was blessed with two sons and one daughter. The daughter, Maria, died while the family was still in Germany, and his wife predeceased him on March 4, 1964. And now the Lord, in whose hands are our times, has suddenly called him from us, on August 9, at the age of 81 years. To his sons, Wolfgang and Hans, their wives and the six grandchildren, we express our sincere and deep Christian sympathy, assuring them that the students who sat at his feet, the pastors with whom he shared his spiritual insights in public presentation and personal discussion, and a grateful Church cherish the memory of their father and grandfather, a pastor and theologian who worked assiduously in the cause of the Lord and his Gospel, while it was day.

Pastor J .H. Biar was in charge of the service at *Immanuel,* North Adelaide, on August 12. Some 75 pastors of the Church were in attendance. Dr. S.P. Hebart, Principal of Luther Seminary, based his address on Romans 8:37. At the graveside in Centennial Park cemetery Dr. L.B. Grope, President of the LCA, spoke on Matthew 10:32,33.

'We are more than conquerors through him who loved us.'

Study Questions

1. Sasse received his Doctor of Theology in Berlin in ____ and his a Master of Sacred Theology Degree after studying at ____.
2. Concordia Theological Seminary, Springfield in 1969 conferred on Sasse ____.
3. How long did Sasse serve in the parish ministry? ____
4. Sasse remained in heart a ____ who cared for____.
5. Sasse and his family arrived in Australia in ____.
6. Where did Sasse serve as a guest lecturer in the U.S.? ____

§

OFFICIAL LUTHERAN PUBLICATIONS IN U.S. IGNORE SASSE'S DEATH

Christian News, September 20, 1976

Dr. Hermann Sasse, one of the world's greatest Lutheran theologians, died over a month ago. We have not yet found a notice of his death in any of the many religious news reports we receive. While we may have missed some small death notice, so far we haven't found any mention of his death in the papers of the major Lutheran bodies in this country. About the only report we have seen appeared in the September 2 *Christian Beacon*. It is reproduced below.

When liberal churchmen die official publications of the major Lutheran bodies are quick to publish a story. The death of such leading conservative Lutheran theologians as Dr. David Hedegard, Dr. Hugo Odeberg, Dr. William Beck and others is hardly mentioned by the liberal press.

Official Lutheran publications give all sorts of publicity to liberal theologians. Few LCMS theologians produced as much of real lasting significance as Dr. William Beck and yet hardly any LCMS professors and officials attended his funeral in St. Louis. The liberal press and Church officials may give all sorts of recognition and publicity to liberal theologians and "yes men" theologians who toe the party line regardless of who is in control, but God knows those who, like Dr. Hermann Sasse, are truly faithful to His Word and who have accomplished something of real value in His kingdom.

From *The Christian Beacon*, September 2, 1976.

Dr. Hermann Sasse Called Home

Word has come from the Rev. Gilbert Cassidy of Adelaide, Australia, that Dr. Hermann Sasse, world-renowned Lutheran theologian and opponent of ecumenism died August 9. A close friend of the late ICCC leader, David Hedegard, Sasse greeted Dr. Carl McIntire on his first ICCC visit to Australia. He was a staunch Lutheran, an opponent of the Lutheran World Federation. He defended the inerrancy of the Scriptures and was fully versed in the developments, not only in the Lutheran world, but in the religious world as a whole. He was a friend to the refugee groups of Lutherans, and he wrote vigorously against the apostasy of the Lutheran Church and its collaboration with the Roman Catholics in Germany. His activities were reported in the United States through *Lutheran News* and later *Christian News,* and he was a close friend of Herman Otten, editor, who has been contending for the historic Lutheran faith. He was an encouragement to the International Council of Christian Churches and was in correspondence with Dr. Carl McIntire, its president.

A great Christian scholar of the old school has left an abiding impact for the cause of Christ.

Sasse went to Australia in 1949, and was a member of the faculty of

Emmanuel Lutheran Theological Seminary in North Adelaide. His book, *Here We Stand,* was a challenge against all encroachments and attacks against Christianity and particularly the struggle in Lutheran circles. He was a Christian gentleman in every sense of the word.

Study Questions

1. When Dr. Hermann Sasse died, how much publicity did the official Lutheran press in the U.S. give to Sasse's death? ____
2. Sasse was a close friend of ICCC leader ____.
3. The *Christian Beacon* said that Sasse defended the ____ of the Bible.
4. Carl McIntire's *Christian Beacon* said that Sasse was a ____ in every sense of the world.

§

IN MEMORIAM - DR. HERMANN SASSE

B. W. Teigen
Lutheran Sentinel, October 28, 1976

On August 9th Dr. Hermann Sasse passed away at his home in North Adelaide, Australia, at the age of 84. Since possibly the name of Dr. Sasse may not be well known to some of the readers of our *Lutheran Sentinel* and since, on the other hand, his name meant a great deal to many others, it is proper that something be said about this servant of God, especially since he had a warm place in his heart for our Evangelical Lutheran Synod. Up to the end of his life, he eagerly followed the work of our synod by reading the *Sentinel,* Synodical Reports, and other periodicals.

Dr. Sasse was born in Germany and spent his youth there when this nation was a prosperous world power, at the turn of the last century. He attended the University, with the intention of becoming a Lutheran pastor; but at the completion of his studies, World War I was raging at its fiercest. As a result, he was drafted as a foot soldier, going through some of the bloodiest battles of the war. It was something to hear him tell in his own quiet way how just as the war was to end nearly his whole company was wiped out, but he was spared. When he was able to get back to civilian life, he became a pastor of a parish Church, strongly committed to preaching to his parishioners the pure Gospel as it is expounded and confessed in the Lutheran *Book of Concord.* By 1933 his talents as a scholar and as a profound student of Christian doctrine and Church history were recognized by his being called to the University of Erlangen as a professor in the History of Doctrine. Here he taught and did scholarly research work in the Reformation, the Early Church, and the New Testament. He was invited to prepare several articles for the monumental

181

Theological Dictionary of the New Testament ("Kittel," as it is called today after its first editor). His essay on "The World," *(Kosmos),* is one of the outstanding articles in this prestigious work. At the same time, Dr. Sasse raised his voice against both the old theological liberalism still found in Germany even after World War I and against the newer Barthian new-orthodoxy which was sweeping Germany during the Depression and threatening to turn Lutheranism into some kind of Reformed Calvinism. He also early saw the dangers of Hitlerism to the state of Germany.

Dr. Sasse exerted an international influence for confessional Lutheranism, not only by training at the University of Erlangen men who eventually became conservative theologians in Germany, Denmark, and Norway, but also by being active with his pen. In 1934 he published a remarkable and popular book on the essence of the Lutheran Reformation and Lutheran Doctrine, as expounded in the *Book of Concord.* The German title to the book was, *Was Heisst Lutherisch?,* which might be translated as "What does it mean to be Lutheran?" The book, however, was translated into English in 1939 with the title, *Here We Stand.* I can still remember as a young pastor reading it early in the 1940's and the profound impression it left with me. He demonstrated that the Reformation was an event in the history of the Church of Jesus Christ, and it would not do to interpret it in economic terms, or nationalistic terms, and much less as an event centered around a great hero. The Reformation, Sasse asserted, was an event in the Church of Jesus Christ because Luther had derived his doctrine from God's Word and had proclaimed the pure Gospel of the forgiveness of sins through faith alone in Jesus Christ.

Dr. Sasse continued to serve as professor at the University of Erlangen until 1941, when he withdrew from the University and the Bavarian Lutheran State Church because that once conservative Lutheran State Church had finally given up the Lutheran Confessional principle by joining the Evangelical Church in Germany, which was made up of both Reformed and Lutherans who had agreed to disagree in matters of Christian doctrine. Dr. Sasse subsequently emigrated to Australia, there serving as a professor in a Lutheran theological seminary until his retirement about seven years ago. At that time, his name as a Lutheran theologian had become world known, especially through the publication of circular letters to Lutheran pastors throughout the world. His great work was undoubtedly his carefully researched study of Luther's and the *Book of Concord's* doctrine of the Lord's Supper, *This Is My Body,* published in 1959.

Sixteen or seventeen years ago, in some way which I cannot now quite remember, we began corresponding and carried it on until a year or two ago when Dr. Sasse became quite feeble. In March 1962, six or seven pastors from our Evangelical Lutheran Synod, together with two or three laymen on our Doctrine Committee, met with Dr. Sasse in an all-day meeting in Minneapolis. It was a good meeting, since he had heard some rather derogatory tales about our synod. He was pleased to know that our synod was committed to proclaiming God's Word in its truth and pu-

182

rity and to confessing the doctrines of the *Book of Concord*. Three years later, Bethany's Convocation Committee invited him to deliver a couple of lectures to the public on pressing problems facing Lutheranism. By that time he was well aware of the doctrinal deterioration that had taken place at Concordia Seminary, St. Louis. His lecture on "The Impact of Bultmannism on American Lutheranism" had a profound effect on the large audience that had come out in the midst of a snowstorm to hear him. Years later he wrote that he had never forgotten "that wonderful day in Mankato where the Old Synodical Conference seemed to be alive. The meeting has always remained a precious memory. God speed the day when a new Lutheran Conference will unite what has remained of the loyal in the faith."

While there was one point on which our Church could not fully agree with Dr. Sasse, namely, his presentation of the doctrine of the inerrancy of the Bible, still we must say that he was one of God's gifts to the Church. Personally, he was a humble, kind, dignified gentleman of the old school. His piety ran deep, and he avoided all sham. His scholarship and the tools God had given him to perform his scholarly duties, he wore with easy grace. We can apply to him what he wrote upon hearing of the death of one of our pastors whom he had met in 1962. He wrote, quoting from a Burial Prayer from an Early Church Liturgy: "For Thy faithful, O Lord, life is changed but not taken away." And then Dr. Sasse added: "The blessing of faithful confession remains with the Church on earth."

Lord of the Church, we humbly pray
For those who guide us in the ways
And speak Thy holy word:
With love divine their hearts Inspire,
And touch their lips with hallowed fire,
And needful grace afford.

Help them to preach the truth of God,
Redemption through the Savior's
blood:
Nor let the Spirit cease
On all the Church His gifts to shower;
To them a messenger of power,
To us of life and peace.

Study Questions
1. During World War I Sasse was drafted as a ____.
2. When Sasse returned to civilian life he became a ____.
3. What happened to most of Sasse's company during WWI? ____
4. Sasse was called to the University of ____.
5. Sasse raised his voice against ____.
6. Sasse saw the dangers of ____.
7. According to Sasse, the Reformation was ____.
8. The Evangelical Lutheran Church in Germany is made up of ____.

9. Where did Sasse go? ____
10. Sasse's This Is My Body was published in ____.
11. "God speed the day when a ____ will unite what has remained loyal in the faith."
12. The Evangelical Lutheran Synod did not fully agree with Sasse on ____.
13. "For The Faithful, O Lord, life is ____ but not ____."

§

THE DOCTRINE OF BAPTISM

From The LUTHERAN (Australia), August 21, 1978.

The writer is the late Dr. Hermann Sasse, and the translator P.H. Buehring. The article is reprinted, with some minor corrections, from THE LUTHERAN OUTLOOK, September 1949, 265-270.

The doctrine of Holy Baptism is a doctrine that has brought out clearly for many of our contemporaries the differences between the confessions that go back to the period of the Reformation.

It is true that, in addition to the controversy about the Lord's Supper, there was even in the 16th century a lively, highly informative debate on the subject of Baptism, especially at the Moempelgard Colloquium between Andreae and Beza. However, since both the Lutherans and the Reformed maintained and defended the practice of infant baptism over against the Anabaptists, the radical difference between the confessions regarding the meaning of this particular means of grace was not sufficiently noted at that time.

It is Karl Barth who deserves the credit for having clearly pointed out what to him is 'a wound in the body of the Church' ('Die Kirchiche Lehre von der Taufe', *Theol. Existenz Heute,* new series 4, 1947). And although his demand that the Reformed Churches revise their doctrine and practice of Baptism has met with determined resistance, the question still remains whether Barth in this respect has not been more Reformed than the Reformed, whether he has not seen more clearly than any Reformed theologian before him certain inconsistencies of Zwingli and Calvin which resulted from their opposition to the Anabaptists of the 16th century.

The need of concerning ourselves about the meaning of Baptism and about Barth's objections to infant baptism is brought home to us Lutherans by the fact that disciples of Karl Barth have attempted to read his doctrine of Baptism into the Augsburg Confession, and that even in the Lutheran dogmatics of our day a considerable uncertainty may be observed regarding the rationale of infant baptism and thus concerning the meaning of the Sacrament of Baptism in general.

1. Baptism A Sacrament

Any discussion of the Sacrament of Baptism must begin with the fact that Baptism is a sacrament, a means of grace in the strict sense, and not merely a more-or-less beautiful, more-or-less justifiable usage of the Church like, let us say, confirmation, or the marriage rite, or the funeral service. This at once makes all arguments irrelevant that are based on the view that Baptism is a symbolical act, a symbol, perhaps, of the *gratia praeveniens* that precedes all human action, or a symbol of the 'community Church' as distinguished from what Troeltsch has called the 'sect' in the sense of a second type of Church that has grown out of the radical, anabaptistic movement of the Reformation period. (Translator's Note: The term 'community Church' is to be taken here in the sense of the German *volkskirche,* not of our well-known American community Churches. P.H.B.)

Today it is customary to say 'free Church' instead of 'sect', and it is claimed that a surrender of infant baptism must inevitably result in the dissolution of the community Church in favor of the Free Church. But disregarding the fact that all free Churches except the Baptists practice infant baptism, certainly the very serious dogmatical question must be raised, whether the Sacrament of Baptism can be used as a means for preserving the community Church, if infant baptism cannot be justified dogmatically. As distinguished from the concept of baptism, which has been a part of Christian dogmatics since the days of the apostles, the concept of the community Church is a concept of religious sociology, barely a hundred years old, theologically legitimate, coined (as far as we know) by Johann Hinrich Wichern (at any rate popularized by him). The theological nonsense of this concept, which no educated theologian should ever use, becomes clear from the constantly repeated statement that one becomes a member of the free Church by a conscious act of the will, while one is 'born into' the community Church. One never becomes a member of the Church by a resolution of the will or by birth — the latter is true only of certain state Churches like Zurich, the prototype of the community Church since the days of Zwingli, where today one can exercise all the rights of a Church member except the strictly spiritual without even being baptized. According to the testimony of the New Testament (1 Corinthians 12:13), one becomes a member of the Church by Baptism. And the only theologically legitimate question, which also determines the right or wrong of infant baptism, is, who may be baptized: those only who can confess their faith in Jesus Crist, i.e., adults and older children who are able to do so, or also minor children, *infantes* in the strict sense?

2. The Early Church

So the question of infant baptism is a theological question, not merely one of practical sociology. Neither is it a question that is to be answered from history. Thomas Aquinas (S. Th., III Quaestio, 68:9) meets the ob-

185

jection that intention and faith are necessary for baptism with a quotation from the last chapter of the 'Heavenly Hierarchy' of Dionysius the Areopagite, according to which the apostles approved the baptism of infants. But that is, to say the least, a tradition that cannot be checked.

However, Joachim Jeremias, *(Hat die älteste Christenheit die Kindertaufe geübt?* 1938) and W.F. Flemington *(The New Testament Doctrine of Baptism,* 1948) have advanced a mass of weighty arguments showing the probability that infant baptism, which is first mentioned *expressis verbis* by Irenaeus (c. AD 185), goes back to the apostolic age, where it was practiced following the pattern of the Jewish baptism of proselytes, which as is well known was administered not only to adults but, in cases where entire families were admitted, to all the members of a household, including the children. The well-known examples of Lydia, the seller of purple, and of the jailer at Philippi (Acts 16) who were baptized together with all those in their households after they themselves had come to faith, come to mind here.*

When Polycarp at the trial preceding his martyrdom testifies that he has been serving the Lord for 86 years *(Mart. Pol.,* 9), the reference can only be to his membership in the Church. Accordingly, his baptism must have taken place in the apostolic age, even prior to the year 70. The statement of Justin *(Apol.* 1:15) that at that time there were many Christians 60 and 70 years old who from the days of their childhood *ematheteuthesan to Christo* can refer only to members of the Church who were baptized as children during the period between 80 and 90 AD. We have already mentioned Irenaeus. He testifies that Christ came to save all, 'all who by Him are regenerated unto God: babes *(infantes),* little children, boys, youths and men' *(Adv. Haer.,* II 22:4). In the Church Order of his disciple, Hippolytus the baptism of little children is mentioned in so many words. They are to be baptized before the adults and their parents or some relative are to take their places at the 'Amen' and confession of faith by speaking vicariously for them.

When Tertullian in his *Treatise on Baptism* directs his polemics against the custom of infant baptism, he certainly is not attacking it as an innovation; even as, later on, Pelagius in his battle against Augustine's doctrine of original sin had to admit the argument that, after all, infants were baptized too; at least he does not deny the fact. Likewise, Origen and Cyprian presuppose the baptism of infants: the former in the claim later transmitted to the Middle Ages by Dionysius the Areopagite that the baptism of infants goes back to a tradition given by the Lord to his apostles *(Commentary on Romans,* 5:9); Cyprian in the well-known instruction given to Bishop Fidus *(Ep.* 64) not to defer baptism to the eighth day analogous to circumcision. Jeremias is right when he claims that a later introduction of infant baptism would have stirred up a great excitement and thus have left definite traces in the history of the Church. The results of Church-historical investigation rather indicate that in the ancient Church, precisely as in our modern mission fields, both forms of baptism, adult and infant, have always existed side by side. If that is true, then infant baptism must go back to the apostolic age. The baptism

186

of children must then be included in the baptism of entire families, of which we have examples in the New Testament, even though the children are not specifically mentioned.

3. A Theological Question

It is obvious from the above that the *historical* question whether the Church of the apostolic age knew and practiced infant baptism must be answered in the affirmative with a very high degree of probability. But that fact in no wise decides the *theological* question concerning the right of infant baptism. After all, the Church of Corinth in the days of the apostle Paul practiced a vicarious baptism for the dead. It is possible, therefore, that we are dealing here with a very ancient abuse. Theologically, infant baptism can be grounded only on Scripture evidence which proves it to be a legitimate form of Baptism.

The argument against infant baptism formerly raised by the Anabaptists and today by Karl Barth is that the essence of the Sacrament of Baptism includes 'the responsible willingness and readiness of the person to be baptized' to receive the divine promise and to accept the divine obligation (Barth, op. *cit.*, 23). In an essay in the Berlin religious weekly, *Die Kirche,* some time ago, a disciple of Barth attempted to prove the correctness of this view by a reference to the story of the Ethiopian eunuch (Acts 8) where, as he maintained, not only an expression of the will of the candidate preceded his baptism but also his confession of faith as a condition for receiving it. Unfortunately, that theologian had overlooked the fact that verse 37 with its solicitation of a confession of faith and the making of that confession is an ancient addition to the original text, as is shown by a study of the manuscripts. The oldest and best manuscripts do not have it and thus confirm the fact that in the primitive Church (cf. Acts 2:41) Baptism was sometimes administered without a spoken Credo.

So the question is what is Baptism according to the testimony of the New Testament? What does it give or profit? What is the relation of Baptism to the faith of the baptismal candidate? Is it necessary for salvation or not? Our first answer must be that, according to the clear teaching of the New Testament, Baptism is 'the washing of regeneration'. The ancient Church, which always actually identified Baptism and regeneration, and the Church of all times with the exception of the Reformed denominations, has understood Titus 3:5 in this sense, and rightly so. There Baptism is said to be 'the washing of regeneration and renewing of the Holy Ghost'.

In Baptism the Holy Spirit is communicated; we are 'all baptized into the one body' (1 Corinthians 12:13). Those who are baptized have been baptized into Christ's death (Romans 6:3). These are all realities that take place, not alongside of Baptism, but in Baptism. In the New Testament, Baptism with water, inasmuch as it is a baptism into Christ, into the name of Christ, is baptism with the Spirit, it is a being born anew and at the same time from above 'of water and of the Spirit' (John 3:5).

Certainly, the New Testament knows of no regeneration without Baptism and independent of Baptism. Baptism, therefore, is not a sign but a means of regeneration. To take it only as a sign of regeneration, that also takes place without it and independently of it is unbiblical.

The Reformed Church in its doctrine of Baptism, precisely as in its doctrine of the Lord's Supper, on the one hand rejects the pure symbolism of Zwingli, as though Baptism were nothing but an 'ostensible' sign of the Christian profession like the white cross which the confederate attaches to his garment in order to show that he is a confederate; but on the other hand it also rejects both the *opus operatum* of the Roman sacramental doctrine and the Lutheran and New Testament identification of sign and substance.

Why does it do this? In the final analysis, it is because of the aversion of Calvin and his medieval theological predecessors to the view that an external, physical act can evoke spiritual effects like the forgiveness of sins. But this is, in the first place, a philosophical prejudice, and in the second place it is a misunderstanding of the significance of the Word of God in Baptism. 'For without the Word of God the water is simply water and no Baptism; but with the Word of God it is a Baptism, that is, a gracious water of life and a washing of regeneration.' Even in Catholic doctrine the Word as *forma* is inseparably united with the sacrament; as Augustine's famous dictum, quoted over and over again by all occidental Churches, puts it: *Accedit verbum ad elementum et fit sacramentum.*

That which separates Luther from the Catholic doctrine of Baptism is best stated in his own words in the Smalcald Articles, where he draws the line between himself and Thomism as well as Scotism at the same time:

Therefore we do not hold with Thomas and the monastic preachers or Dominicans, who forget the Word and say that God has imparted to the water a spiritual power which, through the water, washes away sin. Nor do we agree with Scotus and the Barefoot Monks who teach that by the assistance of the divine will Baptism washes away sins, and that this ablution occurs only through the will of God and by no means through the Word and water.

For Luther, everything depends on the close connection of water and the Word:

God, however, is a God of life. Now, because He is in this water, it must be the true *aqua vitae* that expels death and hell and quickens forever (WA. 52, 102,9).

But that this presence of God or Christ cannot be any other presence than that in his Word will not need to be proved, we trust, in the case of Luther. All effects of Baptism, in the view of Luther and the Lutheran Church, are effects brought about by the Word connected with the water.

Consequently, the Reformed objection to the Lutheran interpretation of Baptism is none other than the objection to the Lutheran doctrine of

188

the means of grace in general. That God gives his Spirit — and with him forgiveness of sin, life and salvation — to no one without the external means of his grace, without the external Word, without Baptism, without the Lord's Supper: that is the point against which this objection is directed. 'The power of Jesus Christ, which is the only power of Baptism, is not bound to the execution of Baptism' (Barth, op. *cit., 14i.).* A favorite distinction made by the older Reformed theologians was the one between external baptism by water and internal baptism by the Holy Spirit and the blood of Jesus Christ which cleanses us from all sin. The reception of both, they said, does not always coincide; it is possible to have the one without the other. Whether an individual receives the Spirit-and-blood baptism together with the water baptism depends upon whether he is one of the predestined or not. This point of view also accounts for the objection to emergency baptism which has been raised again and again since Calvin, especially against the *Weibertaufe* (baptism by women, midwives). Even so late a document as the Union Constitution of the Palatinate contains the sentence: 'The Protestant Evangelical Christian Church of the Palatinate does not recognize emergency baptism' (E.F.K. Mueller. *Die Bekenntnisschriften der Ev.-Reformierten Kirche,* 1903, 871).

After all (they say) Baptism cannot give man anything he would not have without Baptism. Salvation and damnation do not in any sense depend upon Baptism, but only upon the question whether a man has been predestinated unto salvation or not. That is classic Reformed doctrine. And even where, as in the school of Barth, the old predestination doctrine has been softened up or surrendered, the conclusion still stands: Baptism has been instituted by Christ — Calvin agrees with Luther and the universal tradition of the Eastern and Western Churches that the institution is identical with the baptism of Jesus — hence it must also be practised as an ordinance of Christ, but it is not necessary for salvation. According to Karl Barth (*op. cit.,* 15), one can only speak of a *necessitas praecepti,* never of a *necessitas medii.*

4. BAPTISM AND FAITH

When, over against this view, the Lutheran Church maintains the *necessitas medii,* the character of Baptism as a means of grace in the strict sense, it does not of course contradict the ancient Catholic dictum: *Deus non alligatur sacramentis suis* (God is not bound to his sacraments). Our Church has never denied that God has still other ways of saving men; the writings of Luther and the old Lutherans concerning the fate of children who die unbaptized prove that. What we must guard against is the tearing asunder of Spirit and Word, of external and internal baptism. It is the water baptism inseparably connected with God's Word of which Luther sings:

Blind sense but water sees, and spurns:
'Pray, how can water save us?'
Faith marks the Word, and well discerns
Christ's merits that here save us;

189

Faith sees this cleansing fountain red
with the dear blood of Jesus,
which both from sin inherited
From fallen Adam frees us.
And sins we have committed.
(Richard Massie's translation)

And as for the relationship of the miracle of regeneration wrought in Baptism to the fact that some who have been baptized are lost, that question belongs to the secrets of divine predestination concerning which nothing has been revealed to us in the Gospel, but which, as Luther explains toward the end of *his De Servo Arbitrio, we* shall fully understand in the light of glory. We simply hold to the Gospel and to the promises attached to Baptism in the Gospel, when we confess concerning Baptism as the washing of regeneration: 'It works forgiveness of sins, delivers from death and the devil, and gives everlasting salvation to all who believe it, as the words and promises of God declare'.

But what about the faith of the person to be baptized? As we raise this question, we touch the very heart and core of the Reformed objection to the Lutheran doctrine of Baptism, an objection which had its parallel in the Reformed world a century ago in the so-called Gorham Controversy in England, when the denial of baptismal regeneration on the part of the Evangelicals so deeply disturbed the Church of England. For one who stands on the ground of infant baptism, the following alternative seems inescapable. Either there is such a thing as forgiveness of sins and regeneration unto eternal life in Baptism, even without the personal faith of the individual baptized or his personal confession (that is the answer of the Catholic Church, which lets the faith of the Church take the place of that of the infant that is to be baptized); or forgiveness of sins and regeneration are separated from the act of Baptism — which in turn leads to several practical observations.

It is possible, then, to retain infant baptism, as most of the Reformed do, by taking a stand on Colossians 2:11 and viewing it as the New Testament sign of the covenant analogous to the Old Testament sign of circumcision. Or, on the other hand, following the example of the Anabaptists of the Reformation period and of the modern 'congregations of Christians baptized as believers', one can discard infant baptism entirely. Or, again, one can follow Karl Barth along the middle way between these two possibilities and consider infant baptism as valid indeed, but nevertheless as a practice that rests upon false or erroneous presuppositions connected with the idea of the community Church, and that should therefore be revised. That Barth himself in the meantime has probably come to see that none of the great Reformed Churches is inclined to take his advice and give up *a* custom that has been so firmly established since Zwingli and Calvin, is a matter which we need not discuss here.

But on the periphery the question might be raised whether the principles and practice of the Baptists are not after all, the most consistent application of the Reformed doctrine of Baptism, and whether the retention of infant baptism in the Reformed Church is not to be accounted for as a compromise with the force of a tradition of 1,500 years and with the opposition to the enthusiasts of the 16ᵗʰ century. For despite Colossians 2:11, Baptism cannot be taken as a counterpart to circumcision, because circumcision lacks the very thing that makes Baptism a Baptism. They are at least as different from each other as the Old Covenant is from the New, or as the Israel of the flesh is from the Israel of the spirit. If this parallel is insisted upon. Baptism can never be anything else than a symbol of grace. Then it can never be a means of grace in the strict sense, despite every effort of the Reformed to retain this concept of Baptism.

Here too, as elsewhere, Luther walked his lonely way between Rome and the enthusiasts. Over against the latter, among whom he also counted Zwingli and his adherents, and would have counted the Calvinists had he lived to know them, Luther held firmly to the Sacrament of Baptism with all that belongs to it: infant baptism, necessity for salvation, regeneration. Over against Rome he held with equal firmness to the *sola fide:* it is only through faith that we receive forgiveness of sins, life, and salvation. Just as in the Sacrament of the Altar only *he* receives forgiveness of sins and with it life and salvation who believes 'these words' (viz., the promise: 'Given and shed for the remission of sins'), so it is also true of Baptism: 'It works forgiveness of sins, delivers from death and the devil, and gives everlasting salvation to all who *believe* it, as the words and promises of God declare'. And he is not talking here about a future faith which is then confessed in the rite of confirmation, as though the latter were a necessary complement of Baptism.

Bucer, who was the first to introduce pietistic notions into the Church, carried an un-Lutheran element into confirmation (in itself a proper rite), which had its roots not in biblical ideas but in a sociological concept of the Church, and which came to maturity in the age of pietism and rationalism. It is a significant fact that in the 18ᵗʰ century confirmation was never introduced in Wittenberg, where the First Communion was deemed sufficient, but it was introduced in the synagogue. At that time it seemed impossible to conceive of the Church as anything else but a 'society', a 'religious association' which one joined by an act of the will. For Luther, on the other hand, the faith of which we speak in connection with infant baptism is not the future faith to be produced by Christian education; neither is it a kind of germ-faith implanted in Baptism as many 19th century Lutherans thought; but it is *the* faith, a faith with which children come to Baptism precisely the same as adults, with only this difference that in children it is not yet a conscious faith which they themselves can confess.

In his *Large Catechism* Luther quite properly called attention to the fact that even the faith of the adult never suffices as a ground for Baptism.

For I myself also, and all who are baptized, must speak thus before God: 'I come in my faith and in that of others, yet I cannot rest in this, viz., that I believe, and that many people pray for me; but in this I can rest that it is Thy Word and commandment. Just

as I receive the Lord's Supper, trusting not in my faith but in the Word of Christ...' Thus we do also in infant baptism. We bring the child in the purpose and hope that it may believe, and we pray that God may grant it faith: but we do not baptize it upon that, but solely upon the command of God (Jacobs' translation).

And the reason for this, he says, is that all men may err and deceive, but God, who has given the command to baptize, cannot err.

But that God by his Holy Spirit can also give faith to a child, the same as to an adult, no one can deny who remembers how Jesus blessed the little children and set a child before his disciples as an example. In fact, when you examine it closely, even the most heroic faith, even the faith of an Athanasius and a Luther, is no more than the faith of a little child.

Or when would you say that faith begins on the basis of which we should venture to baptize? Perhaps at the present age of confirmation? Or in little children when they can confess with the mouth, as Thomas Muenzer of old would have it? Why, it would be the equivalent of turning the miracle wrought by the Holy Spirit into a psychologically perceptible fact, if any attempt were made here to fix a time-limit for the working of the Spirit.

Here, too, Luther goes his lonely way between Rome with its hierarchical, and the enthusiasts with their psychological sanctions — the lonely way of the Reformer who heeds only the Word and God and trusts that this Word can do all things, even the humanly impossible. In this way, and only in this way, has Luther and the Lutheran Church after him been able to hold both the objectivity of the sacrament and the *sola fide,* not forgetting that justifying faith is not a matter of a single moment but the content of an entire human life. For this faith certainly is not the individual act of surrender to God, consciously felt and experienced at certain moments of our life, but it is the continuing trust — though overshadowed again and again — in the Gospel promise of grace; just as repentance according to the evangelical conception is not a single act but something that goes on continually throughout our life. So too our baptism is not a finished act, but it goes with us throughout our life. To be a Christian does not mean simply to have been baptized sometime in the past, but it means to live in the power of Baptism and to return to it again and again.

As is well known, the *Small Catechism* answers the question: 'What does such baptizing with water signify?' by saying:

It signifies that the old Adam in us, by daily contrition and repentance should be drowned and die, with all sins and evil lusts, and that a new man daily come forth and arise, who shall live in righteousness and purity before God forever.

Just as we who are sinners and righteous at the same time live by daily contrition and repentance and by daily forgiveness of sins, so too our dying and rising again with Christ, that real though incomprehensible anticipation of an eschatological event which takes place in Baptism, is something that determines our entire life.

This, over against Rome and against the enthusiasts, was Luther's understanding of Baptism and of the faith that accepts Baptism. We embrace it not only at one given moment, whether it be at the moment we are baptized, or at the moment of confirmation, or any other given moment of our life that might be named, but we embrace it or should embrace it throughout our entire life, every day anew. This is the reason why Luther recognized no additional sacrament to supplement Baptism, whether it be confirmation or repentance, which would be anything else but a return to Baptism.

5. Conclusion

From this point of view, the question of infant versus adult baptism becomes theologically irrelevant, important as it is for churchly practice. This explains, too, why that question cuts no figure either in the New Testament or in Luther. Aside from the fact that adult candidates for Baptism voice their assent and confess their faith personally. Baptism has always been administered in the Church 'just as though' the persons to be baptized themselves desire Baptism and believe that which is spoken in the baptismal confession of faith. This practice must not be accounted for on the basis of liturgical traditionalism and ecclesiastical conservatism, but it belongs to the very essence of the rite. We baptize infants 'just as though' they were adults, even as we adults believe 'just as though' we were infants. Whatever the difference between adults and infants may signify for us human beings and for our estimate of a man, for God it signifies nothing. A human being is a human being, is a child of Adam or a child of God, without regard to his age. That is the deeper reason why all baptismal rituals treat the infant 'just as though' it were grown up. Only the Nestorian and the Reformed Churches have produced special rituals for infant baptism.

And down to the time of Calvin this, too, was a part of the act of Baptism that it did not take place in the presence of the assembled congregation. In the primitive Church, those who wished to be baptized received the sacrament outside of the space used for worship, while the congregation was assembled there to engage in intercessory prayer for the candidates. This arrangement was not merely one of propriety, for the Baptists immerse their candidates in full view of the congregation. The baptisterium, whether it was a fully developed baptismal chapel or a simple baptismal font, in earliest times always had its place in front of the entrance to the Church. It is more interesting to observe that the same Calvin who, as we believe, destroyed the dogmatic content of Baptism, moved this sacrament out of the area of privacy and individuality, out of the outer court, as it were, into the sanctuary of the assembled congregation. He probably got his idea for this, as for so many other changes, from Bucer in Strasburg, who very likely is also responsible for the corresponding rubric in the Hesse Church order of 1539, which in turn reappears in later Reformed Church orders like that of the Palatinate of 1563 and Bentheim of 1588. There is an internal connection here with the rule that the Reformed Church reserves the administration of Baptism to the clergy and prohibits emergency baptism by laymen or even women, whereas we find that precisely in the New Testament the administration of Baptism takes a subordinate position after the apostolic office.

Moreover, in the Reformed Church, and in that wing of Protestantism in general which is influenced by modern Calvinism, the service in which a baptism is administered is then designated as a 'sacramental service', and it is forgotten that 'sacrament' in the sense of a sacramental service is always the Sacrament of the Altar, the *sacramentum sacramentorum,* the Lord's Supper as such, as Luther's usage abundantly shows. Never would he have called a service in which in conjunction with the Creed a child is baptized a 'sacramental service'. For him the sacramental service was the 'mass', i.e., the combination of the service of the Word and the administration of the Lord's Supper. In this respect he fully agreed with the entire, universal Church. Whatever reforms may still be needed in order to bring back the Sacrament of Baptism to its place of honor in the Lutheran Church, under no circumstances must our Church lose sight of the goal of restoring the real sacramental service of the Church of all ages, including the Lutheran Reformation. A deeper understanding and a new appreciation of Baptism is possible only through a return to that which Luther's Catechism teaches on the basis of the New Testament, and in the simplicity of faith concerning Baptism as the washing of regeneration.

'I still do as a child who is being taught the catechism,' writes Luther in his preface to the *Large Catechism.* 'Every morning and whenever I have time I read and say, word for word, the Ten Commandments, the Creed, the Lord's Prayer, the Psalms, etc. And I must still read and study daily and yet I cannot master it as I wish, but must remain, and that too gladly, a child and pupil of the catechism.' What a difference it would make for us Lutheran pastors, for our Church, if we heeded these words of Luther more attentively and applied them in our life and our ministry! How many false conceptions of Lutheranism would then disappear, quite spontaneously, from our own minds, and how many prejudices against our Church in the world would be removed! *Kyrie eleison!*

* The present English reader can consult further developments of the work of Jeremias in the following English translations of his works: *Infant Baptism in the First Four Centuries* and *The Origins of Infant Baptism* (SCM Press, 1960 and 1963).

Study Questions
1. Karl Barth objected to ____ Baptism.
2. According to the testimony of the New Testament, one becomes a member of the Church by ____.
3. Did the early Church practice infant baptism? ____
4. According to the clear teaching of the New Testament, Baptism is a washing of ____.
5. For Luther everything depends upon the close connection of ____ and

the ____.

6. The Reformed reject the scriptural doctrine of the means of ____.
7. It is only through faith that we receive ____.
8. Even the most heroic faith is no more than the faith of a ____.
9. To be a Christian means to live in the power of ____ and to ____ it again and again.
10. Luther said that "I must still read and study daily ____."

§

Preus's Last Public Appearance

SASSE SYMPOSIUM — "CONFERENCE OF THE DECADE"

Christian News, November 13, 1995

By the Rev. Michael Brockman, Pastor
Christ Lutheran Church,
Hutchinson, Kansas

For the 250+ registered pastors, spouses, laymen and laywomen it was exactly as one speaker described: "The conference of the decade." The Hermann Sasse Symposium, conceived by Drs. Ronald Feuerhahn and John Stephenson, organized by Concordia Lutheran Theological Seminary in St. Catharines, Ontario and generously endowed by the Lutheran Life Insurance Society of Canada, was that conference.

The Sasse Symposium (October 30-November 1) marked the centennial birth year of Hermann Sasse, a German-born clergyman, who ministered and taught both in Germany and Australia. Sasse, a diminutive man has left a huge mark on the Catholic Church. His writings (This Is My Body and Trilogy We Confess Jesus Christ, the Sacrament and The Church, among others, have been available in English; other books, lectures and letters are being translated) are confessionally pastoral; his activities were ecumenically catholic. His life was distinctive and his voice, prophetic.

Since some of the speakers had had Sasse as professor and had known him personally, it was as though the prophetic voice was present. Dr. John Kleinig, lecturer for Luther Campus at North Adelaide, South Australia and former student, warmed the crowd with first-person anecdotes of Sasse on liturgy, Sasse on sacraments and Sasse on holding hands in chapel. Dr. Tom Hardt of Stockholm, Sweden carried on a weekly letter writing offering with Sasse by which he was able to open to the attendees

195

Sasse's thinking on theology and philosophy. Professor Kurt Marquart was a young "brash" pastor when he began serving near Sasse in Queensland, Australia in the 1960s. Marquart sat many a time at the feet of this instructor in the Word and delivered his lecture, appropriately, The Sacramental Word.

The man who has led the renaissance of Sasse studies, Dr. Feuerhahn, laid the foundation for the three-day event with the historical background on Sasse the man and churchman. His book of the same study awaits publishing. Feuerhahn's colleague at Concordia Seminary in St. Louis, Dr. Norman Nagel, closed the symposium with Ave Verum Corpus, a Sassian call to halt the use of the term consubstantiation. Dr. Lowell Green (Buffalo, New York) and Dr. John Wilch (St. Catharine, professor) expanded greatly into the pre-World War II/World War II days of Sasse at Erlangen under the Third Reich.

Perhaps the greatest applause after each 75-minute lecture was given the three youngest speakers.

Two, Dr. John Stephenson and Pastor Thomas Winger, are local, situated for the time being in St. Catharines, Ontario. Stephenson urged the sacrament (the supper) like Sasse urges the sacrament. The sacrament is forgiveness. The sacrament is visible. The sacrament is the Church's earthly present and heavenly future. The renewal of the Lord's Supper is the life and death event for the Church. Winger, the youngest presenter (29), gave the catholic and apostolic defense of the Confessional evening at the banquet, Preus would be thanked publicly by former student Stephenson for Preus' years at the Fort Wayne Seminary where many a healthy confessional pastor and spiritual son of Dr. Robert Preus was prepared for the Holy Ministry. This writer counts himself as one, urged all to do their catholic and ecumenical duties, as Sasse did, in surveying where Lutherans' closest affinities lie, with liberal Protestantism or with Rome.

The banquet speaker, Dr. Edwin Lehman, President of the Lutheran Church Canada, was a great asset to the entire program as were the Matins, Vespers and seminary choir. The Lutheran Church-Missouri Synod is graced with our sister seminary at St. Catharines.

Study Questions
1. The Sasse Symposium marking the 100th birthday of Hermann Sasse was described as "The Conference of the ____."
2. Where was it held? ____
3. Who spoke at the conference? ____

§

THE GOSPEL DIES WITH THE SUPPER

By Hermann Sasse

Christian News, October 26, 1998

In light of everything that we have said about the Lord's Supper on the basis of the New Testament, the fate of a Church that has lost the Sacrament of the Altar is clear. A Church that does not continually gather around the Supper must undergo secularization. It must irreversibly turn into a piece of the world, because the Supper establishes the boundary between Church and world. This conclusion is confirmed by the experience of Church history and especially of the history of worship in the last few centuries. The destruction of the Supper is followed by the disappearance of the living remembrance of Jesus from the hearts of Christians, especially of His suffering and death.

Thus, in the century of the Enlightenment, the fading away of the person of Jesus as the Biblical Redeemer into an indeterminate universal teacher, who might just as well be called Moses or Socrates, was bound up with the decline of the Supper as the celebration of His inextinguishable remembrance. We have already spoken at length about the connection between the Sacrament of the Altar and belief in justification. Where Jesus Christ no longer Himself speaks to us in the Holy Supper the Gospel "given and shed for you for the forgiveness of sins," the message of the Lamb of God who takes away the sin of the world necessarily fades away.

Christ certainly speaks this in His Gospel to us not only in the Supper, but also in each of His words. He certainly does not need the Sacrament in order to impress this message on us, but He is pleased to make use of it. He has not only once offered the sacrifice for the sin of the world, nor does He merely keep on having this fact proclaimed. Rather, He who is high priest and sacrificial lamb in one, gives us a share in His sacrifice here and now. The unique occurrence on the Cross, which is at once a truly historical and truly suprahistorical happening, is rendered present when Jesus Christ, the crucified and risen one, gives us His body sacrificed for us to eat and His blood shed for us to drink. Where this no longer happens because Christians have stopped celebrating the Supper, Christ's sacrifice turns from a reality into an idea, and the vicarious satisfaction for sins turns from a fact into a theory. In the place vacated by faith in the Son of God "who loved me and gave Himself for me," steps the intellectual conviction of the correctness of the doctrine of reconciliation. This doctrine will then very soon turn into a topic for general philosophical discussion, bandied about in apologetics; and it will eventually undermine faith altogether as it fuels doubt. Thus, the Gospel itself dies with the Supper.

From: Church and Lord's Supper

Translated by John Stephenson

Study Question

1. The Gospel itself dies with the ____.

§

A LUTHERAN TRAGEDY AT CHRISTMAS: HERMANN SASSE RECOLLECTS

By Pastor Per Jonsson
Landskrona, Sweden
Christian News, December 25, 1995

Each Christmas many of us who consider ourselves confessional Lutherans, bound by Scripture and our Lutheran confessions, are reminded of a tragedy that occurred one Christmas over a century ago to some of our forefathers. Hermann Sasse, the renowned theologian of Germany and Australia, first wrote of the incident in 1934 and narrated it again in his book In Statu Confessionis (2nd Volume, 1976).

In the early 1800s two emperors of the former province of Prussia attempted to force a union of the Lutherans and Reformed in their territory into one united "evangelical" Church. Fierce were the outcries and the opposition among some of our Lutheran forebears who endured persecution and harassment for their stand. Some of them emigrated to America and to Australia in order to find freedom of worship and conscience for themselves and their descendants.

Word reached the court that in the Prussian hamlet of Hoenigern the Lutheran pastor, one Kellner, was adamantly refusing to use the Reformed Agenda (order for worship), instead sticking to his Lutheran liturgical order. Sasse writes:

"The imperial commission, accompanied by gendarmes, came to crush, once for all, this obstinate resistance which the young pastor had carried on for several years against the decreed Reformed order of Worship. Kellner was a disciple of Scheibel, the theologian in Breslau who fought energetically against the Prussian union.

"Scheibel was one of the theologians who had opposed the Prussian Union from the moment it was announced by the emperor at the Reformation festival of 1817, the 300th anniversary of Luther's heroic stand at Wittenberg. They based their stand on the Lutheran confessions. Without reservation they also rejected the royal decree imposing the Reformed order of worship as a statement of this union and an instrument for its enforcement.

"The congregation gathered in Hoenigern gave Kellner a negative answer when he brought to them the superintendent's demand that he introduce the new order. When he refused to do so, he was suspended from office. The congregation refused to recognize his suspension on grounds that the united consistency had acted without proper authority against a Lutheran pastor.

"The suspended pastor continued to use the Lutheran order for several more months. Then, on the day of Christmas Eve, 1834, the Prussian military came to the village. A 400-man infantry, 50 dragoons, 50 Hussars and two cannons invaded Hoenigern. That morning the soldiers closed the Church while 200 members of the congregation watched. A warning to clear the area went unheeded. The rifles were loaded . . . the doors to the Church and the adjacent school were barred shut. . . .

"Then the authority of the state showed itself ready to reopen the Church under the new Reformed liturgy and the jurisdiction of the Prussian Union."

When Sasse was recalling the events of a century earlier, in 1934, the Church in Germany was facing an enemy even more sinister and powerful than the Prussian Union. This enemy was National Socialism. The government of the Third Reich took the same line as the emperor of Prussia a century earlier: that one "evangelical" union Church must be constituted. Hitler saw to it that one of his toadies was installed as "Reichsbischof" over both Lutherans and Reformed. In this way the Church could more easily show itself as a ready supporter of the national welfare. Because of the inroads of liberalism the Church of the Lutherans was miserably unprepared to resist.

Right after the fall of the Third Reich in 1945 Sasse wrote: "It was not Lutheranism that gave in but a sick Lutheran Church which opened the doors to National Socialism."

If there is one thing which we could generally say today about our Lutheran Church in Sweden, it is that she is a "sick Lutheranism." This Church no longer can be recognized as "Protestant." Today she can no longer take any stand against deviations from the faith. The overriding concern is for "freedom of thought, conscience, and speech." The pastors of the Church of Sweden are not bound to Scripture and the confessions nor will they recognize any such obligation.

(Translated and adapted from Lutherskt Saendebrev, monthly publication of the Lutheran Confessional Church of Sweden and Norway, of which Pastor Jonsson is editor. Translated by Pastor Edward A. Johnson, Cloverdale, Indiana.)

Study Questions
1. Who was the theologian who fought against the Prussian Union?____
2. What was the Prussian Union? ____
3. What happened on Christmas Eve, 1935 in Hoenigern? ____
4. Why was the Church unprepared to face Hitler's demands in 1934? ____
5. What opened the door to National Socialism? ____
6. Pastor Per Jonsson of Landskrona, Sweden wrote that the pastors of the Church of Sweden ____.

§

BETHANY REFORMATION LECTURES:
Hermann Sasse and the Path of Confessional Lutheranism in the Mid-20th Century

Mankato, MN
26-27 October1995

by Dr. Ronald R. Feuerhahn, lecturer
Lutheran Synod Quarterly, December 1995. Vol. 35, No. 4 (Excerpts)

The title, "'Confessing' Church", was itself significant. [6] While for Sasse a confessional Church must necessarily be a confessing Church, it also must necessarily be both. [7] Nothing should be allowed to rob the creed of its doctrinal content. The occasion of confessing must not ignore or be separated from its substantive content. "The essence of a Church confession lies, first of all, in the fact that it bears witness to objective truths." [8]

When Eberhard Bethge described how much Sasse impressed Dietrich Bonhoeffer, he also identified the chief point of difference in precisely these terms of confession.

Bonhoeffer's earlier delight at his discovery that Sasse's resistance and the view he held sprang not from ecclesial conservatism, but from a new relationship to the Confession, had, of course, given way to profound disagreement over the assessment of the function and dignity of historical confessions. Sasse, for his part, had come to see Bonhoeffer as an "enthusiast" because the latter credited the living event of communal, actual confessing with so much power that antitheses dividing Churches dwindled to antitheses, dividing schools. [9]

xxx

In the end, Sasse's confession place him *in statu confessionis.* "It may become my duty to separate from my present Church if she continues to remain a member of the LWF," he wrote Tom Hardt in 1959.XI His was a confession made at great cost to himself and his family. At the pastors' conference and in the presence of the Executive Secretary of the LWF, Carl Lundquist, he would confess.

At the Pastors' Conference I shall confess, at synod I shall not be present. Since 6 years I am *in statu confessionis.* I cannot receive Holy Communion in my congregation or at the Pastors' Conference. The logical step would be to transfer to the ELCA. This would smash all hopes for a union of the two Churches. Besides, it would kill my wife. What shall I do? I confess by word and deed, but I cannot leave my office, my honre [sic. home?] It is a tragic situation. [42]

Dr. Hermann Sasse, whose life was marked by tragedy and loneliness, knew the life under the cross. He was a theologian of the Church. The Church which could hold so many disappointments and tragedies was also the Church in which he found forgiveness and strength in Word and the sacraments. He would doubtless have rejoiced in the words of one of his Church fathers, Wilhelm Löehe:

"Behold the Church! It is the very opposite of loneliness- blessed fellowship! There are millions of saints and believers who are blessed in it, and in the midst of their songs of praise is the Lord. No longer **lonely,** but filled, satisfied, yes, blessed is he who is one of these millions who completely and fully have Christ and with him have heaven and earth! [43]

Footnotes

6 Sasse, "On the Problem of the Union of Lutheran Churches," II, QS 47.4 (Oct. 1950) 273

7 ibid., 277. In a document proposing the nature of a VELKD, Sasse discussed the importance for both, the act and content of confession:

"It is the perception of the necessity of the churchly confession for the Church in the double sense: that a Church which does not confess its faith before the world ceases to be the Church of Christ and it arrives at that not only in the act of confessing, but also in its content. The Church must know what it believes, teaches and confesses; and it must make this confession fearlessly before the world." (HLA/D15V/Nr.16 [148f, et passim.])

8 Sasse, "Church and Confession 1941," in Nagel, I, 74 [emphasis original]

9 *Dietrich Bonhoeffer ...,* 475f .

41 Letter, Sasse to Hardt (17 Sep 1959)

42 ibid., italics added.

43 Loehe, Wilhelm, *Three Books About the Church* (Seminar Editions), trans. & ed., by James L. Schaaf, Philadelphia: Fortress, 1969, 51

Study Question

1. "The essence of a Church confession lies, first of all, in the fact that it bears witness to ____."

2. Sasse came to see Bonhoeffer as an ____.

3. In the end Sasse's confession placed him____ .

4. Sasse wrote: "I cannot receive Holy Communion in my ____ or at the____."

§

WHAT DOES IT MEAN
TO BE LUTHERAN TODAY?

Laurence L. White
The Lutheran Concerns Association
Itasca, Illinois
April 3,1997
Christian News, April 21, 1997

I. Introduction

Our topic—*What Does It Mean to Be Lutheran Today* — is inspired by
a little book by Dr. Hermann Sasse titled *Was Heisst Lutherisch?* The
German original was first published in 1934 and the book was subsequently published in English as *Here We Stand* (1937). The goal of Sasse's
monograph was *to delineate the essential nature of one of the great confessional Churches of Christendom* (Sasse, p. x) at a time when
Lutheranism in Germany found itself locked in *a stern struggle for existence* (Sasse, p. 16). Dr. Sasse was convinced that there was a real possibility that the history of the Lutheran Church in Germany, the great
homeland of the Reformation, *might be nearing its end* (Sasse, p. 16).

Sasse correctly concluded that the Lutheran Church was being called
upon to define and defend her right to exist in the face of two fundamental challenges to her continued existence. On the one hand, German
Lutheranism was imperiled by the Struggle—confronting the malignant
evil of national socialism and the idolatrous demands of a totalitarian
state. 1934 was, of course, the year of the famous *Barmen Declaration,*
in which leaders of the protestant confessing Church publicly declared
their opposition to the demands of the Nazi worldview. Hermann Sasse
was one of a small handful of Christian thinkers who recognized the total
incompatibility of Christianity and the ideology of the Third Reich. He
was a determined foe of the Nazis from the very beginning, and played a
leading role in the theological discussions that led to the Barmen Synod.
Yet, at the last hour, he found himself unable to support the *Declaration*
itself because of its failure to recognize the confessional distinctives of
the Lutheran and Reformed traditions. Church historian Klaus Scholder,
while firmly disagreeing with Sasse's action, offers grudging respect for
the consistency of a strict Lutheran for whom *theological problems were
more important than political problems* (II, p. 144).

On the other hand, Sasse recognized that Lutheranism was also
threatened by Reformed theology which had always been susceptible to
unionism and was being re-energized by Barthian neo- orthodoxy. It was,
in fact, this second threat to which Sasse directs his attention in *Was
Heisst Lutherisch?* The bulk of the book offers a clear delineation of the
essential incompatibility of Lutheran and Reformed theology.

I am convinced that once again Lutheranism finds itself engaged in *a
stern struggle for existence.*

As in 1934, so also in 1997, the threat which confronts us is both theological and cultural. If we fail to recognize the nature of the struggle in which we are engaged and fail to meet the challenge of these days then we too face the distinct possibility that the history of the Lutheran Church in our country *might be nearing its end*. In the limited time available to us this morning and without the advantage of a presenter even remotely comparable to Dr. Sasse and his encyclopedic knowledge of the history and theology of Christendom we will briefly attempt to define the essence of Lutheranism and summarize a few of the challenges which confront us as Lutherans today.

II. The Essential Nature of Lutheranism

The Lutheran Reformation was a rediscovery of the pure Gospel as the message of salvation by grace through faith in Jesus Christ to a degree that had never been reached since the days of the New Testament. Sasse writes: *The Reformation was a renovation of the Church brought about by the rediscovery and renewed proclamation of the pure doctrine of the Gospel of the forgiveness of sins* (Sasse, p. 61).

The insight that the Reformation was renovation not innovation is critically important for a proper understanding of the nature of Lutheranism. Lutherans saw themselves as members of the *catholic,* that is, *universal* Church in the strictest sense of the term, and identified with the orthodox Church in all times and places. Thus the *Conclusion to the Augsburg Confession* declares:

Nothing has been received among us, in doctrine or in ceremonies, that is contrary to Scripture or to the Church catholic (contra scripturam out ecclesiam catholicam). For it is manifest that we have guarded diligently against the introduction into our Churches of any new or ungodly doctrines.

Sasse declares:

The Lutheran theologian acknowledges that he belongs to the same visible Church to which Thomas Aquinas and Bernard of Clairvaux, Augustine and Tertullian, Athanasius and Irenesa once belonged. The orthodox evangelical Church is the legitimate continuation of the medieval Catholic Church, not the Church of the Council of Trent and the Vatican Council, which renounced evangelical truth when they rejected the Reformation. (Sasse, p. 102)

The Lutheran Church was born of a love for the truth of God and an unshakable conviction that God has revealed that truth in His Word. Sasse writes:

Those men of the Age of Orthodoxy excelled the men of our age in at least one respect. They knew one thing which modern man does not know and does not care to know. They knew that, as individuals and as nations, we literally live by truth and literally die by falsehood. Hence they never shared the cold skepticism and wearied resignation of modern relativism, which holds that there are only relative truths, no absolute truths, and that it consequently does not pay to wrestle for the truth. Nor, with a bold "will to believe" did they have to satisfy themselves with half-truth or second-hand truth in order to have some ground on which to stand. Their quest after truth, their struggling for the truth, was conditioned, moreover, by the conviction that there is One who is Truth in person. One who said to the truth-seekers of all ages, "Everyone that is of the truth heareth My voice" (John 8:37). One who promised His Church on earth that His Holy Spirit would guide it into all truth. (Sasse, p. 89)

When the great composer, Felix Mendelssohn, was asked why he who had been born a Jew wrote the magnificent *Reformation Symphony,* he responded: *In those days, men had convictions: We moderns have opinions!* Hence the Lutheran Church, above all other Churches, is a Church that is passionately concerned about the teaching of the truth and firmly committed to guarding against the devil's wiles and false teaching. That is to say, the Lutheran Church is, by its very nature, a confessional Church —a Church that exists for one reason and one reason only, for the sake of the faithful proclamation of the pure doctrine of the Gospel in all of its articles. Of course, historically, that has also been true of other Churches which adopt and then conscientiously attempt to live by confessional statements. But in no other Church has confessional responsibility ever been so clearly and emphatically determinative. The Lutheran Church is the confessional Church *par excellence!*

Lutheranism has never defined itself in terms of polity, piety, or popularity, unlike both Rome and Geneva. Lutheranism is not a matter of institutional loyalty or denominational affiliation. It is, and must always be, a matter of doctrine. Dr. Theodore Schmauk affirms this confessional principle as the essential characteristic of the Lutheran Church:

She is the Church who stakes all on bearing witness. Her office is one of public proclamation and confession of the Truth, as it is in Christ Jesus. The preaching of God's Word, pure and as given in Scripture, is her central activity. . . She is here to proclaim and apply God's Word in Scripture, sermon, and sacrament. She is the Church of faithful, regular, and continuous witness to the Truth. Hence the source of her witness, the Word; the standard of her witness, the Confessions; are central; and she is willing—as indeed she must be, if she wishes to live—to abide by and uphold her confessional principle. (Schmauk, p. 13)

When the Lutheran Church formally declared its existence in 1530, with the presentation of the Augsburg Confession, it had no structure, no episcopal or synodical organization or officials to represent it. But it did have a confession, a doctrinal position. In response to the imperial summons, the confessors at Augsburg fearlessly declared:

Wherefore, in dutiful obedience to your imperial majesty, we offer and present a confession of our pastors' and preachers' teaching and of our own faith, setting forth how and in what manner, on the basis of the Holy Scriptures, these things are preached, taught, communicated, and embraced in our land, principalities, cities, dominions, and territories.

Dr. Sasse offers this eloquent definition of the nature of Lutheran confessionalism with typically Teutonic thoroughness:

The loyalty of the Evangelical Lutheran Church is accounted for by these experiences. We are faithful to this Church, not because it is the

Church of our Fathers, but because it is the Church of the Gospel; not because it is the Church of Luther, but because it is the Church of Jesus Christ. If it became something else, if its teaching were something other than a correct exposition of the plain Word of God, it would no longer be our Church . . . Nor is it the Evangelical Lutheran Church, as a separate Church in Christendom that matters. The moment it becomes anything else than the stand on which the lamp which alone is the light upon our path, it becomes a sect and must disappear. We would not be Lutheran if we did not believe this! Since this is the character of Lutheran confessionalism, it is in harmony with the breadth of genuine ecumenical feeling. We are confident that the Evangelical Lutheran Church which is faithful to its Confessions is truly the Church of Jesus Christ; that its office of teaching the Gospel and administering the Sacraments is an office instituted by Jesus Christ; and that it is effectual by reason of the institution and commandment of Jesus Christ, even if it is exercised by weak and sinful men; that Christ, the Lord, is really and personally present in the Word and Sacraments of our Church, and that the communion of saints, the fellowship of justified sinners, is built up in our midst by this Word and Sacraments. (Sasse, p. 173)

This is the essential nature of Lutheranism as it has been since its inception. It does not change, it cannot change, for the Gospel which is the substance of our confession does not and cannot change.

The primacy of that Gospel is the basic theological concept which dominates the whole teaching of the Lutheran Church and clearly distinguishes it from the Reformed. For Lutherans, the Gospel is the message of the sinner's justification—the gracious promise of the forgiveness of sins for Christ's sake. Without the light of the Gospel the Holy Scriptures cannot be properly understood. The Doctrine of Justification is, as the Confessions note, *the key which alone opens the door to the whole Bible* (Sasse, p. 112). The proper distinction between Law and Gospel is the crucial question which has always separated the Lutheran Church from the Reformed. For Lutherans the Gospel, the saving message of the sinner's justification, is first and foremost — *proprium suum officium,* the real work, the first purpose of Christ; while the proclamation of the Law, which damns and condemns the sinner, is an *alienum opus,* a strange or foreign work, a secondary purpose, which prepares the way for and serves the cause of the Gospel. This distinction between Law and Gospel is, in Luther's view, *the most important thing to know in Christianity* (Sasse, p. 114). The Formula of Concord declares: *The distinction between the Law and the Gospel is to be maintained in the Church as an especially brilliant light, whereby, according to the admonition of St. Paul, the Word of God may be rightly divided.* The theological and practical implications of this distinction are enormous, as C. F. W. Walther has masterfully demonstrated in his classic *Law and Gospel.* Yet it is precisely at this point that Wittenberg and Geneva decisively part company with one another. The individual doctrinal differences which separate Lutheranism and Calvinism — on the nature of faith, predestination, the nature and structure of the Church, and the real presence of the body and blood of

205

Christ in the Sacrament — all flow from our basic disagreement on Law and Gospel. For Calvin and his heirs, Christ is not only a Savior but also a Lawgiver. Karl Barth, speaking for the Reformed tradition, contends:

The Law takes its place alongside the Gospel on the same footing and as a part of the selfsame eternal treasure. The demand for repentance stands on the same level with absolution, sanctification with justification, harmonizing in the same act of revelation and reconciliation. (Sasse, p. 112,113)

In consequence, the Gospel becomes a new law; faith is turned into obedience; Christianity is reduced to moralism; and sanctification ultimately takes priority over justification. The Church is no longer a community of believers, which owes its existence solely to the Lord who is truly present and active in Word and Sacrament. Instead, it is transformed into a community of believers and obeyers which owes its existence not only to Christ, but also to us — the result of who we are and what we do. The Formula of Concord sternly warns — *Thereby the Gospel is again changed into a teaching of the Law, the merit of Christ and the Holy Scriptures are obscured. Christians are robbed of their true comfort, and the doors are again opened to the papacy.*

For Lutherans this Gospel, the precious promise by which God opens His whole heart to the sinner in Christ, must be first and foremost. Sasse contends: *The entire Church life of old Lutheranism, the message of its preaching and teaching, its liturgy and its classic hymnody, give one great testimony to this understanding of the Gospel.* (Sasse, p. 117) This emphasis on the primacy of the Gospel is the essence from which the vitality, dynamic power, and ecumenicity of Lutheranism is derived.

III. Challenges We Face Today

As previously noted, Hermann Sasse wrote Was *Heisst Lutherisch?* in 1934. This was a time when the continued existence of Lutheranism in Germany was threatened both culturally and theologically. American Lutheranism, and specifically we in the Lutheran Church-Missouri Synod, are presently engaged in a similarly *stern struggle for existence.* Once again the threat is both cultural and theological.

A. Modern Evangelicalism/Church Growth

While the influence of classic Calvinism has waned on the American religious scene, its Ariminian step-child has flourished, growing by leaps and bounds. The most significant development in American Christianity in the last half of the 20th century is the emergence of what is euphemistically called *evangelicalism.* This theological black hole of doctrinally indifferent, man-centered, feeling founded, consumer oriented religion threatens to swallow up Lutheran and Calvinist, liberal and conservative alike. Within our circles we tend to refer to this generic Christian consumerism under the heading of the *Church Growth Movement.* The problem, however, is much more pervasive than Fuller Seminary and its impact on the LCMS. David Wells offers this perceptive critique of the state of evangelical theology in his recent book. *No Place for the Truth:*

It is this God, majestic and holy in His being, this God whose love knows no bounds because His holiness knows no limits, who has disappeared from the modern evangelical world. He has been replaced in many quarters by a God who is slick and slack, whose moral purposes turn out to be friendly advice that we can disregard or negotiate as we see fit, whose Word is a plaything for those who wish merely to listen to themselves, whose Church is a mall in which the religious, their pockets filled with the coin of need, do their business. We seek happiness, not righteousness. We want to be fulfilled, not filled. We are interested in satisfaction, not a holy dissatisfaction with all that is wrong. This is why we need reformation rather than revival. The habits of the modern world, now so ubiquitous in the evangelical world, need to be put to death, not given new life. They need to be rooted out, not simply papered over with fresh religious enthusiasm. And they are by this point so invincible that nothing less than the intrusion of God in his grace, nothing less than a full recovery of his truth, will suffice. (Wells, p. 300)

Dr. Michael Horton, in a fascinating book titled *Made in America, the Shaping of Modern American Evangelicalism* contends that the problem is cultural accommodation. He traces the origin of this crisis of truth within the Church to the same forces of individualism, pragmatism, relativism, and hedonism which have shaped American culture as a whole. What has happened is that instead of transforming the world we have been transformed by it. Horton outlines the progression as follows:

We can see how each of the philosophical characteristics of American religion build on each other. First we declared independence from all sovereigns, including God, and established a religion, as well as a culture "of the people, for the people, and by the people." The democratic God celebrated by the American people was a civil servant who was elected by the people to serve their interests. The biblical God was told he could remain in our company only so long as he stayed on the sidelines and served as a public mascot — not as an umpire, nor even as a player, but as a mascot. Then, pragmatism demanded that God serve not only as a mascot, but also as a bellhop. God had to work and his own revelation had to meet the approval of utilitarian interests . . . And now, human centered religion takes another step toward supposed autonomy by demanding that God be a product too ... In this consumer religion Christianity becomes trivialized. Its great mysteries become cheap slogans. Its majestic hymns are traded for shallow jingles, often sung off the image from an overhead projector, much like an advertising executive uses to sell a client on an ad campaign. And its parishioners, now unashamedly called audiences, have come to expect dazzling testimonies, happy anecdotes, and fail proof schemes for successful living that will satiate spiritual consumption. (Horton, p. 64, 70)

He grimly warns that the day is coming when *the bright lights will burn out and the super Churches are turned into warehouses* (Horton, p. 71) because what is being offered to modern man is not the Biblical

207

Gospel of salvation in Christ.

Given the confessional nature of the Lutheran Church, and its clear focus on the primacy of the Gospel, we Lutherans ought to have been particularly resistant to this perversion of authentic Christianity. Unfortunately that has not proven to be the case. The appeal of success, of pews full of bodies and budgets full of bucks has proven to be irresistibly attractive even to conservative Lutherans.

And so we indulge in glib distinctions between style and substance to maintain the illusion that nothing has changed while in fact we have bartered our precious legacy of confessional faithfulness for a porridge bowl of transitory worldly success.

B. Institutionalism/Legalism

Our old evil Foe is a past master at twisting blessings into banes. We would do well to be mindful of that reality as we celebrate the 150th Anniversary of the Lutheran Church-Missouri Synod. The transition from the confessional principle of Lutheranism to the realities of denominational structure and practice is fraught with difficulty. Four years ago Dr. Erling Teigen presented a thoughtful essay at this conference exploring the thesis that: *The idea of conservatism as an ideological stance in the spiritual realm is antithetical, or at least inimical, to Lutheran Confessionalism.* (Teigen, p. 7) He characterized conservatives as those who place a high value on the status quo, are disinclined to rock the boat, and tend to preserve existing power structures. Teigen observed:

While conservatism may be construed as a desire to preserve that which is good, it doesn't necessarily work that way. The fundamental nature of conservatism is to preserve power structures, and status quo. That, in fact, is the fundamental nature of any bureaucracy, and not any less of Church bureaucracies. The Chureaucrat has to preserve the power structure within which he intends to function, for without the trappings of power, he is lost. Business and bureaucracy are fundamentally conservative in that sense, and the more our Church leadership pattern themselves after the business world, the more conservative they will become. To think of ourselves in terms of "conservative" strikes me then as dangerous and a stance that has taken us down the wrong path. (Teigen, p. 9)

Confessionalism, in distinction to conservatism, is dynamic, not static — ready to make radical change — constantly evaluating teachings and teachers in terms of the Biblical and confessional standard.

The evolution of the LCMS over the past 50 years from a confessional Church body in which the preservation of genuine doctrinal unity was the first priority to a conservative Church body in which the preservation of institutional unity is the first priority seems to demonstrate the validity of Teigen's thesis. That same contrast can be readily observed in the patient pastoral leadership of our synodical president whose efforts to reassert the confessional nature of the Synod have been opposed and often frustrated by administrators and power-brokers throughout the synodical structure. In many ways Dr. Barry exemplifies the qualities of Missouri's earlier years when we were content to walk together governed

208

only by the power of the Word of God and convincing — when our leaders were chosen because of their commitment to the Word of God. At that point, we did not seek leaders who were razzle-dazzle administrators or men with special management skills but humble pastors who loved the Lord, His Word, and His people — men who were well versed in the doctrine of the Lutheran Church and absolutely committed to that doctrine. Writing in 1896, Dr. Franz Pieper, expressed Missouri's unique perspective:

Our entire synodical arrangement has the very opposite purpose. Through it we work to assist one another so that the Word of God and nothing but the Word of God rules in our midst. The visitors see to it that in their circuits everything is done in the congregations according to God's Word; the District Presidents have a similar duty in the entire district, and the synodical president in the entire Synod. Therefore also we elect as visitors and presidents not people who are perhaps clever with documents or are better versed than others in our Synodical Handbook, but people who are well experienced in God's Word and are better able than others clearly to present and apply it in reference to existing circumstances. The supervising offices established by our synodical order are not to supplement God's Word, but serves God's Word, so that it—God's Word—might hold sway . . . The Church structure of the Synod should not be erected as a rule alongside of and ultimately over the Word of God but the entire structure of the Synod must serve the one and only rule of the Word of God. (Pieper, p. 40-41)

Our increasing dependence upon handbooks, bylaws, and human regulations is indicative of our decreasing dependence upon and confidence in the Word of God. Pieper warns that the cry for ever stronger government within the Church and greater power for Church officials is symptomatic of a fundamental misunderstanding of the Church's nature and purpose. He noted that this misunderstanding has led to *a long line of false Church governments from the papacy to the American Synods with legislative powers.* (Pieper, p. 45)

Institutional conservatism leads to legalism, coercion, and endless struggles for denominational power. At the same time, it stifles the confessional impulse and turns our attention inward upon ourselves and our own intramural battles. The fathers of our Synod were confessional ecumenists — without any of the unsavory connotations which attach to the concept of ecumenism today. Their aversion to unionism and Syncretism is renown. Their unwillingness to compromise or water down Lutheran doctrine was absolute. Yet they maintained a lively awareness of and interest in theological developments throughout Lutheranism and Christendom. They were ready and eager to break new ground in finding ways for substantive doctrinal discussion — constantly pursuing opportunities to offer the good confession. They founded Church publications like *Der Lutheraner* and *Lehre und Wehre* in which doctrine was fearlessly, forthrightly, and constantly discussed. They organized free conferences and anticipated in theological discussions throughout the United States. They were initiators and innovators, aggressively advancing the faith once de-

209

livered to the saints. They recognized that their confessional obligation did not allow them to withdraw into their own parochial little world. They were also fully cognizant of the fact that the history of Christendom did not begin in 1847 and that they were part of a broad stream of orthodox teaching and practice that stretched back across the centuries.

In my personal experience that attitude of confessional ecumenism was uniquely personified by Dr. Robert Preus — in an unshakable commitment to the historic doctrine of Lutheranism— in a worldwide vision that spanned continents and denominational boundaries with a resolve to confess the truth of God. When a question of doctrine or practice was posed to Dr. Preus, the answer never came in the form of legalistic hairsplitting or diplomatic doubletalk — the answer was always theology, pure, powerful, wonderful theology. Our Synod's disgraceful treatment of this great man of God — that which was done and that which was tolerated— is a profoundly tragic illustration of the difference between confessionalism and institutional conservatism. As Missouri celebrates her 150th anniversary, the distinction is one we would do well to ponder.

C. Cultural Disengagement

I would like to briefly address one final challenge which confronts us as confessional Lutherans today. Unlike the others which have been discussed, this challenge comes not from inside the Church but from the culture in which we live.

The failure of the Lutheran Church in Germany to recognize and oppose the evil of National Socialism is a tragedy that has done much to discredit Lutheranism in the eyes of the world. The popular myth, endlessly repeated, is that this failure was the direct result of the Lutheran doctrine of the two kingdoms. The falsehood of that myth should be evident to anyone who actually understands Lutheran theology. The specific demonstration of that falsehood is beyond the scope of today's presentation. For us it must suffice to listen again to the words of Dr. Hermann Sasse, one of the few who courageously opposed Hitler and his henchmen from the very beginning. Sasse's opposition to Nazism is all the more significant in that it was explicitly confessional.

It was Sasse's contention, that not Lutheran theology, but a Lutheran Church which had watered down and abandoned its theology, which fell prey to Nazism.

No, it was not Lutheranism as such, but a sick Lutheranism that gave National Socialism an open door into the Church. It was a Lutheran Church which was no longer capable of standing guard over the souls of its people because it had fallen asleep itself. It had lost its power over demons because it no longer possessed the power of distinguishing between "spirits". . . We have noble families in which the grandfathers were conservative and confessional Lutherans; the fathers were German nationalists and members of the Union Church; and the sons are members of the SS. (Hermann Sasse, p. 50, 51)

It is, of course, a great deal easier to look back over 60 years of history and condescendingly conclude what people should have done then than it is to decide what we ought to be doing now surrounding by bewildering and often contradictory trends within our own culture. Be that as it may, the negative experience of German Lutheranism ought to at least indicate the peril of confessional disengagement from the culture in which we live. I would submit to you that recognition of and response to trends within the culture is an important part of our confessional obligation. The Lutheran doctrine of the two kingdoms affirms the Lordship of God over every dimension of human life while insisting that God has chosen to rule differently within the two kingdoms. In the kingdom of the left hand, the political realm, He rules by reason and the sword. In the kingdom of the right hand, the spiritual realm, He rules by the power of His Word.

We live in a culture that is self-destructing— reverting to barbarism and chaos. The most basic standards of human decency are being cast aside in the mindless pursuit of the immediate gratification of our every desire. Violence fills our streets because we lack the moral will to distinguish between right and wrong and then to appropriately punish the wrongdoer. We sanction the vilest perversion as acceptable alternate lifestyle while pestilence stalks the land. At the festering core of the moral disease which infects America is the horror of abortion. Over 4,000 innocent unborn children are slaughtered every day in a 24 year long holocaust that makes Hitler look like a humanitarian.

Luther rightly teaches that God established civil government to *bind the devil's hands* and restrain the rampant destructiveness of sin. The devil is running loose among us, wreaking havoc on every side. A confessional Church and her pastors must clearly identify the false gods who summon our people to bow down before them every day of their lives. Confessional preaching does not come in the form of safely vague pious platitudes. When we speak to these issues, we do so not as political agitators or social reformers, but as faithful servants of the Lord Jesus Christ. To withdraw into the comfortable isolation of our padded pews is a denial of our nature as confessional Lutherans.

Dietrich Bonhoeffer, another Lutheran—although not nearly so confessional as Hermann Sasse —bitterly denounced his Church for its failure to rise to the challenge of the times. Writing in 1940, at the height of Nazi power and military success, Bonhoeffer said:

The Church must confess that she has not proclaimed often or clearly enough her message of the one God who had revealed Himself for all time in the person of Jesus Christ and who will tolerate no other gods beside Himself...She must confess her timidity, her evasiveness, her dangerous concessions. . . She was silent when she should have cried out because the blood of the innocent was crying not raised her voice on behalf of the victims and has not found ways to hasten to their aid. She is guilty of the deaths of the weakest and most defenseless brothers of the Lord Jesus Christ . . . The Church must confess that she has desired security, peace and quiet, possessions and honor... She has not borne witness to the truth of God. . .By her own silence she has rendered herself guilty of a failure to accept responsibility and to bravely defend a just cause. She has been un-

willing to suffer for what she knows to be right. Thus, the Church is guilty of becoming a traitor to the Lordship of Christ. (Bonhoeffer, pp. 113-115)

Those grim words could have been written today. They ought to sear the conscience of every Christian in America.

IV. Conclusion

In conclusion, we return to the question with which we began. What does it mean to be a Lutheran today. It means what it has always meant—in 1530, 1847, 1934, and 1997. To be a Lutheran means to offer the good confession. It means to proclaim the Gospel of salvation. It means to defend the truth of God's Word and to contend for the faith once delivered to the saints. It is our heartfelt prayer that God may bless us and our Church that by His grace we may rise to meet the challenge of these days, and thus may be worthy of that most honorable name—Lutheran—today.

Sources:

Bonhoeffer, Dietrich, Ethics. New York, Macmillian Publishing Company, 1979.

Herman, Stewart, W. *The Rebirth of the German Church,* New York: Harper and Brothers Publishers, 1946.

Horton, Michael. *Made in America — The Shaping of Modern American Evangelicalism.* Grand Rapids: Baker Book House, 1991.

Pieper, Franz. *Kirche und Kirchenregiment — Dreiundzwamigster Synodal Bericht der Allgemeinen deutschen ev. luth. Synode von Missouri, Ohio und andern Staaten.* St. Louis: Concordia Publishing House, 1896.

Sasse, Hermann. *Here We Stand.* New York: Harper and Brothers Publishers, 1938.

Schmauk, Theodore. *The Confessional Principle and the Confessions of the Lutheran Church.* Philadelphia: The General Council Publication Board, 1911.

Scholder, Klaus. The *Churches and the Third Reich, Volume II* Philadelphia: Fortress Press, 1988.

Teigen, Erling. *Confessional or Conservative — The Confessional Principle and Church Fellowship* published in A *Call to Confessional Faithfulness and Understanding.* Brooklyn Center, Minnesota: The Lutheran Church of the Triune God, 1993.

Wells, *David. No Place for Truth.* Grand Rapids: William B. Eerdmans Publishing Company, 1992.

Questions for Study

1. Sasse was convinced that the history of the Lutheran Church in Germany was coming _____ .
2. Sasse was a determined foe of _____ .
3. Lutheranism was also threatened by _____ .
4. The Lutheran Reformation was a discovery of _____ .
5. The Lutheran theologian acknowledges that he belongs to ____.
6. The Lutheran Church was born out of ____.

7. The Lutheran Church is the confessional Church ____.
8. The Evamgelical Lutheran Church which is faithful to its Confessions is truly the ____.
9. The Gospel does not and cannot ____.
10. What doctrine opens the door to the whole Bible?____
11. The most important thing to know in Christianity is the distinction between ____.
12. For Calvin and his heirs, Christ is not only a Savior but also a____.
13. What threatens to swallow up Lutheran and Calvinist, liberal and conservative alike? ____
14. What is the Church Growth Movement? ____
15. What has proven to be irrestively attractive even to conservative Lutherans? ____
16. Confessionalism in distinction to conservatism is ____.
17. The entire structure of the Synod must serve ____.
18. The increasing dependence upon bylaws, and human regulations is indicative of ____.
19. Institutional conservatism leads to ____.
20. The fathers of the LCMS were ____ ecumenists.
21. What is the tragic illustration of the difference between confessional and institutional conservatism? ____
22. We live in a culture that is ____.
23. What makes Hitler look like a humanitarian ____.
24. What does it mean to be Lutheran today? ____

§

THE LONELY WAY

Christian News, February 11, 2002

The Lonely Way — Selected Essays and Letters. **Hermann Sasse. Volume 1 (1927-1939). St. Louis: Concordia Publishing House, 63118. 2002. 502 pages.**

The back cover of *The Lonely Way* says:
"This is a book by a pastor for all of God's people. While Hermann Sasse became an eminent theologian, he always remained a pastor at heart. His theological writings — and these include many circular letters to pastors — are always concerned with issues relevant to the parish pastor and his flock.

"All Christian readers will appreciate Sasse's lively and engaging style plus the depth of his theological insight. Reading Sasse is like reading Luther." Among the many issues treated here are the office of the ministry, the centrality of the Lord's Supper, the nature of the true Church, and ecumenical relations. These issues are often thorny, as Sasse said in 1943:

As Luther once went *the lonely way* between Rome and Spiritualism, so the Lutheran Church today stands alone between the world powers of Roman Catholicism on the one hand and modern Protestantism on the other. Her doctrine which teaches that the Spirit is bound to the means of grace is as inconceivable to modern people in the twentieth century as it was to their predecessors in the sixteenth.

"The straight and narrow way is always less traveled, but Sasse would remind us that our Lord Jesus Christ is present with us at every step."

Matthew C. Harrison writes in the translators preface:

As much as he criticized Rome, Hermann Sasse envied the Roman Catholic Church's sense of time. On a trip to Rome he stopped to visit Augustin Cardinal Bea. Sasse was apologetic for taking the cardinal's time with such a visit. Bea responded, "I always have time, only no time to waste."

It seems to Sasse that the Lutheran Churches of the world were always rushing matters, establishing dogma without proper historical and exegetical deliberation. And Sasse was witness to more than a few such decisions, such as the Barmen Declaration, which ultimately compromised the confession of the Church. On the other hand, it was the corrective of a broad perspective of dogma through the ages which Sasse, throughout his career, strove to give the Church. His message was always urgent but never faithless, for he was convinced that the Church has a future because Jesus Christ has a future.

Sasse's perspective is needed in the Church today. It certainly was helpful to me as a pastor. As a young and eager seminary graduate, I headed off to my first parish, St. Peter's Lutheran, Westgate, Iowa. In my own struggles to bridge the gap between zealous orthodoxy and wise pastoral practice, Sasse became a godsend, the single most influential literary resource for the molding of my own pastoral practice. Sasse helped me move from talking about the Gospel to delivering it. Sasse taught me what there is no contradiction between confessional Lutheran fidelity and true ecumenicity. Sasse made it all so profoundly simple, concrete, and practical.

At the seminary my dear father in Christ, Professor Kurt Marquart, had introduced many of us to Sasse, who had been his own colleague, father in Christ, and confessional Lutheran mentor during Marquart's Australian years. I then spent a year studying at Sasse's seminary (years after his death) and read every bit of Sasse I could get hold of in my STM studies at Concordia Theological Seminary in Fort Wayne, I delved into Sasse's German. So I developed the habit of translating several pages of Sasse's work nearly every day over the course of a four-year pastorate in a little Iowa farming village. This I continued, albeit less regularly, as I continued my pastoral ministry at Zion Lutheran Church, Fort Wayne.

Through all of these studies and pastorates, Sasse provided perspective. His sweeping historical-dogmatic treatises, at once utterly orthodox and truly ecumenical, gave me doctrinal confidence, confessional depth,

214

and historical sensibility as I dealt not only with my own people, but also with the clergy and laity of other denominations. All of what I was reading in Sasse, like the Lutheran Confessions themselves, emphasized the point of all orthodox dogma and practice as loving pastoral care. Sasse's breadth helped provide a very young and inexperienced pastor with what he sorely needed to be a true pastor of Christ's people: Confessional fidelity and patience.

There is a long history to the Church's dogma and practice. Where that dogma and practice have gone awry, only patient teaching and loving practice can possibly right it again, and this only as God grants by his grace. Entire eras have their movements and weaknesses and inabilities to perceive the truth of this or that reality of NT and confessional Lutheran Christianity. In such eras the faithful pastor must have the biblical and historical tools to be able to recognize the circumstances in which he finds himself, to diagnose the malady, and then patiently to meet the challenge, leaving the results to Christ.

The Sasse essays included in this first volume were profoundly influential to me in all the aspects I have mentioned. Many of these papers were written in the white-hot heat of the *Kirchenkampf*— the struggle of the Church under Nazism. And if Sasse could maintain such confessional fidelity, evident ecumenical spirit, and faithful confidence in the Lord of the Church, even under Hitler, then I could patiently meet the challenge of lovingly standing firm in the comparatively meager challenges I faced in the parish.

In June of 2000 I visited the grave of Sasse on the south side of the city of Adelaide, South Australia. The stone bears this epitaph: *Tuis fidelibus Domine, vita non tollitur, sed mutatur* ("For your faithful, O Lord, life is not taken away, it is changed"). He had chosen the words himself. Hermann Otto Eric Sasse was taken to be with Christ in 1976. We rejoice now that far from being taken away from the Church which he so loved, Sasse's voice now continues to live, even if changed by translation through this publication. And it just may be that Sasse's voice will be heard today for the cause of confessional Lutheranism to a far greater extent than ever before. Such posthumous service is all the more meaningful and appreciated in light of what was for him most often a very "lonely way."

My heartfelt appreciation to the many that have in many different ways made this project a reality. Ron Feuerhahn has for over a decade now been a dear friend, mentor, and *Amtsbruder*. He has provided us all with an invaluable wealth of information on Sasse, and happily, he kindly consented to continue to do so for this volume. Sincere thanks also to Dr. Norman Nagel for his decades of interest in Sasse and for his constant encouragement. I am deeply thankful to and for my dear brother in Christ Paul McCain, whose enthusiasm for reading fresh translations of Sasse has never flagged. He made time to edit some of the essays of this work and approached the Marvin M. Schwan Charitable Foundation for a grant. My sincere thanks to the Schwan Foundation for enabling us to produce, at reasonable cost to the reader, this volume and the second

215

which will soon follow. And here too I must thank our sainted President A. L. Barry for his support for the project. May his legacy of confessional fidelity endure like Sasse's. I heartily thank the others who gladly provided translations for this volume: Maurice Schild, Lowell Green, Gerald Krispin, Robert Bugbee, and John Stephenson. The capable staff at CPH has been a pure pleasure to work with, especially Fritz Baue, who has guided this project through the long process of publication, and Julene Dumit, who meticulously copy-edited the manuscript. I should be remiss were I to fail to mention the constant companionship and strength I received from one Kathy Harrison, the greatest single First Article gift of my life. Though the many essays of this book look toward the past, they do so with the intent of building a bridge to the future of a confessional Lutheran Church, and that for the sake of my dear sons, Matthew M. L. and Mark M. C. Harrison, as well as generations to come.

Translating is challenging business. Thankfully, Sasse's German is straightforward. Others have checked the translation here and there, but I shall not mention their names so that responsibility for any deficiencies, and I am sure there are plenty, falls squarely in my lap. Those who actually knew and heard Sasse will find my translations less than true to Sasse's own unique literary and oral style. I plead the indulgence of such brothers. I never knew or heard the man. That stated, I should like to dedicate this volume of translations to the Reverends Bruce Adams, John Kleinig, Andrew Pfeiffer, Avito DaCosta, David Buck, and Mark Hampel (all beloved brothers in Christ) and to the entire ministerium of the Lutheran Church of Australia. The way may be lonely, but *ne desperemus!* The Lord still prays for his Church.

* * *

Like Luther and Walther

Concordia Seminary, St. Louis, Professor Ronald Feuerhahn writes in a biographical sketch that "For depth of insight and clarity of expression, Sasse is like Luther and Walther."

Feuerhahn notes:

"Instead, the formation of the *Evangelische Kirche in Deutschland* was a great disappointment for him. In his view it suffered the same misconception as Barmen: It was the triumph of unconfessional Barthian ecclesiology.

"The Erlangen professor finally withdrew, resigning his post as *Ordinarius* (full professor) and his membership of the Bavarian Church. He joined the *Evangelisch-lutherische (altlutherische) Kirche,* an independent or 'free' Church which had formed in reaction to the Prussian Union. A day (literally, hours) before receiving a call to Concordia Seminary, St. Louis, he accepted the call of the United Evangelical Lutheran Church of Australia (UELCA) to be professor of Church history at its Immanuel Seminary (later renamed Luther Seminary), North Adelaide, Australia. He was installed in this new office on October 12, 1949" (19).

"Once Sasse moved to the English-speaking world, he discovered a lacuna in his theological work — the doctrine of the sacred Scriptures. He devoted himself to that study more and more in this period.

It would prove to be one cf— if not *the*— most controversial subjects in his work. It became a work in process. *Brief* number 14, 'On the Doctrine *de Scriptura Sacra*' (August 1950) was so controversial that it was the only writing which Sasse withdrew.

"His personal correspondence was voluminous. He wrote Church presidents (e.g., John W. Behnken of The Lutheran Church-Missouri Synod), university professors (e.g., Leiv Aalen, Oslo), seminary professors (e.g., F. E. Mayer, St. Louis), pastors, and students. One of the most remarkable exchanges was that with a young pastor and graduate student in Sweden, Tom Hardt. Between the first exchange in 1958 until Sasse's death in 1976 Sasse wrote almost weekly.

"Sasse developed friendships with many churchmen in Australia and became honorary president of the Inter-Varsity Christian Fellowship. He was a member of the committee in dialog with the Roman Catholic Church in Australia and was invited to the Vatican by Augustin Cardinal Bea. An extensive correspondence followed, especially with Bea's secretary, Father Schmidt. Some have conjectured that Sasse's intense interest in the Roman Church was due to the fact that his younger son, Hans, converted to Roman Catholicism in Adelaide. In addition, Sasse maintained close contact with The Lutheran Church-Missouri Synod, especially with its Springfield (now Fort Wayne) seminary, which awarded him an honorary doctorate on January 20, 1967. The following sentence from the citation on that occasion gives a good summary of his life: 'Dr. Sasse is recognized as one of the outstanding leaders of confessional Lutheranism in the modern Ecumenical Movement.'

"Most of those who encountered this man were never quite comfortable unless they were willing and able to hear his call of repentance to the Church: For conservative Lutherans as well as liberal Protestants, Hermann Sasse was a voice of catholic Christianity. He had a particular talent for 'opening up new perspectives and offering penetrating insight'" (21).

The LCMS

Here are a few statements from Sasse in *The Lonely Way*:

"There is in America perhaps no more active Church than the Missouri Synod, which is the most dogmatically rigorous Lutheran Church in the country. The history of the organization of this Church demonstrates that Lutheranism can exist in forms other than a state Church or a Church dependent upon the state (as we hear happily repeated time and again in Europe). Lutheranism is never more vibrant than where it is free from all guardianship by a secular authority" (55).

"*Only Lutheranism can pose the question of truth over against the Roman Catholic Church* [emphasis added]. For it belongs to the essence of Lutheranism to raise the claim to truth, not for a human authority, for an infallible teaching office, rather for the *Verbum Dei* ['Word of God'], which it possesses. It acknowledges that every Church possesses the truth in so far as the Word of God is present. The greatness and uniqueness of the Lutheran concept of the Church is in this connection between its view of the Church and its view of the Word of God.

"The difference, however, over against the Fundamentalist fellowship is in the view of the Word of God. The Fundamentalists too pose the question of truth over against all Churches on the basis of their strict biblicism. But what a difference there is between their view of the Bible, which elevates the letter of the Bible to law for human thought and dealings, and the Lutheran doctrine of the Word of God! Over against the mechanism and clandestine materialism of that way of explaining the Bible stands genuine Lutheran theology as something completely different. Lutheranism conceives of the Word of God as something more living, because it considers it first as the spoken and incarnate Word, and only secondly as the written Word" (55-56).

The Social Doctrine of the Augsburg Confession

"The basic concept of the Lutheran social doctrine is the clear *separation of the world and the kingdom of God* in the sense of Christ's words: 'My kingdom is not of this world' [John 18:36]. Thus Lutheranism is opposed to any attempt to draw the kingdom of God into this world, be it the attempt of the Roman Church *to ecclesiasticize the world* or the attempt of fanaticism and Protestantism influenced by fanaticism *to Christianize the world*. The Roman Church too knows of the difference between the world and the kingdom of God, and in its doctrine of natural law it speaks of state and government and authority very often in a manner similar to old Lutheranism, which to a great extent took over Roman ecclesiastical traditions. But because the Roman Church asserted the lordship of Christ — and that means for it the lordship of the Papal Church — over all areas of life, because it subordinated the state to the Church, the apparent ecclesiasticizing of the world became in reality, a secularization of the Church. That is the great doctrine of medieval Europe" (96).

The Church and the Word of God

"Over against both opponents the Churches of the Reformation have emphatically asserted that any alleged revelation which goes beyond the Scriptures goes beyond Christ, who is the truth in person, and thus is no revelation, rather illusion. Nor can John 16:12-13 be cited in this regard. All the great heresies of ancient (Montanus, Mani, Muhammad) and modern times have done this. Where the Word of Scripture has been forsaken by proceeding beyond it, there the unadulterated office of proclamation has also been lost. But then that which is preached does not long remain the revealed Word of God. For the revealed Word, the proclaimed Word, and the written Word of God are only forms of the one unique Word, in which God has revealed himself to humanity and upon which the Church is founded" (158).

Church Government and Secular Authority

"In order to avoid any possible misunderstanding, let it be firmly stated here that neither Luther nor the Lutheran Confessions know anything of a 'Christian state.' Such would be a state which as state confesses

Christianity and sees in Christendom one of its fundamental elements, so that it necessarily is of the *essence* of its governing authority that it be Christian. In distinction from the theocratic view of Zwingli, who bound the authority of the governing authority to its Christian faith and consented to the overthrow of the governing authority in the event that it was no longer obedient to the commands of Christ,* the Lutheran Confessions expressly teach that the confession of faith does not change the character of governing authority as such: The Gospel does not introduce any new laws about the civil estate, but commands us to obey the existing laws, whether they are formulated by heathen or by others" ('Nec fert evangelium novas leges de statu civili, sed praecipit, ut praesentibus legibus obtemperemus, sive ab ethnicis sive ab aliis conditae sint,' Ap XVI 3 [55]; the English translation is from Tappert, BC, 222-23). *[In support of his statement about Zwingli, Sasse cited this:] 'But if it is untrue or exceeds the bounds of Christ, it may be overthrown with [the help of] God' (*Schlussreden,* 42, in Muller, *Bekenntnisschriften,* 5, 4). HS" (203 footnote 43).

Study Questions

1. While Sasse became an eminent theologian, he always remained ____.
2. Reading Sasse is like reading ____.
3. The Barmen Decleration ultimately compromised ____.
4. Who introduced many to Sasse ____ .
5. The grave stone of Sasse says that____ .
6. How does Sasse's voice continue today ____.
7. Who approached the Schwan Foundation for a grant to publish Sasse's writings ____.
8. Sasse became honorary president of ____.
9. Sasse's son Hans converted to ____.
10. What belongs to the essence of Lutheranism? ____
11. Lutheranism is opposed to any attempts to ____.
12. Neither Luther nor the Lutheran Confessions know anything of a ____.

§

SASSE'S VOICE

Christian News, February 11, 2013

This issue includes "The Lutheran Church-Missouri Synod's President Explains Why Hermann Sasse is an Important Voice Today," (p. 1), by Paul McCain of CPH. It is an interview with LCMS President Matthew Harrison.

Christian News may have been the first publication in the U.S. to give Sasse's writings wide publicity. Some of the Sasse writings *CN* published are in *A Christian Handbook on Vital Issues* and *The Christian News Encyclopedia.*

The *CN* editor met Sasse in San Francisco in 1959 where Sasse was a key speaker at an LCMS convention and theological convocation prior to the convention. After discussing the theology being taught by various liberal professors at Concordia Seminary, St. Louis with Sasse and the president of the Australia Lutheran Church and the president of this Church's Queensland District, they spoke with LCMS President John W. Behnken. Behnken invited Otten to meet with him in his office in St. Louis. He showed Otten a call he had received from the Queensland District in Australia asking for Herman Otten. Behnken urged Otten to get certified by the seminary. The president of the LCMS's Western District also told Otten he would get him a call to a congregation in his district which would pay far more than the $150 a month he was receiving from Trinity, New Haven. All Otten had to do to get certified, the LCMS leaders told him, was to say that all the professors at the seminary were teaching sound Lutheran doctrine and that he had not told the truth when he reported to Behnken and others that there were liberals teaching at the St. Louis Seminary who maintained Moses did not write the Pentateuch, evolution is OK, Adam and Eve are not historical, man does not have an immortal soul, and there are no direct rectilinear messianic prophecies in the Bible. When Otten refused to say all the professors were orthodox, Sasse came to Otten's defense. Sasse knew that Otten had told the truth about theological liberalism being tolerated at the St. Louis seminary. Behnken, after he retired, similarly recognized Otten had told the truth.

When Sasse's *The Lonely Way*, a collection of essays and letters edited by Harrison, was published, the February 11, 2002 *CN* published much of Harrison's translator's preface. Harrison mentions that "my dear father in Christ, Professor Kurt Marquart, had introduced many of us to Sasse." Harrison spent a year studying at Sasse's seminary years after Sasse's death. In the year 2000 Harrison visited the grave of Sasse in Australia. He says "I am deeply thankful to and for my dear brother in Christ, Paul McCain, whose enthusiasm for reading fresh translations of Sasse has never flagged. He made time to edit some of the essays of this work and approached the Marvin M. Schwan Foundation for a grant." Harrison wrote: "The capable staff at CPH has been a pleasure to work with, especially Fritz Baue." *CN* then published statements by Sasse in *The Lonely Way*. Reproduced in this issue is "We Shall Miss Him," from the August 30, 1976 *Christian News,* published at the time of Sasse's death, and "In Defense of Sasse," from the February 11, 2002 *Christian News* when *The Lonely Way* appeared.

Study Questions
1. When and where did Otten first meet Sasse? ____
2. Sasse knew that Otten told the truth about ____.
3. Who introduced Harrison to Sasse? ____
4. Who financed the writings of Sasse's published by CPH?____

§

HERMANN SASSE REJECTED ABSOLUTE SCRIPTURAL INERRANCY?
From RPDigest, February, 2002
Christian News, February 11, 2002

The "Questions and Answers" section of the Wisconsin Evangelical Lutheran Synod's website, http://www.wels.net, just added one on long-deceased German theologian Hermann Sasse, to-wit, "What is the WELS position on the writings of Hermann Sasse? Are they worthwhile for a WELS layperson?

"There is much that we can admire in the writings of Hermann Sasse (1895-1976) and some things we can't. The Wisconsin Lutheran Quarterly, the theological journal produced by our Wisconsin Lutheran Seminary, printed some of his articles a half century ago. However, in time, it became apparent that Sasse differed with our synod on the inspiration of Scripture and Church fellowship.

Sasse rejected the absolute inerrancy of Scripture. His doctrine of inspiration allowed for factual errors in the Bible in things that do not pertain to faith. His doctrine left room for human weaknesses and errors on the part of the biblical writers.

He believed that differing doctrines of inspiration and inerrancy were not to be divisive of fellowship."

Interim Concordia Publishing House Chief Executive Officer Paul T. McCain is recommending that a newly translated book of Sasse's writings into English be purchased for Valentine's Day.

Study Question
1. The Wisconsin Evangelical Lutheran Synod said that "Sasse differed with our Synod on _____."

§

"Here We Stand" pg. 55
- HERMANN SASSE
Christian News, August 2, 2004

"A religious teaching with which a whole nation agrees— perhaps, enthusiastically—certainly has nothing to do with the Word of God. For this Word speaks of a 'sign which is rejected.' Consequently, the bitter struggle over the Gospel, which began in Germany, did not alarm Luther.

221

On the contrary, the vehemence with which the controversy was carried on served him as evidence that the powerful and living Word of God, before which the spirits parted, was operative. Hence he could say that 'it is most cheering to see parties, dissension, and discord arises because of the divine Word.' It was not that he derived pressure from discord itself. He, too, shared the feeling which the Evangelicals expressed when they declared that 'God, who is the Ruler of all hearts, knows that we find no pleasure or joy in this frightful discord.' But unity can never be purchased with a lie, nor can discord ever be eliminated by sacrificing the truth of the Gospel."

Study Question
1. Discord can never be _____ by sacrificing the _____ ."

§

LOGIA – BONHOEFFER – SASSE

Christian News, November 19, 2012

Dear Rev. Otten,
Just read an interesting article in Logia Reformation 2012 titled "Bonhoeffer and Sasse as Confessor and Churchmen: The Bethel Confession and its intended but unfulfilled purpose" by Rev. David Jay Webber. Have you read this article? If you don't have a copy, I'll make you one. I thought Dietrich came out looking pretty good. What did you think?

Got a laugh out of a quote by Sasse (pg. 10). "The longer he (Bonhoeffer) lived the more Lutheran he became."

I think you met Dr. Sasse in San Francisco in 1965. Did he say anything to you about Bonhoeffer?

God Bless

- - - - - - - - - - - - - - - - - - -

November 9 , 2012
Brother:
Please send the article on Sasse you mention. I did meet Sasse in S.F. in 1959 and have a good number of personal letters from him. We did not discuss Bonhoeffer, who at one time worked with Sasse but then they parted. Sasse opposed his liberal theology. Read what is in my *Bonhoeffer and King* about Sasse, check the index. Logia and so far other publications and blogs which praise Bonhoeffer have refused to review *Bonhoeffer and King*. It clearly shows that Bonhoeffer in his last writing opposed historic Christianity and such doctrines as the physical resurrection of

Christ.

The November 5 *CN* reviewed "The collected Sermons of Dietrich Bonhoeffer" just published by ELCA's Fortress. Note what Bonhoeffer writes about fairy tales and legends in the Bible, among them the creation account in Genesis and the raising of Lazarus. I know of no confessional Lutheran who has actually read *Bonhoeffer and King* who still defends their theology.

God's richest blessings,
Herman Otten

Study Question
1. Bonhoeffer in his last writings opposed _____ .

§

THE LUTHERAN CHURCH—MISSOURI SYNOD'S PRESIDENT EXPLAINS WHY HERMANN SASSE IS AN IMPORTANT VOICE TO HEAR TODAY

Christian News, February 11, 2013
From Cyberbrethren: A Lutheran Blog
By Paul McCain

The following is an interview with Matthew C. Harrison addressing the importance of Hermann Sasse and his Letters to Pastors to the current life of the Church. The book is also available in Kindle eBook format.

Until the end of World War II, Sasse was a pastor and professor in Germany; then he emigrated to Australia, where he served as a professor at Immanuel Seminary in South Australia. He came out of a very liberal education prior to the end of World War I, but gradually and decisively turned toward confessional Lutheranism. Sasse was very active in the ecumenical movement before he was forbidden to travel by the Nazis. He was the first in the German Church to publicly take the Nazis to task for the "Aryan paragraph" in the party platform. Sasse contributed to Kittel's *Dictionary of the New Testament* and wrote the greatest book in English on Luther's doctrine of the Lord's Supper (*This Is My Body: Luther's Contention for the Real Presence in the Sacrament of the Altar*). He fought tirelessly for solid Lutheran-ism. When his own Church, the Bavarian Church, joined a union of Lutherans and Reformed Churches (the Evangelische Kirche in Deutschland [Evangelical Church in Germany or EKiD]), Sasse joined the German free Church. Ultimately he left Germany to teach at the seminary of the Lutheran Church of Australia. He

223

spent the rest of his life writing public letters, books, and treatises rally-ing confessional Lutherans around the world and rousing particularly The Lutheran Church—Missouri Synod (LCMS) just as it was drifting from its historic confession. He died in 1976.

Describe the relationship between Sasse and the LCMS. Why are his writings of importance for the ongoing life of the Church?

Sasse saw the LCMS as the "last hope" for world confessional Lutheranism. Yet post-World War II Missouri Synod (and particularly the seminary in St. Louis) was bent on a path of Lutheran union in the United States. Sasse believed the danger to the LCMS was either a confessionless entry into the Ecumenical Movement and the loss of doctrinal substance, or evangelical fundamentalism. His writings are largely historical/doctrinal treatises on pertinent topics of world Christianity and Lutheranism that apply even in our day. LCMS President John Behnken (1884–1968, president 1935–62) very much wanted Sasse to teach at Concordia Seminary, St. Louis, but the administration of the seminary was strongly opposed.

What was the genesis of the group of documents gathered together as *Letters to Pastors*? Who received these letters and how were they communicated more broadly?

In 1948, Sasse wrote to Herman A. Preus: "The only thing I can do is write letters." As he was preparing to enter self-imposed exile in Australia, Sasse began writing treatises on what it means to be a confessional Lutheran, commenting on basic issues of Bible and confession, the Lord's Supper, Church fellowship, Baptism, the Office of the Ministry, Church governance, Luther's teachings, and much more. The letters, written in German, were dispersed in mimeographed form in the early years by Sasse's friend Rev. F. Hopf, who had remained in Germany. Americans began translating the letters immediately. Now, for the first time, we have translated all seventy letters and are publishing them in a series of three volumes.

There is great controversy surrounding a couple of the letters in this volume. Why publish them?

Upon his arrival in Australia, Sasse was immediately placed on a committee working toward the unification of the country's two Lutheran bodies (one associated with the American Lutheran Church and the other with the LCMS). The issue of Scripture, its inspiration and inerrancy, was central in the discussions. Sasse had studied under the most notorious liberal of the late nineteenth and early twentieth centuries—Adolf von Harnack. While Sasse had moved far away from Harnack's rejection of all the supernatural content of the Bible, when Sasse wrote "Letter 14" and then "Letter 16", he was convinced that the inerrancy of the Bible did not include all issues addressed, but only issues of faith and belief. There was a tremendous backlash, and eventually Sasse retracted "Letter 14". However, many in the LCMS who were arguing against absolute inerrancy and for higher criticism picked up on this letter in particular. I have included these significant letters along with other supporting doc-

224

umentation so readers can see that Sasse moved significantly on the issue, and so readers can see, in part, what was at stake in the great battle for the Bible in the LCMS. At the same time, Sasse's concern that the Missouri Synod might lose a fundamentally Lutheran view of Scripture and Church because of its participation in America's evangelical/Protestant context remained a real concern. Although we must disagree with Sasse at this point in his career, we can also see the validity of his concern.

How do you hope this volume will benefit the Church?

Sasse is tremendously lucid. He is a profound Lutheran historian. Jumping on his back, as it were, gives one a tour of the 2,000-year history of the Church. He's clear. He's scriptural. He calls for repentance and faith. He's courageous. At times he's a curmudgeon. He often says what is unpopular, though he says it in a gentle and generous manner. He's uncompromisingly Lutheran yet sees what is good in other Churches. Sasse touches on so many of the issues that challenge us today: the Office of the Ministry, the priesthood of believers, relationships with other Church bodies, closed Communion, understanding the Roman Catholic Church, mission/evangelism, theological education, and so much more. Through it all, Sasse brings us back to basics, to the very Gospel itself.

Study Questions
1. Sasse came out of a very liberal ____ prior to the end of WWI.
2. Sasse fought tirelessly for ____ .
3. When did Sasse die? _____ .
4. LCMS President John W. Behnken wanted Sasse to teach at_____.
5. Who used Sasse retracted "Letter 14"?_____ .
6. Sasse brings us back to _____ .

§

THE *BRIEF STATEMENT* AND INERRANCY IN DEFENSE OF SASSE

Christian News, February 11, 2013

The Lonely Way - Selected Essays and Letters, by Hermann Sasse is reviewed on page one of this issue.

The website of the Wisconsin Evangelical Lutheran Synod recently noted: "Sasse rejected the absolute inerrancy of Scripture. His doctrine of inspiration allowed for factual errors in the Bible in things that do not

225

pertain to faith. His doctrine left room for human weaknesses and errors on the part of the biblical writers. He believed that differing doctrine of inspiration and inerrancy were not divisive of Church fellowship."

"We Shall Miss Him," *CN*'s August 30, 1976, editorial at the time of Sasse's death reprinted here together with some letters Sasse wrote *CN* about this matter. They are in *CN*'s *Christian Handbook on Vital Issues*.

CN has enough letters Sasse wrote *CN* and articles Sasse sent to *CN* for a book. Some of them should be of far greater interest to LCMS pastors and laymen than some of the material in *The Lonely Way*. *CN* published a good number of Sasse's articles and a few of the letters he sent *CN*. Some of them are handwritten and are more of a personal nature. The editor probably has more letters from Sasse than most of the current hyper-euros who are now regularly quoting Sasse. As far as *CN* knows, few of them ever quote what Sasse said about *CN*. Nor do they mention that Sasse was a strong supporter of the editor and his congregation in their cases with Concordia Seminary, St. Louis and the Missouri District of the LCMS. Some want to know why the foundation which helped finance the publication of *The Lonely Way* would not finance publication of the material and letters Sasse sent *CN*.

The anti-Walther and pro-Loehe hyper-euros, who now try to use Sasse in their opposition to the LCMS's *Brief Statement*, are misrepresenting Sasse. The editor's congregation was one of those which promoted Resolution 9 of the LCMS's 1959 convention. This resolution backed the LCMS's *Brief Statement* and its binding nature. The editor spoke with Sasse in San Francisco in 1959. He was delighted that the convention reaffirmed the *Brief Statement*. This official LCMS statement, which the hyper-euros now oppose in part because the *Brief Statement* does not state that ordination is a sacrament, is in *The Christian News Encyclopedia*. Among other doctrines, it affirms the inerrancy of the Bible, the historicity of the Genesis account of creation, including, a six-day creation.

Sasse did express some misgivings about a few phrases in a *Brief Statement* and recognized the need of translating it into present day language. *CN* has often pleaded for a 20th and now 21st Century *Book of Concord* which covers the burning issues of our day. Sasse mentioned the *Brief Statement* in a letter he wrote to the editor on December 24, 1959: "As to Scharlemann's paper, I agree with you. It is very superficial and untenable, Anglican rather than Lutheran. I enclose our Theses on that question. This is mainly my work. I think the *Brief Statement*, written by Pieper 30 years ago, does not answer all of our questions and contains even such doubtful statements as that Adam had a perfect scientific knowledge of nature. It must be translated into the language of our time. But if Scharlemann has objections he the (?) way as indicated in San Francisco ...In the whole controversy I am on your side against Scharlemann and Piepkorn. It is a grave violence of Christian love to (?) the young student of Missouri. Your leaders know that grave mistakes have been made. I am just receiving the volume of documents. I am shocked by the treatment you had to undergo. Are you still being victimized?

226

Please let me know about your present position and your whole situation. If necessary I shall intervene with Dr. Behnken. You cannot be punished for the sins committed by Dr. Sieck. God bless you brother, I shall help as I can."

Dr. Louis Sieck was president of Concordia Seminary, St. Louis, when some liberals were called to the faculty. Dr. Martin Scharlemann, who was the *CN* editor's most outspoken opponent on the faculty, later changed his position. He affirmed the inerrancy of the Bible, and helped the editor with An American Translation of the Bible. He told the editor that he was withdrawing all charges against *CN* and would fight for the editor's certification. Dr. Ralph Bohlmann, however, blocked him and would not give him the opportunity to get the faculty to reverse its position. Dr. Sasse's letter of December 24, 1959, which comments on the *Brief Statement*, is photographed here for the Sasse scholars and those who maintain that he opposed the *Brief Statement*.

Dr. Ralph Gehrke, who is mentioned in Dr. Sasse's letter of June 17, 1967, is the translator of Dr. Sasse's *De Scriptura Sacra*. This is the essay Sasse withdrew. Gehrke was later found guilty of false doctrine after Pastor Walter Otten pressed a case against him for a good number of years. Gehrke is about the only LCMS liberal who was removed for doctrinal reasons. He had been a professor at Concordia, River Forest. Information about his case is in the *Christian News Encyclopedia*.

On February 22, 1970, at a testimonial banquet for *Christian News* at the Marriott Motor Hotel in Chicago, attended by some 850 Lutherans, keynote speaker Dr. Alvin Wagner, who had been a member of the LCMS's Commission on Theology, read a letter from Dr. Sasse where Sasse wrote: "Somebody should rise and thank Herman Otten for his brave fight." "Why was it left to a young man to speak where others should have spoken?" Wagner then said: "That from one of the world's ablest Lutheran scholars can hardly be tapped a REPUDIATION. It is APPROPRIATION of the highest order coming as it does from one of the keenest observers of the historical Church scene past and present. When he hears —as he undoubtedly will — that you the concerned of Illinois, did rise and publicly thank Herman Otten and his gifted wife Grace for their 'brave fight,' his heart will rejoice."

LCMS President Jacob Preus and the entire Council of Presidents in 1969 repudiated *Christian News*. *CN* was told that Preus was miffed that so many attended the banquet and heard what Wagner said.

Preus wanted to be known as the great hero who turned the LCMS around and back to theological orthodoxy. Preus later ordered *CN* to cease publication. He tried to destroy *CN* financially and did not want major donors to support *CN*.

One of the Greatest Confessors

The editor of *CN* concluded an essay he delivered to the 1988 convention of the Institute for Historical Review, where many non-Christians were gathered: "I commend to all revisionists and everyone else nothing more nor less than historic Christianity. God by 'raising Christ from the dead has given everyone a good reason to believe' (Acts 17:31).

"In spite of the many attempts to falsify history, the Christian Church has always struggled for the truth. This was true for the first Christians. It was also the basic issue of the Reformation. One of the greatest confessors of faith in this century, Dr. Hermann Sasse, who was also avidly anti-Nazi, points out in his book *Here We Stand* that the 'reformation emphasized the profound seriousness of the truth.'

"The subject of the holocaust is not my primary concern in life. It is not my main message. As stated in the masthead of the paper we founded and have served as editor for the past 26 years, we preach Jesus Christ and Him crucified. Nevertheless, Christians must not only strive to proclaim the saving Truth of the Gospel. We are obligated by this same Gospel to tell the truth in all areas of life, including events of politics, economics, war, and Church and secular government.

" 'These are the things which you should do: Speak the truth to one another; judge with truth and judgment for peace in your gates.' Zechariah 8:16." (*CNE*, p. 3990).

Dr. Sasse was among the orthodox theologians like William Oesch, Siegbert Becker, J.T. Mueller, Paul Burgdorf, David Hedegard and others who hoped *CN* would receive major financial support in order that it might reach more in the U. S. and other nations.

Dr. Sasse wrote to the editor of *CN* on October 7, 1974:

"Dear Brother Otten:

You may have wondered that you did not hear from me for so long a time. The reason is my state of health which made it almost impossible for me to attend to my correspondence. That little time I could spare was entirely taken up by my duties here — even an emeritus has to be a busy man — and by urgent theological work. But I must thank you for the Christian patience with which you took my silence.

"When you started your paper you could not anticipate what a tremendous work you were undertaking. Future generations only will be able to gauge the share you have had in the attempts to revive Lutheranism from its sleep. You will also find the recognition on the part of future Church historians who will have to write the sad chapter in the history of our Church.

"You had the freedom to speak out what the official Church paper — this refers to all papers in all Churches of our time — had not the freedom to say even if their editors wanted to tell the truth, the whole truth and nothing but the truth. Also you had not the *charisma numquam deficientis veritatis* on which the *theologia gloriae* of official Church papers rests. But you have never been ashamed to correct and retract what turned out to be untenable and even wrong. We all owe you a great lot of gratitude, hoping that the volume of collections which you have published will be followed by continuations."

Dr. Sasse was not the only oversees was theologian who supported *CN*. In Germany there was Dr. Wilhelm Oesch, in Sweden Dr. David Hedegard, and in Norway Dr. Carl Wislof. There were others in other countries.

"SPECIFICATION OF DOCTRINAL ISSUES" (pp. 12-13) was one of the documents in the Concordia Seminary, St. Louis vs. Otten case which the editor sent Dr. Sasse. Dr. Arthur Carl Piepkorn was the St. Louis professor who defended position B in the section on the doctrine on election. The editor had almost every undergraduate and graduate course Dr. Piepkorn taught. He took issue with Piepkorn's position on the historicity of Adam and Eve, the inerrancy of the Bible and the doctrine of election. Sasse did not agree with Piepkorn. Dr. Robert Preus and Dr. Albert Merkens accompanied the editor, at the request of LCMS President John W. Behnken, in some meetings with Dr. Piepkorn on the doctrine of election. Preus and Merkens agreed that the editor had correctly presented Piepkorn's position.

***

Lutheran Forum recently had some articles on Dr. Arthur Carl Piepkorn. *Lutheran Forum* should have published "The 25th Anniversary of a Conversation With Dr. Arthur Carl Piepkorn" by Rev. Carl Bornmann, which appeared in the July 13, 1998 *CN* and "Arthur Carl Piepkorn: R.I.P." which was published in the December 31, 1973, *CN* at the time of Piepkorn's death and reprinted in the July 13, 1998, *CN*. "Arthur Carl Piepkorn" in the July 13, 1998, *CN* noted: "...it appears to us that if Dr. Piepkorn was living today he would still much prefer to be a member of the LCMS than the Evangelical Lutheran Church in America. What Pastor Bornmann writes about his last conversations with Dr. Piepkorn seems to confirm this." The liberals promoting Piepkorn should read *CN* and the hyper-euros, who oppose *CN* and regularly quote Sasse should read and publish what Sasse said about *CN*.

Study Questions
1. What did the website of the WELS say about Sasse?_____ .
2. Why have the publications of Sasse writings financed by the Schwan Foundation never included any of the letters Sasse wrote to *Christian News*? ____ .
3. Sasse was delighted that the LCMS in 1959 reaffirmed the _____.
4. Martin Scharlemann later changed his _____ .
5. What did Sasse write in a letter read at a testimonial banquet for *Christian News* on February 22, 1970? _____ .
6. Who tried to destroy *CN* financially _____ .
7. Sasse in his book *Here We Stand* wrote that the Reformation emphasized the profound seriousness of _____ .
8. Sasse was among the orthodox theologians who hoped *Christian News* would receive _____ .
9. Sasse wrote that Otten had the freedom to _____ .
10. Who agreed that Otten had correctly presented Piepkorn's position? _____ .

§

HARRISON AND THE LCMS
NEED A LIVING SASSE

Christian News, February 18, 2013

President Matthew Harrison has edited several books with articles and letters by Dr. Hermann Sasse. The latest is *Letters to Lutheran Pastors, Volume I, 1948-1951. CN* highly recommends this great 480 page book. It is available from *Christian News* for **$31.50 plus s/h.**

Shortly before *Christian News* began, Dr. Wilhelm Oesch, a prominent Lutheran theologian in Germany, advised LCMS President John W. Behnken that he needed a "theological watchdog" to keep him regularly informed about what was going on theologically in the LCMS. It would be the watchdog's responsibility to read all publications in the LCMS and also many others. Once *Christian News* began, Oesch recognized that *CN* had become "an important and necessary" unpaid watchdog.

The LCMS's organized conservatives now commend Harrison for his apology and want *CN* to close.

Ed. Harrison apologized for asking an LCMS pastor to apologize for participating in an interfaith service in Newtown, Connecticut where leaders of non-Christian religions participated and President Obama spoke. Christian News, February 18, 2013.

Sasse supported *CN* and backed the editor in his case with the St. Louis seminary. Today organized conservatives oppose *CN*. They have taken a holiday from history. Sasse wrote to *CN* on October 7, 1974:

[See previous article for this statement from Sasse]

x x x

Here is one of the fine statements by Harrison in *Letters to Lutheran Pastors, Volume I, Hermann Sasse*: "Sasse's concern that theology is constantly swept aside by bishops and Church presidents (i.e. 'Church politicians'), and that theologians who dare to have opinions are 'thrown away,' is at once evidence of personal frustration and also a stern warning to those who lead" (p. 367).

Right from the beginning of his presidency, Harrison should have had a living Sasse at his side giving him sound scriptural advice. He then would not have had a bishop, Walter Obare, wearing a mitered hat from an LWF Church which promotes an unscriptural apostolic succession, preach the sermon from the pulpit at Concordia Seminary at his installation. Instead he would have had a theologian like former Lutheran Hour speaker and former LCMS Vice-president Wallace Schulz, a theologian who was "thrown away" from the LCMS because he dared to hold a scriptural position and acted accordingly in the pulpit. Schulz rightly suspended LCMS District President David Benke for worshiping with pagans. Benke maintained "the god of the Muslims is also the true God." Schulz, like Sasse, knows from first-hand experience in Europe that the

LCMS should beware of the LWF. Harrison, right from the outset, should have shown that he will follow the stand taken by Sasse and his other Australian mentor, Kurt Marquart. He would not have banned the editor of *Christian News* from participating in the communion service when he was installed. One critic said instead of banning Otten after Harrison used *Christian News* to get elected, he should have had Otten sitting right up in front with the COP Harrison praises. He would have considered the charges of false doctrine against such an outspoken evolutionist as Matthew Becker instead of going along with the COP which refuses to take any disciplinary action vs. evolutionists, supporters of women pastors in the LCMS and those who deny the inerrancy of the Bible on the LCMS clergy roster. Harrison rightly says in a footnote in *Letters to Lutheran Pastors*: "Where absolute inerrancy has not been regarded as Church dogma, or where it has been asserted but where fellowship has been granted with those who do not hold to it, such Churches cease to be confessionally Lutheran" (p. 342, ft. 8). What does that say about the LCMS remaining in fellowship with Matthew Becker?

(Ed. --Becker resigned from the LCMS, joined the ELCA and continued teaching at Valparaiso in 2015. Harrison appointed Benke to be the chairman of the Committee on Missions of the LCMS's 2013 convention. Benke and Harrison now say they are in agreement. Harrison has expressed no disagreement with the theological position of Dr. Frederick A. Niedner, a colleague of Matthew Becker's in the Theology Department of Valparaiso University. Niedner has long defended the same anti-scriptural position taken by Becker (Christian News, November 23, 2015).)

Had Harrison had a living Sasse as an advisor, he would not have had an Anglican, who rejects the inerrancy of the Bible, the scriptural doctrine of justification, supports evolution, and whose wife is an Anglican priestess be the keynote speaker on Reformation Day at an International Conference of Confessional Lutherans sponsored and paid for by the LCMS with the help of Thrivent and praised by the Steadfast Lutherans. Instead Sasse would have advised him to have a confessional Lutheran such as David Menton, Alvin Schmidt, or John Warwick Montgomery speak.

If Harrison had followed what Sasse said about the "unionistic" Dietrich Bonhoeffer and his "pure *Schwaermertum* which ends in blasphemy" (*Letters to Lutheran Pastors, Hermann Sasse*, pp. lxiii-lxiv, ft. 45) Harrison would be urging the Bonhoeffer fans to read *CN*'s *Bonhoeffer and King* which documents Bonhoeffer's denial of the resurrection of Christ and his demythologizing of the Bible. Instead, Harrison, in his election promotion, according to *Forum Letter*, *Little Book on Joy* goes along with the Bonhoeffer bandwagon. Sasse would have advised the derailing of the bandwagon even if it might arouse the wrath of the LCMS's a-theological COP which need to get off their computers and should be reading *Letters to Lutheran Pastors, Hermann Sasse*, along with all LCMS pastors.

Study Question

1. Wilhelm Oesch advised LCMS President Behnken that he needed _____ .

2. Harrison should have had a ____ at his side.
3. Who preached the sermon at Harrison's installation at Concordia Seminary in 2010? ____ .
4. Dr. Wallace Schulz rightly suspended ____ .
5. Who did Harrison ban from participating in his installation communion service? ____ .
6. Who was the keynote speaker on Reformation Day at a Conference of Confessional Lutherans sponsored by the LCMS ____ .
7. Harrison in his *Little Book of Joy* goes along with ____ .

§

CHRISTIAN NEWS TOLD THE TRUTH
BARMEN DECLARATION, BARTH, BONHOEFFER, AND SASSE

Christian News, September 16, 2013

Bonhoeffer and King includes "An Evaluation of Dietrich Bonhoeffer's Life and Theology After Half of a Century" by Raymond Surburg. It first appeared in the September 19, 1995 *Christian News*. The Barmen Declaration is mentioned.

Defenders of Bonhoeffer often insist that Bonhoeffer must be a confessional Lutheran since he was associated with Hermann Sasse, contributed to the Barmen Declaration written primarily by Karl Barth. *Letters to Lutheran Pastors*, edited by Matthew Harrison and published by CPH in 2013, notes: "Bonhoeffer proclaimed that Barmen was the voice of the Spirit of God, and Sasse cried, 'Schwärmgeisterei!"(lxiv)

"... after the Barmen Synod, Barth and Asmussen trumpeted this declaration as a new 'Confession' and the basis for a new Union, though they knew what Bonhoeffer *(Ev. Theologie* 1938, Heft 6, p. 227) says today in plain language, namely, that with this view of the synod and its declaration 'the *Augustana* has already been decisively abandoned. Here Bonhoeffer was as imprudent as Asmussen. He, shall we say, let the cat out of the bag a little early; and he did this also by openly declaring that the Barmen Confession is God's Word! 'If we take this message of the synod with absolute earnestness, we must then confess that God the Lord Himself is responsible for this message: Then he asks: 'What has God said regarding His Church and the way it is to go, if He has spoken through Barmen and Dahlem?' This is pure *Schwärmertum,* which ends in blasphemy. This is the result if the Barmen Confession is declared a binding doctrinal decision. We can only declare to the 'Provisional Leadership' that what they understand by 'Confessing Church; namely, a Church comprising Lutheran, Reformed, and United [Christians] based upon the Barmen Confession, which appeared in Barmen as a result of a divine miracle, is a sect, and indeed one of the worst we have experienced in

Germany. We understand something different when we speak of the Confessing Church" (Wider die Schwarmgeisterei; *Lutherische Kirche 1936 15* [August 1]: 237ff.). (p. lxiv)

"Is Only the Loser Guilty" by Dr. Walter Bodenstein in the section on Germany in the *Christian News Encyclopedia,* pp. 2272-2275 comments on the Stuttgart Declaration. Bodenstein wrote: "Stuttgart was based on the theology of the Swiss Calvinist theologian Karl Barth, who played such an important role for the Allied war propagandists." "What a scenario! Eleven German Protestant churchmen without a German government, took a position in the name of the entire German people."

"The Allies not only repatriated to Stalin with certain death the soldiers of the so-called Russian Liberation Army of General Vlassov, who fought against Communism with the Germans, but also helpless Russian prisoners-of-war and the evacuated Russian forced laborers in Germany, who averted starvation during the war by working for the Germans."

"It may interest Americans and Canadians that in 1986, it is illegal for Germans to teach in the schools that these 15,000,000 were uprooted. One must teach that they left voluntarily. So history is falsified 40 years after the war."

CN has noted that many of the Bonhoeffer champions are uninformed about Church and world history, particularly the history of WWII. They refuse to read the facts in *CN* and the *CNE.*

Here is the introduction to Bodenstein's "Is Only the Loser Guilty" originally published it in the September 1 and September 15, 1986 issues of *Christian News:*

"IS ONLY THE LOSER GUILTY?" This is an English translation authorized by the Lutheran theologian, Dr. theol. Walter Bodenstein. He was born 1914, studied in Goettingen and Erlangen, served in France and on the Eastern Front during World War II. In 1957, he became pastor in the Lutheran Church in Hanover, then Superintendent in West Berlin, and since 1969 Professor for Religion Pedagogue at the Hochschule (University) in Kiel. This lecture was given on May 26, 1984 for the Zeitgeschichtlichen Forschungsstelle (Contemporary History Institute) in Ingolstadt, Germany. The Director is Dr. Alfred Schickel. The lecture was published both by the Forschungsstelle and by the MUT Verlag, of Asendorf, West Germany, in 1985. The address of Bodenstein is Buelowstrasse 16, 2300 Kiel, West Germany. The authorized translation was made by R. Clarence Lang, Ph.D. Seguin, Texas, 78155.

We first got into difficulty with some churchmen in 1949 when as a teenager we made some of the same observations which Dr. Bodenstein in a far more scholarly manner makes in this address. We noted during a speech on the causes of World War II at Concordia Collegiate Institute, Bronxville, New York, that the allied powers were not entirely guiltless, had ruthlessly and unnecessarily bombed civilian populations and had forced hundreds of thousands, who were fleeing from the Communists back to the Soviet Union and almost certain death. We maintained that

President Franklin Roosevelt was at least in part responsible for the Pearl Harbor disaster. . . .

We know of many Germans who opposed Hitler. Our own grandmother almost got into serious difficulty because she refused to salute Hitler. She insisted she had only one "Heiland" (Savior) and she was not going to say "Heil Hitler." When we toured Europe as a 20 year old seminary student in 1953, we still saw much of the destruction of cities and the almost endless crosses marking graves near major battlefields of WWI and WWII. We saw hundreds of gold stars in Churches marking the death of soldiers who were members. The graves in one cemetery had a section where young teenage soldiers, forced to fight, were buried. They were killed in the last days of the war because of Hitler's idiotic policies and Roosevelt's demand of unconditional surrender. When we preached our first sermon in Germany in 1953 we said that the time had surely come for both sides to repent and now work together in a spirit of harmony and peace. The kind of attitude expressed in the Declaration of Stuttgart (a city we also visited) is wrong and certainly not helpful. We hope our readers have time to read this article by Dr. Walter Bodenstein.

(These articles are available with an on-line archive subscription to Christian News. www.christiannewsmo.com)

Study Questions
1. What did Sasse say when Bonhoeffer declared that Barmen was the choice of God? ____
2. The Stuttgart Declaration was based on the theology of ____.
3. The Russian Liberation Army of General Vlassov fought against the ____ with the Germans.
4. How was history falsified 40 years after WWII? ____
5. Who was Dr. Walter Bodenstein? ____
6. Is the attitude expressed in the Declaration of Stuttgart helpful? ____

(* Note for page xi) The *CN* editor wrote to LCMS President Matthew Harrison on August 20, 2015:

"*CN* will shortly be publishing a book of some 275 pages titled "Missing Letters to Lutheran Pastors". It includes your letter to me of October 30, 1990 and mentions you in the preface. I will send you a copy before it is sent to the printer. Note particularly what is said about you and Kloha in the preface. If I have misrepresented you in the preface and you disagree with Kloha's use of Sasse, please let me know so proper corrections can be made."

When *CN* wrote to Harrison on August 28, 2015 if he found any false doctrine in Kloha's writings, he responded: "Sorry you are not a responsible journalist." LCMS bureaucrats like Harrison, who used *Christian News* to get elected, once in office considered *CN* irresponsible since they could not control *CN*. *CN* told them they could always depend on *CN* to tell the truth but not to play any political games. Sasse, wrote to Otten in 1974: "You had the freedom to speak out against what official Church papers – this refers to all papers in all Churches of our time— had not the freedom to say even if their editors wanted to tell the truth, the whole truth and nothing but the truth" (p. 143).

INDEX

238